"I've had the privilege of being Da
After nearly 25 years in the pastorate
say that I've never heard a more rem_____ _____ _____ ____ ___ _____,
redemption, freedom and fruitfulness are all personified in David Foster."

Steve Berger,
founding pastor, Grace Chapel,
Franklin, Tennessee

"For anyone who has any sexual regrets (and who doesn't?), this book is
a gift. Here is a modern and very personal retelling of a story as old as
the Gospel, a story of creation, fall, redemption and restoration. If you
need to understand a wandering prodigal—yourself or someone else—by
all means read this book."

Nate Larkin,
founder, Samson Society;
author, *Samson and the Pirate Monks*

"In *Love Hunger*, we are able to see into the life of a 'man after God's own
heart.' David shares his story with transparent vulnerability—an unusual
mix. We are rarely willing to be both vulnerable and transparent about
family, sin, pitfalls and triumphs at the same time. Most often we try to
control one or the other. This humble man invites you to see into all of his
life so that you might experience the power and glory of *His* life in you."

Rick Kardos,
co-founder and executive director,
Nathan Project, www.nathanproject.net

"Not only the world, but God's Church, so heavily sunk and trapped in
sexual bondage, desperately needs to hear this story! David's testimony
candidly reveals how the Lord took him deeply and fully into forgiveness
of his father, and how each struggle against compulsive behaviors drove
him into knowing beyond doubt that only God's patient grace ever truly
delivers us, not our striving to be free. I plead, dear people, read this book
with a heart humbly driven into the persistent love of our Father for even
the worst of sinners—and for you."

John Loren Sandford,
author; founder, Elijah House

"In my work in Christian media, I have found David Kyle Foster to be
a fascinating interview. He once said he had more than a thousand gay

sexual encounters before the Lord saved him. Here is his amazing autobiography, including his experiences in Hollywood in the 1970s. This book is a fascinating read. David is a modern-day trophy of the grace of God."

Jerry Newcombe,
TV producer; author; co-host, *Kennedy Classics* and *Truth That Transforms*

"David Kyle Foster's story is profoundly personal and completely transparent. From the lurid details of wrestling with sexual predators and an exploitive drug culture in Hollywood, Foster lifts the reader gently into the transition to a transformed life of Christian hope and healing, without sparing the Church and theological institutions from their own honest and difficult struggles. He makes both struggle and salvation real. His story is challenging yet joyfully heart-lifting."

Rev. Dr. Henry L. ("Laurie") Thompson,
dean of doctoral studies and advancement,
associate professor of liturgical studies,
Trinity School for Ministry, Ambridge, Pennsylvania

"Each time I have heard David Kyle Foster share his story, I have been deeply impacted. It's not so much the details of the journey but more significantly the way David describes his movement closer to knowing God and His redeeming love. This isn't just knowing about God's Father-heart for him, but experiencing it and appropriating it in every part of his life. I pray this book will be a catalyst by which many hurting and imprisoned souls will find healing, freedom and restoration."

Rev. Paul Watson,
Ellel Ministries Australia

"*Love Hunger*, the title and theme of David Kyle Foster's new book, is itself the major root of the sexual identity confusion he experienced (and the level of brokenness that is so common in our modern day). Though never glossing over sin, it is with clarity and tenderness combined that David shows us the power of redeeming love. Thank you, David, that your life, as well as your work, demonstrates that God's miracles can last for years."

Betsy and Chester Kylstra,
Restoring the Foundations,
Hendersonville, North Carolina

LOVE HUNGER

LOVE HUNGER

A HARROWING JOURNEY
from SEXUAL ADDICTION
to TRUE FULFILLMENT

DAVID KYLE FOSTER

Chosen

a division of Baker Publishing Group
Minneapolis, Minnesota

Published by Chosen Books
11400 Hampshire Avenue South
Bloomington, Minnesota 55438
www.chosenbooks.com

Chosen Books is a division of
Baker Publishing Group, Grand Rapids, Michigan

Printed in the United States of America

Library of Congress Cataloging-in-Publication Data
Foster, David Kyle.
    Love hunger : a harrowing journey from sexual addiction to true fulfillment / David Kyle Foster ; foreword by Neil T. Anderson.
        pages cm
    Summary: "After searching for love in all the wrong places, a Hollywood actor shares his harrowing struggle with sexual addiction and his journey to true fulfillment"— Provided by publisher.
    ISBN 978-0-8007-9580-1 (pbk. : alk. paper) 1. Foster, David Kyle—Mental health. 2. Sex addicts—United States—Biography. 3. Actors—United States—Biography. 4. Sex—Religious aspects—Christianity. I. Anderson, Neil T., 1942 writer of preface. II. Title.
    RC560.S43F67 2014
    362.2'7092—dc23   2013047095
                                                                                      [B]

Cover design by Dual Identity

This book is dedicated to the memory of my father and my mother, the Reverend Philip Kyle Foster and Betty Carey Foster (Price). Neither could have imagined the kind of wild child that they would get in having me, but they did their best before God. I am not only a testimony to the unbelievable grace of God, but also a testimony to the power of the prayers of parents whose loved one(s) have gone astray. I will be forever in their debt for their unwavering and persevering prayers.

CONTENTS

FOREWORD

Christianity can be separated from any other religion or cult on the basis of one question: By what means are you accepted? Only Christianity offers unconditional love and acceptance with no hoops to jump through, but that is not always how the Church is perceived, nor is it always practiced by those who profess to be Christians. Such was the case for David Foster, who was the son of a preacher. He desperately wanted the love and acceptance of his father, but he never got it growing up. Rules without relationships lead to rebellion, and that is the path David chose, like so many other troubled teens.

Overbearing authoritarianism often drives children to escape the inevitable conflicts at home. Attempts at running away or taking one's own life can be a cry for help, but those often lead to severe punishment and even tighter restraints. Children caught in that cycle do not feel good about themselves, so many turn to alcohol and drugs to numb the pain. When asked why he used drugs, one teenager said, "That is the only time I feel good about myself." If this happens in a supposedly "Christian" context, God appears to be a distant judge rather than a loving Savior. Such rebellion is not just against parents, but against any authority figure, including God.

The sexual revolution was well underway when David left home for college, and the liberal "Christian" college he attended was a hotbed for sex and drugs. Rebellious and insecure teens have little or no defense against such peer pressure, and David fell right into it. David, like many who struggle with sexual identity confusion, was not sure when and where same-sex attractions started to surface, but there is always a cause and an effect. For many it begins with sexual abuse. Legalistic authoritarianism and parental role reversals are often mentioned by those who struggle. For many it just begins as a battle for their minds. Misguided people can tease someone and make accusations and subtle suggestions, which ruminate in the mind. We also have been warned that in later days, people will pay attention to deceiving spirits and be led astray from their faith (see 1 Timothy 4:1). I know from experience that this is happening all over the world.

Same-sex attraction may begin as nothing more than a tempting thought, which could be brushed aside. If the tempting thoughts continue and are entertained, however, they will eventually affect how a person feels. If people in that condition start to wonder, *Why am I thinking these thoughts?*, they may start questioning their sexuality. Such people believe the lie when they conclude that they are gay, because it would be hypocritical not to believe what you feel. That is the devil's definition of hypocrisy. Christian hypocrisy is to profess to believe something and not live accordingly. If people act upon their homosexual impulses, they are using their bodies as instruments of unrighteousness, thus allowing sin to reign in their mortal bodies (see Romans 6:12–13). Once David stepped over that line, he was trapped in sin. Eventually he discovered that men would pay him for sex, though all the while, he knew it was wrong. The fact that someone wanted him fed into his need for acceptance.

God created us male and female, which is primarily a gender statement. A person's gender can be ascertained by a DNA sample.

The body is telling the truth and the truth cannot be altered, but the soul of someone who questions his or her sexual identity has been damaged. That can be repaired. And what about someone who sells his or her body for sex? Is there freedom and healing for that person? Absolutely, and that is what this book is all about. David's early disappointment in Christianity made him vulnerable to any cult that would accept him, so he was seduced by a false messiah. Meanwhile, his parents came into a fresh, new experience with the Holy Spirit. That same Spirit was leading David out of the wilderness, calling him into ministry and preparing him for one of the most difficult challenges facing the Church today.

When God pulls us out of the quicksand, we are free, but mud and grit are still hanging all over us. The journey toward wholeness does not happen overnight. It is a struggle to renew our minds, because the flesh patterns are still there even though we are new creations in Christ. We had learned to live independently of God, and now we must learn to trust and depend on Him. At first we stand at the edge of the pit and fight the temptation to fall back in, and we fear that we will. God has accepted us, but immature Christians shy away from this modern-day leprosy and wonder whether someone who has come up out of the pit is still "unclean." Liberal "Christians" disavow the testimony. Militant homosexuals are blasphemous and condemning.

David is not gay. He is a child of God. It takes a lot of courage for David to write a book like this. He has been and will be persecuted for his faith. I admire him for taking a stand for righteousness' sake. He wants everyone to know that if God can love, accept and restore someone like him, then God can and will do the same for anyone who will put his or her faith in Him and accept the challenge of becoming like Jesus. To God be the glory.

Dr. Neil T. Anderson,
founder and president emeritus,
Freedom in Christ Ministries

13

ACKNOWLEDGMENTS

This manuscript has been a work in progress since 1987, when I attempted my first draft. Always the perfectionist, I wrote a second draft some years later and sat on that for a while, still unsatisfied. About ten years later, I decided to include a second party in order to give the story some distance from my own feelings and emotions. Danny Carlton helped me compile that third draft. I appreciate his help in giving me some unbiased distance from the material, which, as you might suspect, includes some highly charged and emotional moments for me. By the time that draft was done, however, I was heavy into the "ministry" part of my life, so I let the manuscript sit for another six years before inviting Lela Gilbert to assist me in creating a fourth and final draft—one that would include the many awesome things that God has done in the aftermath of my massively broken life before Christ. I am deeply grateful to Lela for her work in helping me finish the project.

PART ONE

THE EARLY YEARS

My father and I shared a frustrating and futile family ritual. Time after time I would commit some rebellious act against him. Again and again he would fly into a rage, ripping off his belt and whipping me. Convinced that he hated me, and quite sure that I hated him, as each incident exploded, a little more of my soul died within me.

One particular day when I was twelve years old, the ugly cycle intensified and spun out of control. It began because I had unsuccessfully tried to run away from home. Once discovered, I was at the mercy of Dad's legendary fury. I could see how his wrath distorted his face as he tried to grab me by the arm. I shook him off and fled up the stairs. He was at my very heels in hot pursuit.

Once again I was trapped, running for my life. But on that terrible day, something inside me rose up in fierce resistance. I wheeled around on the steps. My defiant eyes met my father's. And in a burst of desperate energy, I shoved him with all my might, hurling him backward, down the stairs. In that split second, I did not care what happened to him.

He fell back as if in slow motion, and in those seconds I wondered what kind of hell I had brought upon myself. I watched as he stumbled and tumbled helplessly down several steps. He landed on the living room couch, with the side table and lamp flying and crashing behind him. He was unharmed, but angrier than I had ever seen him, or ever would again.

Since my father was not dead after all, I could only assume that I soon would be. In a state of panic I locked myself in my room. Almost immediately he was pounding on the door. I knew that either he would break it down or I would let him in. Mentally, I bargained that I might suffer fewer lashes if I unlocked the door, so I did. He flung it open and stormed into the room.

Throwing me over his knee, he started beating me with his favorite leather weapon, demanding with each blow that I apologize. I cried out in pain and fear, but had no apologetic words to say. To express regret for what I had done would be a joke. So he kept hitting me.

Dad managed to scream one word with every blow: *"IF . . . YOU . . . EVER . . . TRY . . . TO . . . DO . . . THIS . . . AGAIN . . . YOU . . . WILL . . . REGRET . . . IT . . . FOR . . . THE . . . REST . . . OF . . . YOUR . . . LIFE!"*

I was screaming even louder than he was, both from the blows and from the emotional trauma of it all. Continuing to beat me, he shouted, *"NOW PROMISE ME you will NEVER try to run away again! Do you hear me? I said PROMISE ME. . . ."*

Now he was asking me to lie to him, which, in my confused state of mind, was a sin worse than wanting him dead. I had every intention of running away as soon as he left the room, so I still did not say anything. And he kept whipping me and repeating his demand.

This went on for what seemed like ten minutes, though it was probably half that long. As the violence continued, one clear thought in my head was drowning out his voice: *You don't love me, so I don't love you! You are not my father, and I am not your son!*

Finally, he gave up, barked some orders restricting me to my room and left.

I had already decided to run away again. I crawled out onto the roof and slithered over to the safest place from which to make the jump. *I'll hitchhike to Ocean City, or maybe Baltimore or D.C., or maybe even New York!* I promised myself.

Just as I was about to leap, Dad reappeared outside, glaring up at me. He had heard me moving around on the roof, and his anger was white hot. "Go back into your room! Now!" he snarled.

After obeying, I wrestled with the idea of going back out on the roof one last time and jumping anyway, but of course I knew that he would instantly be back on me. For the time being, I gave up.

But deep in the darkness of my battered soul, there were two new fractures. From that moment on, I disowned myself from my father. I was no longer his son; he had lost me. And because I had tried to harm him, I believed that God had disowned me and that I was destined for hell.

In the months and years that followed, I gradually began to live as if I were both fatherless and Godless. I managed to convince myself that, in light of my perilous but liberating independence, I would have to find my way through life entirely on my own. And I would just have to make up the rules as I went along.

— 1 —

The FAMILY

I have always loved baseball. As a young boy, I felt a particular sadness knowing that I was never all that good at playing it. Still, I loved the game with a passion. First it was the Yankees— Mickey Mantle, Bobby Richardson, Roger Maris, Whitey Ford. They were the best. I will never forget the day Roger hit his 61st home run. I knew it was gone the second the crack from the bat reached my ears. The only downside is that it did not happen to Mickey.

Then, thanks to living in Maryland, I became an Oriole fan. Yeah, the Birds. They were fantastic—Boog Powell, Frank and Brooks Robinson, Dave McNally—what a lineup. It helped that Brooks was the best third baseman in baseball history and that Frank and Brooks regularly hit back-to-back home runs. My first opportunity to attend a live game was at Baltimore. It was another world. It was a movie. It was a Spielberg moment, watching the ball hovering surrealistically in the air high above home plate.

Many a night, I would fall asleep listening to a twi-night doubleheader, earplug from my trusty transistor radio permanently fixed in my ear. I dreamed that I was the star who hit the grand slam home run in the ninth to win the World Series. Those were epic moments when I could be one with my heroes, floating in their world, mystically united, beyond the reach of my pain.

Unfortunately, it was not baseball that shaped my childhood memories. Instead, at the heart of my story lies a litany of hurts and heartaches, wounding me both as a child and as a young adult. It is this story that fills some of the pages that follow. I do not write about it to seek sympathy or to elicit excuses for the choices I made. I write about it not only because it is true, but because, thankfully, I eventually found health and hope. And I have recorded my painful recollections because I know there are countless others who have walked along similar paths, felt similar hungers and made similar bad choices.

Some children are lighthearted and are emotionally equipped to shake off the rejection brought on by parental injustices and playground humiliations. Others of us are not so fortunate. In my case, because of my deeply felt sensitivities and my perceptions of being unloved, I lived with a ceaseless pain that eclipsed all else, intensifying as I grew older and leading me along an increasingly self-destructive path.

I will begin my story in the small town of Easton, Maryland, in the late 1950s. I was seven years old.

A Preacher's Kid

My father, a Presbyterian preacher, had moved our family to Easton from Florida to plant a new church in the small Maryland community. Dad and I were not exactly soul mates, no matter where we lived. But tensions between us were not the only problem. In my early days in Easton, the stereotypical neighborhood bully played a role in my misery, too. Surrounding Easton were numerous housing developments. Creativity, research and hard work had gone into making these neighborhoods pleasant for those who would live in them. The house plans were geared toward families with children, just as the layout of the streets was carefully conceived. The landscaping in the public areas was maintained meticulously. But in spite of this collaboration of engineering, architecture and civil planning, there was one thing the city planners did not take into consideration—a kid everyone called T.J., who ruled our Calvert Terrace neighborhood with an iron fist.

The day after our family moved into our pristine new home, I went to check out a playground I had seen just a block away. Before I knew what was happening, I felt a whack across the back of my head. For the first time, I heard what I would soon recognize as T.J.'s signature form of abuse—both verbal and physical.

"What are you doing here, punk?" he demanded.

"I just moved here."

"Where from?"

"Florida."

"So what do you think you're doing coming over here?"

"I was told this was the playground for everybody in the neighborhood."

"Well, you were told wrong." With that, he grabbed me in a headlock and began pounding the top of my head.

After a minute or so, while I screamed and cried, T.J. pushed me to the ground. "Now get out of here and don't come back!"

This scenario repeated itself in different forms over many days and weeks. I was clueless about how to defend myself. Instead, I fled from T.J., scurrying back home in tears, pleading with Mom and Dad to do something to help me. For a long time, they never did. Even when Dad finally stepped in—it must have been a year or more later—he made matters worse. He confronted T.J. while I was sitting mute and miserable in the backseat of the car. Dad stoutly lectured him about being a bully. And being a pastor, my father certainly could lecture.

For months I had been wishing he would deliver just such a reprimand. Of course, I did not expect to be there at the time! I sat frozen in place, imagining the reprisal that would surely come once Dad was *not* with me.

I tried to avoid T.J., but no matter how careful I was to make sure he was not around before I cautiously entered the playground, he always seemed to be on the prowl. He would suddenly appear and beat me up. Meanwhile, like neighborhood kids everywhere, the Calvert Terrace boys laughed and cheered while I was being pummeled. They were well acquainted with T.J. and knew that applauding his bullying was the best way to avoid having him direct his violence at them.

Meanwhile, our family life had also begun to unravel. Dad spent most of his time launching the new church. At first, Mom's time was consumed with organizing the house, but the next thing I knew, she had also given birth to yet another brother—Rob. It was up to my older brothers and me to adapt ourselves to our new brother, new school, new teachers and new friends. For better or worse, we were on our own.

There are families who live quiet, simple lives, rarely raising their voices, and there are families who yell a lot. We were a quarrelsome bunch, with an undercurrent of anger fueling our many confrontations. My brothers and I had always fought among ourselves, and now that intensified. My parents' firstborn was four years older than I. He had always tried to tell me what to do, a habit of his that very much annoyed me. My second brother, the next in line, tried to stay out of most of our clashes.

Our family atmosphere bore little, if any, resemblance to such upstanding TV models as the Andersons in *Father Knows Best* or the Nelsons in *The Adventures of Ozzie and Harriet*. In fact, one frequent source of conflict was the television. Brother #1 would come into the TV room while Brother #2 and I were watching something. He would either immediately change the channel or announce, "What are you watching *that* for? There's something I want to see instead!" If we resisted and Mom and Dad were not around, he would change the channel anyway. A major fight invariably would ensue. Often it would be a slugfest, including desperate wrestling on the floor. When I was younger, Brother #1 would easily win because he was four years older. But as I grew older and bigger I fought with all my might, so that even if he won, he would still lose. Why? Because I was good at feigning major injury for my parents' benefit. You could say that it was my first acting job.

After several years of this madness, my parents finally solved the problem by creating a TV-watching schedule. But TV was not the only thing. Brother #1 baited me unmercifully by finding fault with me and criticizing my words and actions. I suppose, looking back, that he was simply mimicking the approach my parents modeled. For obvious reasons, whether emanating from them or from him, that did not engender close relationships.

On the other hand, Brother #2, who was just a year older than I, maintained a cool disinterest in the fray. His aloofness both frustrated me when he did not fight alongside me, and impressed me, revealing him to me as someone wise and good. We shared a room until college, and we usually talked at length after going to bed at night, often through the vacuum cleaner hose stretched between our beds. In those early years at Easton, I confided in him freely. As my actions and traumas grew darker, I told him less and less. In a way, Brother #2 was my only father figure. He always listened, but his emotional distance prevented me from ever being sure he actually understood or cared about my various conflicts and struggles.

I rarely confided in my parents. Mom and Dad generally stuck to the common ethos of not spoiling a child with undue attention. "Spare the rod, spoil the child" and "Children should be seen and not heard" were real-life mottos our parents applied without compromise as they tried to raise their offspring properly. I am sure it was all well intended, but the tight controls they imposed on every aspect of our lives created an unmitigated disaster for me.

My father was the scion of Scots-Irish and McIntosh Clan Scots. He proudly traced his genealogy through Andrew Jackson, back to the old seventeenth-century Covenanters. These Presbyterians were a stern, legalistic bunch who thought it unseemly to be emotionally expressive, physically affectionate or even intimate with others. To praise or affirm children was to lead them into pride. Hugs were few and far between. In fact, I cannot remember my father ever initiating an embrace with me. If he touched me, it was to discipline me. I so wanted to win his heart. But what could be more unfulfilling than to live and breathe to please someone who thinks that showing approval and affection is against the rules?

Mom was a beauty. She was also a complex mix of seeming contradictions. Although she and Dad had endured the same kind of stoic, strict, Depression-era parenting, her father was also an alcoholic. And because a booze-addicted father had raised her, she grew up believing that the keeping of family secrets was her sacred duty. For example, she never told my brothers and me that she had been widowed before marrying Dad. Her first husband was killed near Pearl Harbor in the war, and we found out about it in the most unlikely way. My oldest brother was working as a door-to-door salesman in Mom's hometown. One day, he noticed a wedding photo in an older couple's home. He stared in disbelief. "That's my mother!" he exclaimed. The people were Mom's late husband's parents, her former in-laws. It was an awkward moment, to put it mildly. But such secrets are the hallmark of alcoholic families.

Because of my oft-wounded feelings, I was more conscious of the hurts I felt than of my parents' rare expressions of affection. And in our rough-and-tumble home, there were many more unpleasant conflicts and confrontations than times of peace and love. Still, my parents tried to express love through such events as the family trips we took camping and visiting exciting places, which I enjoyed thoroughly. We also had wonderful Christmases together, when they tried their best to give us the gifts we wanted most. Sometimes when I was quite small, Dad called me "Davy," which made me especially happy. I liked the nickname partly because I shared it with my hero Davy Crockett, but mostly I liked it because of the affection it implied.

My parents tried to teach their four sons to have faith in God and love for Jesus—though in my eyes, at least, there often seemed to be a clash between what was preached and what was practiced in our home. We were never taught that the Bible was the infallible Word of God or that you had to be born again, yet I still remain grateful to my parents for surrounding me with an atmosphere where I learned about Jesus and His love on a regular basis. I have fond memories of Mom reading Bible stories to us and teaching us songs like "Jesus Loves Me."

A Presbyterian Dynasty

As far as I can tell, the Foster Covenanter dynasty first hit U.S. shores from Ireland in the early 1800s. Samuel Foster became a ruling elder in the Reformed Presbyterian Church in Cedarville, Ohio. One of his sons, Dr. James Mitchell Foster, served

My grandfather Rev. Samuel Turner Foster (1880–1953), pastor of First Presbyterian Church, Carbondale, Pennsylvania. He was a stern and towering figure in the family. Like his father, he also was known widely for his published sermons and articles.

for 37 years as pastor of the Second Reformed Presbyterian Church in Boston, Massachusetts, and wrote many books that you can read online to this day. One of his sons was my grandfather, the Reverend Dr. Samuel Turner Foster. He stood a full head taller than Dad, who himself topped out at over six feet. Grandfather was also a successful and well-known Presbyterian minister whose sermons were sometimes published in the Cedar Rapids, Iowa, newspaper.

Following in the footsteps of these towering figures, Dad had big shoes to fill. And like many religious leaders, Dad exhibited two distinct personalities—one for the public and another at home. He was gentle and good-natured with his congregation. With his sons—and it seemed particularly so with me—he was stern, strict and stoic. Like his father before him, he was a graduate of Princeton Theological Seminary, which, by the time he attended, had begun its slide into theological liberalism. Dad was more conservative than most Princeton grads, but he definitely was not an evangelical.

In many ways, there was a great deal to admire in Dad. He was a virtuous man and was brave enough to be one of the first white preachers in his generation to publicly stand up for black people in the small, segregated Florida town where I was born. This was exceptional in the late 1950s and early '60s.

The other side of that equation was, of course, my own real-life experience of being a "preacher's kid." I can still hear faint echoes of my father's impatient command: "Hurry up, boys! We'll be late for church!" Since we always arrived at church an hour early, being late was all but impossible. But that did not change the family mood on Sunday mornings. It was disagreeable at best. Frustration seethed from our collective pores as our car rushed toward the church that was, for some reason, all the way across town from our manse. We would screech into the church parking lot, which was always empty at that hour.

My father, Rev. Philip K. Foster (1915–1982), pastor of Easton Presbyterian Church, Easton, Maryland. He seemed to be a kinder and gentler figure than his forebears, but it was still difficult for his sons to know him at any deep level.

Even before moving to Easton, I had already started to hate church. This was, in part, because church work was forced on us. But it was also because of my father's cold severity. Somehow I knew that he was supposed to represent God to me. But I also noticed that he only seemed interested in me when I served as a compliant family member, performing well for the parishioners.

Our first church service in Easton was held in a suite of basement rooms in the Talbottown Shopping Center. That service was packed out, held in a room that seated perhaps a hundred people. Everyone showed up to check out the new pastor, his wife and kids and his fledgling church. Shy and cautious, I stayed on the fringes of the crowd, hoping I would not have to talk

Our family at church in 1962. My parents, Philip and Betty, stand behind my older brothers, Carey and John; my younger brother, Robert, stands next to me in the front. Our best times together were at Christmas and on summer vacations.

to anyone. Since I was only seven, it was unlikely that anyone wanted to talk to me anyway.

According to family rules, we all had to attend every church service, Sunday school class or youth group meeting. There was, quite simply, no excuse for absence. As Dad would say, "There are no ifs, ands or buts about it!" We went early and stayed late, setting up and tearing down the chairs, helping mimeograph the bulletin, folding various mailings, singing in the youth choir, serving as white-robed acolytes or otherwise being part of what I judged to be the ongoing "show."

All of this performance was particularly galling to me because of the contrast between our "nice Christian family" image at church and the ceaseless strife in our home. Again, punishment at our house was frequent and often meted out with the aid of a belt, Ping-Pong paddle, switch or wire coat hanger. Even now, I recall having spent far too much of my childhood banished to my room by my mother for some misdemeanor, waiting for Dad to come home and mete out the *real* sentence. I grew to view my father as *the enforcer* rather than as a loving and gracious parent, and my resentment knew no bounds. In fact, I would war with God over this injustice for decades.

Today we use the word *affirmation* to define an important element in parenting. But that term does not do justice to the deep craving children feel for appreciation, or to the wounds they incur when they are treated as if they are stupid or worthless. In those days, I hungered for a loving word, a smile or a hug.

My heart ached to have someone let me know that I was worth something. I do not think this was a particularly inappropriate desire on my part. God gave each of us a desire for meaning and worth. Ultimately, He is in our lives to meet those needs. Still, during childhood we are unable to comprehend God's love if it is not conveyed by those closest to us.

We all knew that Dad was busy serving God. He was distracted by innumerable demands and made irritable by difficult people. Starting a church really is a lot of work. But we boys did not know that at the time. If we had, it might have alleviated some of the anger, but it still would have left us desperately in need of his affirmation, affection and attention.

— 2 —

The GREAT SADNESS
BEGINS

During my earliest days in Easton, one of the joys of my life was a special attachment I formed with a girl who lived nearby. Her name was Helga. She had a ponytail and wore white boots, and I quickly fell head over heels in love with her. Nearly every day, we played after school. We spent many an afternoon together, as well as Saturdays. Our friendship was a bit unusual and even potentially embarrassing because boys did not typically spend playtime with girls. But she was irresistible and seemed to like me as much as I liked her.

Helga, the shining light of my life, had somewhat alleviated the hunger I felt for approval from my parents. We would play and talk for hours. As eight-year-olds, our relationship was one of happy, compatible pals, although her genuine affection for me made it feel like something more.

I cannot remember what triggered the conflict, but one day after I came home from school, I said or did something that offended my mother. She punished me, decreeing that I should stay inside and do chores the rest of the day, and she was in no mood to fight with me over it. I tried to argue back, but the more I complained, the more adamant she grew. Finally, in desperation I said, "But Helga's coming over!"

Mom was unfazed. "Well, that's too bad. When she gets here, you can just tell her you're being punished, what you're being punished for and why you can't come out to play."

I was absolutely horrified. Helga was important to me in more ways than I could understand, much less explain. I so wanted to impress her, to please her. And I never wanted to jeopardize our time together. Stunned and sorrowful, I started to cry.

"If you don't get in there and do those dishes, I'll give you something to cry about!" Mom threatened. It was her usual response to my tears during those days.

Hoping to salvage the situation, I began washing the dishes as compliantly as possible. Before long, Helga appeared at the back door next to the kitchen. She knocked with her familiar little *tap, tap, tap*.

"Now, you go out there and tell her what I told you to say," Mom demanded.

"I can't." My eyes flooded again.

"David, don't you *dare* disobey me. Now get out there and tell her exactly what I told you to say!"

Defeated, I made my way out to the breezeway door. By now tears were coursing down my cheeks. Soapsuds dripped from my hands and fell on the floor. As I looked at Helga, I felt overwhelmed with humiliation and shame. I called out to her, "My mom says I can't come out because I'm being punished."

Helga's voice was warm and compassionate. "Okay, but can you play later?"

Suddenly, white-hot fury boiled inside me—anger so intense that it unavoidably spilled over onto Helga, scorching her, too.

Because I could not find words to explain myself, instead I pushed her away: "No! Just go home! *I said I can't play with you.*"

I rushed back into the kitchen without waiting to hear her reply.

My tears mingled with the soapy dishwater as I looked out the window. Walking away, Helga took one glance back. I could see tears on her cheeks. I felt so humiliated by being unable to explain to her what had happened. As far as I was concerned, my mother had destroyed the most cherished friendship I had ever had. To make matters worse, not long thereafter, Helga's family moved away and I never saw her again. Two decades would pass before I was able to forgive my mother.

An Audacious Streak

At the same time, I was still battling the constant pressure of T.J.'s mocking and mistreatment. I knew it was dangerous to enter the playground, but I also realized that somehow I had to stop being his favorite victim. One afternoon, I ventured onto the outskirts of the property and watched the other kids. It did not take long to see that not all of them were happily playing— T.J. was taking his aggression out on some other children. One by one, they retreated to their homes, finally leaving just him and me. I was still some distance away, but he zeroed in on me like the predator he was.

"*So what are you doing here, punk?*" he yelled.

"Nothin'."

"*I'm coming after you next!*"

He ran directly toward me. I dodged him the first time, so he took another run at me. I dodged him again, which I understood was unwise. It was usually better to let him catch me early and get it over with, because if any of us humiliated him in any way, his cruelty increased.

No one else was around, and I knew I was about to suffer not only humiliation but physical pain. I tried something desperate—I dropped my pants and danced around in front of him. This came as such a surprise to him that he froze in his tracks. Then he began to laugh—insanely. Sensing success, I stripped all the way and streaked around the pavilion in the center of the playground at top speed, waving my pants in one hand like a flag. By then he was bent over in laughter.

It had been a huge risk. If a neighbor had seen me and had told my parents, I would have been beaten half to death and confined to my room for the remainder of the century. Thankfully, no one saw me but T.J., and not only had I sent him into hysterics; I had also gained his approval by playing the bad "preacher's kid." I must have made a mental note that day that I could purchase appeasement and applause by taking off my clothes. It was a lesson that would open the gates to even more perverse behavior some years later.

Once I had finally achieved "friend" status with T.J., I was invited to participate in various neighborhood games. That autumn, the sport of choice was football. Apart from the fact that I could not pass, could not kick, could not catch and could not block, I was happy to be included. T.J. assigned me to center, which was a horrible position because oncoming tacklers trying to get to the quarterback repeatedly knocked me down with all their might. The trampling was so bad that even T.J. disapproved. He moved me to fullback.

It was my moment to shine.

No one would have guessed that I would be any good at such a strategic position, but what I lacked in toughness, I made up for in evasive tactics. Instead of plowing my way through tacklers, as most fullbacks do, I found myself a natural expert at avoiding them altogether. Even I was surprised by my skill. T.J. received the snap and handed the ball off to me. I took off like a shot, avoiding one guy, then another and then the next. Three downs later, I was in the end zone, bathing in the sweet sounds of T.J.'s victory hoot. He actually patted me on the back. I had arrived! A few touchdowns later, he began slapping me on the backside—the ultimate sign of approval between guys in sports. I had found my niche. I was a player! And I had not removed even one article of clothing.

"Go Call for Help!"

Whatever success I found in our neighborhood football games, my father never heard about—there would be no accolades from him. And whatever self-confidence I gained in my unexpected gridiron accomplishments was soon forfeited during what may have been the most confusing childhood experience of my life.

Late one Sunday afternoon, my brothers and I were sprawled out over the couch and floor in the TV room, watching a show. We were absorbed by the program, and the volume was, as usual, turned up as loud as we could get it. Noise was also coming from the kitchen, including the clanging of pots and pans and the slamming of kitchen cabinets.

Suddenly I felt a vibration and heard some unexpected sounds coming from the guest room, where my paternal grandmother—we called her Beamie—was staying. It felt to me as if something had fallen. An ominous feeling gripped me.

I left the TV room and moved rather slowly toward the front guest room. My heart was racing. I knew that Beamie had had several heart attacks. Somehow, I intuitively sensed that I was about to be forced to witness another one.

Arriving at Beamie's bedroom door, I slowly pushed it open. She was struggling to pull herself up off the floor. She was a heavy woman, so there was no way she was going to succeed. I knew I could not lift her. Horrified, I wanted to rush back to the TV room and pretend it was not happening. Of course, that was out of the question. I ran as fast as I could to the kitchen.

"Dad! Beamie's fallen on the floor!"

"Where?"

"In her room."

Dad dropped what he was doing and ran to her side. I was close behind him. I watched, immobilized with fear, as he struggled to lift Beamie up off the floor. Then he turned to me, glared angrily and yelled, *"Don't just STAND there! Go call for help!"*

I assumed he wanted me to use the telephone, but whom was I supposed to call? There was no 911 in those days. I did not know what to do. Meanwhile, my brothers were still lounging in the TV room, oblivious to what was taking place. Why didn't I tell them to go help Dad? Or ask them whom to phone in an emergency? In my panic I was frozen in place, staring helplessly at the telephone.

A few minutes later, Dad rushed into the room and asked me if I had called for help. I could barely talk. "I don't know how . . ." My voice broke.

"FOR CRYING OUT LOUD!" Dad screamed at me, grabbing the phone and immediately calling the doctor. I fled, scrambling halfway up the stairs and out of sight, but within hearing distance.

When the doctor arrived, I followed him and Dad into Beamie's room, where Dad had laid her out on the bed. The doctor frantically tried to revive her, but he was clearly unable to feel a pulse from her neck or wrist. As he began to pull up her dress to try to find an artery inside her thigh, Dad roughly ordered me out of the room.

I sat forlornly at the foot of the stairs. It felt as though a lot of time passed before Dad emerged.

"Is she okay?" I asked quietly.

"No. She's gone."

A tide of sorrow washed over me. Not only had I lost my grandmother, but I also felt I had lost even more of my father's heart. Children often blame themselves when tragedy strikes their family. That was certainly the case with me. I was sure that my failure to call for help quickly and effectively had been the cause of my grandmother's death. Dad never said a word about my botched attempt to assist him, but based on my already frayed bond with him, I could only assume that he would never forgive me.

Bad Tricks, Dangerous Treats

Now that I was part of T.J.'s gang, my life had become increasingly exciting—and far riskier—than it had ever been before. Since I had virtually lost heart about pleasing my father, I was not all that concerned about how our childish mischief would displease him. Once Halloween rolled around, T.J., the other boys and I were all looking forward to doing more than just enjoying ourselves. We had big plans to make some local people very unhappy with our trick-or-treat shenanigans. We were thinking almost entirely in terms of tricks.

We began at sundown—the kinds of things we had planned were far better accomplished after dark. We had been plotting for days and had our bags filled with soap, fresh cow manure and other unpleasantries that we planned to visit on anyone whose path happened to cross ours.

We had decided to begin outside our neighborhood, where it was less likely anyone would recognize us. I think we soaped just about every car in town, scrawling rude words and phrases on at least two windows per car. If the car belonged to someone we did not like, such as a hated teacher, we gave it the royal treatment, which could include everything from thickly soaped windows (car and house), grape juice in the windshield-washer fluid dispenser and radio turned up all the way to blast the ear-drums when the unfortunate driver turned the ignition key in the morning. Besides the car, our tricks included cow manure carefully positioned to target the person's first step upon exiting each door of the house, toilet paper throughout the greenery, and smashed jack-o'-lanterns (either flattened with a hammer or blasted with a firecracker or cherry bomb). We added to those a stink bomb thrown inside the car or possibly even thrown in an open window or unlocked door of the house. And to launch our activities at each residence, we rang the doorbell so that our victims could discover our works of art in the confusion of darkness—especially the manure under the doorsill. Of course, we watched the festivities from a safe distance.

One Halloween, we put detergent in the fountain in front of Easton's brand-new bank. Before long, soapsuds were floating down the streets, and the police got involved. They tried to determine who the vandals were, because our prank ended up costing the bank a fortune to clean up and repair the fountain.

As for me, thanks to my newfound friends, I had become somewhat of a minor juvenile delinquent. As time passed, I grew increasingly rebellious, angry, distrustful and disrespectful of authority. When the 1950s ended and the '60s began, that same sort of defiant spirit was creeping across the nation. I was too young to really understand much about it, but I was certainly being primed to become an eager participant.

My insolence, combined with a sense of unmitigated hope-lessness, made me highly susceptible to anything that would momentarily relieve the turbulence in my soul. Not surprisingly, at around that same time—in the autumn of my ninth year—I smoked my first cigarette, courtesy of T.J. I became addicted quickly. The cigarettes were not just meant to impress my friends with how mature, worldly and non–preacher's kidlike I was. Nicotine soon became something I physically required.

I remember secretly smoking alone, scrounging for money to buy cigarettes and thinking how bizarre it was that a kid as young as I was could be addicted to anything. Cigarettes were only a quarter a pack in those days, and it was easy to get them from vending machines at the local Tastee-Freez. I often found the money I needed by searching the change return slots in pay telephones and vending machines.

There was nothing like the sound of a quarter dropping into a cigarette machine and the smooth pull of the lever for the chosen brand. It gave me a sense of power and maturity. And, as self-conscious as I was, in my imagination I dreamed that some really suave older guy was watching me and thinking how cool a kid I must be. My guess today is that anyone witnessing my actions probably would have been thinking just the opposite.

In those days, however, it was not all that difficult to rationalize smoking. The Eastern Shore of Maryland was a major tobacco-growing region, so everyone supported it. Movies and advertisements made smoking seem sexy and hip, and I practiced various ways to hold a cigarette in front of the mirror, hanging it from my lips at just the right angle so that I looked like James Dean or Marlon Brando.

It also was easy to justify my habit because my parents smoked. And the woman next door came to our house to gossip every other day, puffing like a chimney. I could not see much difference between other smokers—including my parents—and me. Meanwhile, I thought at the time that there was no greater sign of male bonding with one's buddies than to light their cigarettes from yours. It was "guy intimacy" of the first order.

After discovering my nicotine habit, my mother tried to work some reverse psychology on me by offering to let me smoke as long as I did it in the house. Deciding to call her bluff, I went up to her in the kitchen a few hours later and asked her for a cigarette. She was less than pleased. Reverse psychology looks good in books, but does not always work in real life. My parents quit smoking permanently not long after that, but I was hooked. I did not give up tobacco until my early twenties, when it was rendered superfluous by other more serious drug addictions.

Dodging the Truth

At about this time, I decided to run away from home and leave all the hurt and frustration behind. I was convinced that my parents were clueless about what I was feeling, what was going on inside of me or why I was being so difficult. I had toyed with the idea of running away before, but had never had the courage to actually do it. After all, I was only nine years old, and I lived in a small town in the middle of nowhere. Where would I go? What would I do? With my luck, some murderer would probably pick me up, and I would be worse off than before. Or I would be sent to a reform school, or—worst of all—an insane asylum. All these possibilities were mentioned in the tales of incorrigible children I often heard from my mother and Mom-Mom—my maternal grandmother.

By this point, the seemingly nonstop yelling and anger in our family was causing me to retreat to empty rooms in the house, secreting myself on the floor behind a bed or couch for hours at a time. In some cases, I would go out to the car in the back driveway and lie on the floor of the backseat.

Masturbation had taken hold at this time, as well. I discovered it by mistake while climbing a pole one day on the playground. The pleasure took me out of this world and into a place of peace. Sadly, that became a bondage that would last for thirty years.

But on this occasion, none of those escapes would suffice. I needed to get out of there in order to keep my sanity, so I made my plan. In my good-bye note to my parents, I wrote, "I'm running away. You don't care about me, and I don't want to live here anymore. Sincerely, David."

I left the note on my bed, sneaked down the stairs and slipped out the front door. I could hear the rest of the family watching TV in the back of the house. *If they only knew what they've done to me*, I thought. It was not so much about my most recent episode of being overdisciplined. It was the buildup of something I perceived as a coldhearted lack of concern. My parents had never once asked me about my thoughts or feelings, and instead made snap judgments and spouted orders without a moment's consideration. I felt like a thing and not a person.

I had not, however, chosen the best possible night for my brave expedition. It was about nine o'clock by the time I left, and it was literally freezing cold outside. The minute I stepped onto the icy sidewalk, I almost gave up. *No*, I thought to myself, *I'm really going to do this. Once I'm gone, they're going to be sorry that they never loved me. They'll feel even worse when I'm found murdered on some highway. Or frozen to death.*

I walked up one street in the neighborhood and down the next, eventually finding it impossible to go any farther. I felt as if an unseen force with very cold hands was holding me back. When I started shivering uncontrollably, I realized that this was absolutely the worst time of year for running away. I thought, *Maybe I had better rethink my plan.*

I skulked back to the house and hid out in the furnace room inside the garage. Crouching down on the floor, I was quickly won over by the heat. I also realized how ridiculous I looked and how humiliated I would be when they found me.

About an hour later, my oldest brother came tearing into the garage, looking for me. My family had found my note, but my brother felt certain that I would not go far. After reporting my presence in the furnace room to Mom, he returned with orders for me to go to her bedroom. I had expected the worst sort of smug humiliation from him, but oddly enough, he did not seem to be gloating. Later, I would learn that he had struggled with his own sense of being unloved by Dad. Perhaps, for the moment, he was sharing in my suffering.

Mom was sitting on the bed as I entered. Dad was curiously absent. I realized that the two of them had decided to take a soft approach. What a relief! This was completely unprecedented. Clearly it was an experiment on their part—perhaps something Mom had read about in a parenting book.

"David, if there's anything that's bothering you, I want you to know that you can come to me," she started.

Oh yeah, right, I thought to myself. *She's using child psychology on me again. If I tell her what's really bothering me, she'll lay into me for being a self-centered, spoiled brat.*

I remained silent. There was no way I could articulate the overwhelming distress that had built up in my heart. At that age, a child knows he or she feels unloved deep inside, but cannot find the words to explain it. Nor could I imagine, no matter what I told her, that she and Dad would change their ways.

Once that session ended, I retreated to my room, thinking, *Man, what a total waste of time*. Even as I left Mom without answering her, I desperately wanted to explain myself. But young as I was, I was already unwilling to risk having my emotions dishonored or discounted. In any case, that was the first and last time I got the "good cop" treatment.

At the beginning of these pages, I described a traumatic confrontation I had with my father after trying to run away from home a second time. Like all kids, I was trying to get attention. But I also genuinely wanted to run away from my household and its explosive, exhausting way of life. I wanted to start over somewhere else and become someone else. Perhaps I also wanted to say—without words—that my father's idea of parenting did not match up very well with his super-saint church persona.

It was not long after that terrible confrontation with Dad that another idea impressed itself on me—suicide. It is often said that those who survive suicide do not really want to die; they simply want help in living and encouragement in being alive. Did I really want to die? Part of me certainly did. Maybe the son-of-my-father wanted to disappear. Maybe the highly sensitive youngster wanted to evade the slings and arrows that made his life unbearable. All I knew was that the pain in my heart from feeling rejected and unloved had risen to such a level that I was ready to do anything to make it go away.

By this time, my sense of being unloved had become a conviction that I was unlovable. Self-hatred had begun to seethe from every pore. Often, I would come home from school and stare into the mirror, berating myself for being ugly, short, defective and just plain bad. I would look at my image and say things like, "I hate you!" If no one was home, I would yell it at the top of my lungs.

One thing is clear, though. In the years that followed, on the many occasions when I tried to take my own life, a stronger Hand than my own thwarted me. I do not believe I hoped to be rescued. To the contrary, I believe God intervened and saved me *in spite of* my best efforts to kill myself.

It was shortly after that second runaway attempt that I considered for the first time the possibility of taking my life. I cannot remember what form my disobedience took the day I first thought about it, but as usual, I had been sent to my room. Lying on my bed, I pleaded with God to make my parents love me—to make *anyone* love me. I had been praying this prayer for years now, and God did not seem to be listening.

The more I thought about it, the more disheartened I felt. I concluded that I was simply defective—too fallen a creature to be loved, even by my Creator. Perhaps it was because of my continuous disobedience, but for some unknown reason, I felt that God did not seem to care much about me.

Despair overwhelmed me. I sat on my bed and cried for an hour. As the minutes ticked by, I gradually convinced myself that I should just kill myself to end the pain. The idea took root in my imagination, and I began to deliberate on how I might be able to do it.

I could hang myself, but what if it doesn't work? I considered. *I might end up paralyzed, so that's out. I could poison myself, but I don't have any poison. My only option*, I finally decided, *is to throw myself down the stairs and break my neck.*

I ran for the stairs, but as I got closer, fear gripped me and I slowed down, barely teetering on the edge. Backing up, I took a second run at it. Again, fear overwhelmed me as the possibility of paralysis threatened this method, too. One last time, mustering all the misery I could summon, I ran to the top of the stairs. I threw myself, half-falling and half-sliding, down to the bottom. I landed on my side and made a lot of noise, but I was basically unhurt.

At that moment, Mother appeared and began screaming at me, "*You've been sent to your room! How DARE you leave it!*"

She went on and on. What a nightmare. She had not a clue what I had really been up to. Then she began hitting me, which jolted me out of my stupor. I hightailed it back up to my room and tumbled into bed, where I thought I would never stop crying.

Naturally, as always, I fell asleep and was back at school the next day. Before long, I found myself involved in our usual schoolyard activities—all pleasant diversions from the grief that ebbed and flowed inside me, just below the surface. At recess, a group of us often got together to play dodgeball. There were few sports I was consistently good at, but this was one of them. It was almost impossible to throw me out. T.J. was the only guy with an arm fast enough and strong enough to do it. He also knew my moves from our times on the playground.

As good as I was, though, to be honest I would say that our friend William was slightly better. William was the only one who could stay in the dodgeball ring as long as I could. In fact, he was the only one who sometimes stayed in longer. As such, he threatened to rob me of my lone championship role. If he had not been such a great guy, I would have hated him.

One particular day, I was in top form. In fact, I was king of the universe—at least in dodgeball. William was going down. The circle gathered, with about twenty on the outside and fifteen on the inside. The first few volleys picked off the noncontenders, and we were quickly down to five. One by one the next three were hit, as the outside circle increased with the numbers of those who had been thrown out, some of whom were good throwers.

Finally, it came down to William and me. At this point, whoever caught the ball on the opposite side of the circle, after it had been thrown, automatically tossed it to one of the top throwers. So William and I were continuously targeted by the big guns—nonstop, fast and furious. Then it happened—I masterfully dodged a wickedly brilliant throw from T.J., and the guy who caught the ball caught William asleep and nailed him. What a great moment in sports history—at least in *my* sports history.

Looking back, I can trace the metaphor our game embodied. Expertise at dodgeball mirrored my growing proficiency at dodging reality. Deep down, I knew being rebellious at home was wrong, but I justified it in my mind by citing the hypocrisy in our household. Together, my friends and I dodged the truth. We knew cigarettes were bad for you. We knew lying to our parents was wrong. We knew pulling mean-spirited pranks on people was wrong. And when some of us set the woods on fire one afternoon and acted like innocent bystanders instead of calling the fire department, we knew it was bad. Instead of facing reality, we dodged the truth.

Yes, we played it well, but how long could we stay in the game?

— 3 —

DIVERSION and DISTRACTION

Diversion and distraction often feel like great assets to wounded people. Even chronic depression can be lifted temporarily by activities that refocus our attention, and especially by actions that include an element of risk. As a boy, I was already learning the basics of the avoidance game, which included addictive behavior. For me, that addictive behavior started out with movies, music and girls.

For a while, I found ways of escaping reality that did not put me much at risk. Returning from a trip to New York, my parents brought back the soundtrack from the Broadway play they had attended, *The Music Man*. I played that album over and over, memorizing every single word. In doing so, I opened a door into the world of creative imagination, a great escape hatch during times of turmoil.

I did not like Robert Preston as the Music Man. He was too old for the part and not pure enough to be a knight in shining armor—a role I fancied myself playing one day. The role he played was that of a scoundrel—a liar, a con man and an older guy trying to deceive a young girl. Still, I was captivated by the love story about how a reluctant girl could be won over by a persistent suitor. It was the satisfying fulfillment of my own attempts at attracting less-than-enthusiastic girls.

This musical embodied so many aspects of my own secret world. It was a surprising revelation to me that anyone on earth could know and understand the hopes and dreams that I thought were mine alone—let alone depict them in a play. Yet there they were, portrayed up on the stage, my hopes and dreams of falling in love with a beautiful girl, of being loved by her and of being a charismatic personality whom people would look up to and follow.

After enjoying that album obsessively, I eagerly awaited the soundtrack of every Broadway musical that came along. Fortunately, my mother also loved Broadway shows, so we ended up with quite a selection of soundtracks.

Then there were the movies. Easton's sole movie theater was called the Avalon, and it soon became my sanctuary. When it opened in 1921, it sparkled with leaded glass doors at every entrance and an 18-foot dome that glowed with 148 lights. There was a 300-pipe electric-pneumatic organ, an electric player piano and a ballroom on the second floor. When the Schine Chain Theatres bought it in 1934, they closed the ballroom and redesigned it with an Art Deco theme. Over the years, three world premieres took place at the Avalon, including *The First Kiss* starring Gary Cooper and Fay Wray, which was filmed in Easton and Saint Michaels, Maryland.

The Avalon was my favorite source of alternative reality. Except for Disney films, which cost 35 cents, movies cost only a quarter in those days—the same as a pack of cigarettes. Once I had sunk into one of the velvety seats, with an imagination like mine, I was able to transform myself into anyone I wanted. I would remain transfixed for six or seven hours at a time. By then I had thoroughly soaked up the essence of the leading characters, and their lives became mine. *This* was my world, not the one in my unhappy home.

One day I would become John Wayne, swaggering and pontificating in *The Longest Day*. Another day I would turn into Lawrence of Arabia, sweeping across the desert on my camel, my Bedouin garb billowing behind me. Or I was Henry Higgins, properly instructing Eliza Doolittle about how to enunciate her words. Or I transformed into Omar Sharif as Doctor Zhivago, struggling against the forces trying to tear him away from his one true love.

Unfortunately, when the final curtain closed, I had to return to my house and all it represented. My father did not like my preoccupation with movies, and he expressed his disapproval by leaving me standing outside the shuttered theater late at night, sometimes for an hour or more, before coming to pick me up. Many a cold Saturday night, I would find myself leaning against the theater building until midnight, the streets dark and empty, waiting for Dad.

I could not have imagined that in a few short years, I would be standing on other street corners, waiting for men I had never met to notice me and pick me up.

Movies and music were a little like drugs—I used them to escape my daily life rather than trying to figure out how to deal with it. But once the movie ended or the song stopped playing, I would return to the real world and find it just as unpleasant as it had been before. At the same time, the arts were building into me a passion for the dramatic, along with a yearning for a happy ending. That set the stage for me to truly "live the fantasy." Before long, an idea began to materialize: *Wouldn't it be great to be in show business?* Perhaps the merging of my fantasies with real life would put a stop to my endless frustrations and disappointments—especially those with girls.

Like Sally, for instance. That year Sally had swept into our classroom from out of nowhere. She was bright and vivacious, a pretty blonde with blue eyes. I took note that she was a little taller than I, but so was everyone else. I loved her smile, her energy and her tremendous sense of humor. Of course, with all her charms she instantly became popular, and thus beyond my reach.

Nevertheless, I thought about Sally all the time. At night in my room, instead of studying, I dreamed about her for hours on end. Who could study with such a girl on his mind? It was impossible. My feelings were too intense, however, and I was too vulnerable to risk potential rejection. I never mustered the courage to actually phone her and try to get to know her, as I had done with so many other girls.

Instead, I decided to mail an anonymous love letter to Sally. I was captivated with the romantic idea of being a secret admirer. And what a relief it was to pour out my feelings toward her at last, knowing that she could not possibly reject me when she did not know I was the author. I was content with the idea.

Once I found the courage to actually mail the letter, I fantasized about Sally reading it and falling in love with whoever had written it. I imagined her finding out I was the writer and taking pleasure in that discovery. I envisioned a moment when I would offer her a friendship ring. Maybe we would soon be going steady, and we would eventually become king and queen of the prom.

One secret letter turned into two, then three, and probably five or six before it all came unraveled. That happened because I made a mistake, describing my house to her under the assumption that she had never seen it. She lived out in the country, so it never crossed my mind that she would figure out which house was mine.

One afternoon while I was standing beside my desk at school, I heard giggles and the chatter of female voices emanating from the cloakroom. I could not determine what they were talking about, but they seemed giddy with excitement. Suddenly, one of the girls in my class rushed up to me.

"David," she smiled, "do you live in a gray house?"

I must have looked puzzled. "Yes. . . ."

"Is it a two-story house?" she continued.

Again I answered yes, still oblivious to what was happening. I had never imagined that the girls would all commiserate, combing my letters for clues as to the authorship. But that is what had happened. One of the girls realized from the description of my house that I might be the one. When I unwittingly confirmed their suspicion, the mystery was solved.

I suppose I had known all along that Sally would never date someone like me. But my dream world melted into a dark pool of woe when she emerged from behind the cloakroom and stared at me with a look of disgust and incredulity. It was not the expression of delight that I had dreamed of. It was a look of bewilderment and disappointment, and it devastated me. Without a word, she communicated that she had nothing to say to me. And what was even worse, all the girls in the class were delighted witnesses of my supreme humiliation. It was a grace of sorts that Sally never spoke to me again. Coming from her, words of rejection would have been unbearable.

But another year, another Sally. This Sally was petite, dark and beautiful, and she somehow made me think of a Hawaiian princess. For months, we talked on the phone after school about absolutely nothing at all, and we did so for hours at a time. I was in love again, and once again it was with a girl entirely out of my league. As usual, despite the amount of time we spent on the phone, my love was unrequited. But with such lovely dreams and fantasies spinning around in my mind, I chose not to notice.

Our phone calls involved chitchat about school and music, including the Beatles and other popular bands. I asked her for a date on several occasions, but she always declined. I never knew why, and she never would say. For that matter, I did not know why she continued to talk to me if she did not share my affection. She lived only two blocks away, but I never went to her house and she never came to mine.

Rather than giving up, however, I upped the ante. In addition to the phone calls, I began to write letters to her. These were love letters, as before, where I could say things I would never say directly to her for fear of rejection. In one final letter, I poured out my heartfelt love and asked her to go steady with me. I even enclosed a friendship ring that I had carefully picked out from McCrory's department store.

What did I expect? As usual, I was too enraptured to think clearly. The day after she received that last letter, she flounced into the classroom and sat down at the desk in front of me. She spun around and opened her closed fist, dropping the ring on my desk. Then she left the room as quickly as she had entered. She never said a word. But once again the message was clear—I was not good enough.

Girlfriends (real and imagined) came and went. Each rejection hardened my heart a little more. Then I turned twelve, and it was a banner year of sorts. I was a Boy Scout, and I had recently added *Playboy* magazine to my reading list, along with *Archie*, *Dennis the Menace* and *Mad* magazines. The combination of pornography and masturbation had become my favorite escape from reality—a combination that would increasingly control my thoughts and actions for decades.

A Holy Moment

Meanwhile, I had struck an unspoken bargain with God. I would ignore Him if He would ignore me. It was a difficult truce to keep, however, because my anger toward Him was always simmering beneath the surface—all the more so as I entered adolescence. How could a loving God give me a father like mine? And why didn't He help me with the strange feelings and sexual obsessions that were tormenting me? Girls did not want me, and I felt unaffirmed and unacceptable as a male.

I found myself staring at other boys, trying to figure out why many of them did not accept me, either. I wondered what I needed to do to change that. I studied their walk, the way they talked to girls, the way they combed their hair—anything that might give me a clue about why they were so popular and successful as males. Meanwhile, my obsessions grew darker and more confusing every day, as did my estrangement from God.

Then one Sunday morning, God broke our truce. I was sitting in the front row at church. With no one in the row but me, I could swing my legs back and forth without getting pinched by Mom, and I could scribble on the guest cards with one of the little pencils that were in the back of every pew.

But what happened that Sunday took me completely by surprise.

For me, church meant boredom. We were Presbyterians after all, which meant there was no display of emotion in our services, but rather a precise and uninterrupted movement through the morning worship hour, precisely as it was laid out in the Sunday bulletin. If God Himself had walked into the sanctuary during the service, He would have been asked to wait to be seated until the next hymn. And the service had to end at 12:00 noon—sharp. No variations, no surprises.

It was the week before Christmas, and the anthem for the service, as usual, was my favorite Christmas song, "O Holy Night." But on this occasion, the vocalist sounded like an angel sent from heaven.

As I sat there enraptured by her voice and the words of the song, something extraordinary happened—something unprecedented.

Jesus Christ became present in the sanctuary. I was suddenly surrounded by His love, which was pure, affirming and completely irresistible. Did anyone else feel His presence as I did? I will never know. But in that moment, my heart was taken captive by His love.

I had always loved Jesus. It was God the Father I hated, because of the association I had drawn between my own father and God. I did not understand that Jesus, God the Father and the Holy Spirit were One. I only knew that I loved Jesus, now even more deeply.

As it turned out, the experience and timing were God's grace shoring up my capacity to survive the perceived torments and trials of my young life. The words of the song touched me: "A thrill of hope, the weary soul rejoices, for yonder breaks a new and glorious morn. . . ."

The new beginning, the "glorious morn" I longed for, was still years away. But Jesus' loving presence enabled me to endure the deep psychic pain that was intensifying in me with every passing day. And somehow, that brief encounter strengthened me for the future and for the traumas that lay just ahead, arriving all too soon in the ensuing years.

PART TWO

HIGHER EDUCATION

What kind of life does a person have when its greatest moment involves making a great play during a softball game?

Okay, I am from a small town where great moments may not all have been earthshaking, but as Peggy Lee asked in her song title, "Is That All There Is?"

Yet even from such a lowly height as that, it is amazing how quickly a person can fall headlong into the deepest and darkest of chasms.

College inaugurated my descent into hell, beginning with the darkest of sexual awakenings and ending with darker things still.

What mix of emotions and events conspire to convince a person to end his or her life?

And how can someone ever rise again from such hopelessness?

— 4 —

INTO the FOG

Most parents experience varying degrees of anxiety as they send their children away to college. Innumerable stories describe berserk freshmen tasting, and then devouring, every kind of forbidden fruit. Do all parents have reason to worry? To some degree, yes. Did mine? They could not have imagined how many taboos I would break, how quickly and with what enormous enthusiasm, once I "got out of Dodge."

Florida Presbyterian College (FPC) in St. Petersburg was the site of my grandest escape yet. It provided the ultimate "run away from home" adventure, in which I would be leaving my loveless household once and for all. I was determined to discover what the real world had to offer. Nothing was going to stop me. And yet, even though freedom was at hand, my father managed to ruin my first semester of school—even though he was not actually there.

My college days arrived during the height of the hippie era. Naturally, my parents were opposed to any style, idea or trend that reflected the counterculture. Since my short hair had begun to grow dangerously close to my ears over the summer, Dad demanded that I have a crew cut before he would deliver me to campus.

Like most college freshmen, I was concerned with making a stellar first impression on my new classmates. I more than suspected that a crew cut was going to sabotage any hopes of fitting in and being accepted. I had tried to tell my father no, but the effort was, as usual, futile. Instead, I entered the dormitory looking like a fresh military recruit for the Vietnam War. This sent an unfortunate message to everyone I met for the first time—that I was for the war, a jock, or worse, a nerd.

It was 1969, and the students were an intriguing mix of long hairs (freaks) and short hairs (jocks). They were primarily white middle-class kids who did not know what they wanted to do with their lives. Those were the years of the Vietnam War, and a good number of young men simply wanted to avoid the draft. An even larger number of "long-haired hippie freaks" were into the latest "tune in and turn on" lifestyle.

What neither my parents nor I realized was that this small church-sponsored college was a notorious hotbed of sex, drugs, rock 'n' roll and rebellion against the established order. Even some of the professors were radical rebels. I was leaving the world of "yes, sir" and "no, ma'am" and entering a universe of "far out," "dude," "power to the people" and "if it feels good, do it."

The cafeteria was called Slater's, after the company that ran it, and the food was questionable at best. Opposite the entrance to Slater's was a small structure on which students periodically painted peace symbols or scribbled slogans such as "Stop the War!" or "Impeach Nixon!" or more esoteric things like "God is in your mind" or "I am the walrus." Everyone except the jocks had long hair, and most of the girls did not wear bras. Almost no one wore shoes.

The school was located on Florida's central West Coast, so the weather was almost always hot, humid and sunny. We sat under old oak trees laden with Spanish moss, while some of the kids played their guitars and sang just for fun. The cars of choice were '57 Chevys, '65 Mustangs and VW Beetles and vans. FPC introduced an odd and interesting array of guest speakers to the campus. They hosted the imperial wizard of the Ku Klux Klan there my first year (1969), but except for William F. Buckley Jr., no other conservatives were invited. It was a liberal campus, welcoming the likes of George McGovern, Angela Davis and Stokely Carmichael.

In 1972, Jack Eckerd, a well-known drug store magnate at the time, offered FPC $12 million. The college basically responded by saying, "Forget the Presbyterian Church; we'll take the money!" The name was changed to Eckerd College. The irony of the name change was soon displayed in a T-shirt surreptitiously sold in the campus underground. It displayed the Eckerd Drug Store logo on the back, with the words *Eckerd Drug College* underneath. And it was true. Our campus was a haven for drug dealers and users. For public relations purposes, the administration forbade the police from coming on campus uninvited, so drugs were everywhere. Even the dean of students grew marijuana plants at his house.

This was the place where my strict Covenanter parents had left me. They had assumed, of course, that FPC was an institution that would continue fostering the discipline and values they had drilled into me at home. Instead, they left me at a recruiting station for pretty much everything they found detestable.

It was fine with me. I had finally made my great escape!

When I first arrived at FPC, my roommate was not there yet, so I settled in on my own. Being fairly shy about meeting new people, I elected not to visit the neighboring rooms. Instead, one by one, guys would appear in the doorway to say hello. One of them, Josh, had dirty-blond hair pulled back into a small ponytail. I had been so sheltered that I had never imagined someday meeting a man with a ponytail.

Finally, my mystery roommate appeared. He was tall and thin, with a bandanna wrapped around his long hair. He walked with a low glide, as though trying to sneak past everyone. He did not make a sound when he walked, so you never knew, without turning around and looking, whether he was there or not.

"I'm Marshall," he introduced himself, looking at my crew cut with a mixture of fear and suspicion. He had a nasal-sounding lisp.

I had my own suspicions about him, too. *The guy's on drugs,* I warned myself. *How am I going to handle this?*

Marshall came and went during the next week or so, as I dutifully sat at my desk and studied every afternoon and evening. One afternoon, I returned to my room to find that it had been evenly divided down the middle by a tie-dyed sheet. I felt a little hurt, but Marshall was so eccentric that I was not altogether surprised. On any given day, the most he could muster was a reluctant "Hi," grunted more than spoken. Why was he so silent and secretive, not to mention weird? Half the time, he came in through the window rather than the door.

The following week, I entered our room to find that the simple tie-dyed sheet divider had become an entire canopy, with a roof and door made from sheets and blankets. Marshall had completely enclosed himself, and I felt humiliated. We had not even had an argument, but it was clear that he wanted nothing to do with me. He, along with the others in my dorm, stirred up old feelings of loneliness and depression. I had dreamed that college would allow me to escape a sense of constant disapproval, but there it was again.

Still, I sat at my desk every afternoon and evening, reading my books and writing my papers. It was quite a challenge, especially when a strong, foreign odor began emanating from Marshall's tent. *It must be incense*, I thought at first. *But what if it's marijuana?* I soon learned that not only was it marijuana, but Marshall and his equally freaky friends were blowing smoke out the cracks of the tent so that I would get a contact high.

Within six months, Marshall moved out, and Josh next door got busted for having a marijuana plant in his room. Everyone was convinced that I was the narc who turned him in.

Joining the Freaks

Despite the disappointments of the past, I wanted to meet some girls. In my romantic fantasies, I dreamed I would find "the right one," and she would provide the lifetime of love and acceptance for which I hungered. At least, I imagined, I might experience for myself some of the magic that young lovers were sharing all around me.

One night I made my way over to a dance being held in a nearby auditorium. What an awkward scene! With a cluster of unattached guys, I stood watching the couples dancing. We were all scoping out the fringes of the crowd for attractive, available girls. For me, the fear of approaching a girl, only to get turned down in front of everyone, was almost paralyzing. Finally, I noticed that one girl was dancing with a different guy for every song. It looked as if she might be

My sophomore year at Florida Presbyterian College in 1970 soon after growing my hair out and becoming a part of the community of hippies who dominated the student body.

Several years later my college had changed its name to Eckerd and I had acquired a very hard shell from taking dangerous levels of drugs and two suicide attempts after a dark fall into extreme sexual immorality.

open to meeting someone new, so I took my chance.

"Hi. You want to dance?" I asked.

"Sure," she replied with a shrug of her shoulders.

I was so relieved that I began to think about scoring on an entirely different level. I was, after all, free from all parental restraint. Would I ever have this chance again?

She seemed to like me, so as we danced I pressed myself against her. Wonder of wonders, she pressed back. After a few more dances, I asked her if she wanted to come back to my room to listen to some music.

"Sure," she said again. This time she did not shrug.

I thought I had won the lottery.

We went back to my room and were soon making out on my bed. It was clear that she wanted to go all the way. Suddenly it hit me—I did not have a clue what to do next. Just then, the ladies' man of the dorm strolled into my room unannounced. He had on nothing but his underwear.

"Hey man, what's happening? Oops! Sorry, dude, I didn't know," he said. Then he glanced at the girl and said, "Oh, hi, Jill. How are you? Haven't seen you in a while."

My first thought was, *If she's friends with him, and he's in his underwear and she doesn't care, she is one loose chick. In fact, she probably has VD.* My excitement was over. After a few more courtesy kisses, I asked if she wanted me to walk her back to her dorm. She got the message and politely declined, and we never saw each other again.

This unsuccessful encounter made me more than aware that, as usual, I was utterly alone. I was getting nowhere in my endless quest for love. I had no close friends, and no one seemed the least bit interested in being friendly with me on more than a superficial level.

At the same time, my boyhood had taught me more than enough about rebellion, and my present surroundings offered me nearly unlimited opportunities to spurn my family's values. Perhaps it was inevitable that I would choose to immerse myself in the one thing that offered the most effective escape from pain and loneliness.

I decided to join the freaks.

The room was dark, and as I entered, someone drew back an inner curtain to let me pass. I remember thinking how exotic and clandestine the whole setup was. Inside, a lit candle burned. Twelve people were seated in a circle. I did not know it at the time, but there was great expectation in the room because I was a "virgin"—a new initiate and therefore long sought after as a conquest.

I was jittery inside, and my heart was racing. *What if this stuff kills me?* I thought. *What if it causes me to lose control and act like an idiot?*

I found an empty space in the circle and sat on the floor. No one greeted me. Had I heard a few snickers? I was glad the room was too dark to distinguish faces.

Soon came an anticipated nudge. I took the joint between my fingers, as I had seen the others do, pursed my lips and sucked in the hot smoke. I made sure not to take in too much so I would not cough, choke or otherwise make a fool of myself. Yet at the same time, I was careful to make enough of a drawing sound so it would appear that I had taken a giant hit—puffing out my chest and holding my breath for the obligatory ten seconds, then making a great show with a hearty exhale.

One by one, the others took their turns as I watched. The circle was large enough that it was a full minute or more before the joint came around again. This time the guy next to me turned to face me. It was Josh, the well-mannered, pony-tailed hippie freak from Tennessee who lived in the room next to mine. He was the one who had gotten busted for growing marijuana in his room. Maybe he wanted to make sure that if I was the one who had turned him in, I would never do it again. He inverted the joint and placed it halfway into his mouth, and then he moved toward me as though he were going to kiss me. Totally confused, I leaned away from him. Muffled laughter erupted all over the room.

"Come on, man. Don't pull back. I just want to give you a 'shotgun,'" Josh protested, half smiling. Not wanting to seem uncool, I remained still while he brought his lips within an inch of mine. With the joint still inverted in his mouth, he blew. An intense, steady stream of smoke poured into my open mouth.

And, out of nowhere, an unexpected erotic thrill shot through me like a bolt of lightning.

The marijuana was much too potent a dose for my virgin lungs to tolerate, and I went into spasms of coughing that lasted a full two minutes. The rest of the group broke into laughter. But by then, the marijuana had already begun to take effect. In a relaxed, happy way, I perceived everyone's laughter as sounds of acceptance. As soon as I could stop coughing, a smile appeared on my face for the first time.

By the third joint my heart was racing, and I started to perspire profusely. Suddenly anxious, I was afraid I would have a heart attack. Then, as if returning to normal time, I seemed to regain consciousness, though in an altered form. It was as if I were in another world, floating on clouds of smoke. I felt marvelous!

This was just what I wanted, the perfect escape from reality. It was like a movie playing in my own head. The dope had me.

Days, weeks, months and years of pain and loneliness simply disappeared, and I felt wonderful. Would the heartache eventually return? I did not care. No fear of the future crossed my mind. Instead, in an instant, I became firmly chained to the pleasure of the "now," immediately enslaved by this new alchemy of mind alteration. Gazing up at a poster on the wall, I began to hallucinate. The old woman rolling a joint in the image gradually morphed into the lusty face of a familiar sexpot.

"Hey guys!" I pointed to the poster. "It's Marilyn Monroe!"

Josh was one of the few coherent people in the room by that time. It took him about ten seconds, but he finally burst into laughter.

"Hey, dudes . . . Foster's seein' Marilyn Monroe!"

It gave them all great pleasure to watch my innocence being corrupted. It was the supreme high for them, and I was only too happy to give them what they wanted. Only later did I recall that I had done the same for T.J. when I had dropped my pants almost a decade before. In each case, I just wanted the pain to go away. And in each case, I noticed the extreme pleasure that people seemed to experience in the act of taking away my innocence.

From that point on, I was able to relax into the interior fantasies conjured by various drugs and forget the pain of my childhood—at least until the high wore off. Marijuana was the perfect drug for me because it took me into a fantasy world where everything was peaceful, everybody was peaceable and I felt good about myself for a change. Even if things were going wrong, marijuana gave me an attitude of not caring so much, thereby providing relief from everyday pressures. As I grew deeper into my addiction, I would smoke hash or weed (or eat it baked in brownies) from the time I awoke till I went to sleep early the next morning. Staying stoned was the answer to all my troubles.

Before long, LSD was added to the mix. That was much more frightening—everyone knew that bad trips on it were extremely unpleasant. I was afraid at first, but my friends convinced me I would enjoy it, and I knew it would give them pleasure to see my innocence lost once again. Some of the trips really were amazing, but I had a few others during which everything became evil and frightening. When you are on LSD, it remains active in your system for twelve hours. If you find yourself on a bad trip, you just have to live with it. That feeling of being trapped with no way to do anything about it was too reminiscent of my childhood, so I only did LSD when pressed by friends.

We also did PCP, psilocybin, crystal meth, opium, hashish, speed, reds (Seconal), yellow jackets (another barbiturate), Quaaludes (which made you highly sexual), cocaine and even marijuana treated in heroin, which we called herojuana. Taking straight heroin, however, was a red line I would not cross, in large part because I hated needles. But I also feared the drug itself and the people I would have to associate with to get it.

Life is strange. Though my new friends would never have accepted me had I not done drugs, some of them became the best and closest friends I have ever had. We were partners in pain, even though we never spoke about our wounds to one another. We simply fled our losses together, in silence. We who were deeply broken on the inside were tired of pretending otherwise, so we admired each other for what strength we had and celebrated our hurts in a bizarre ritual of friendship. Those friendships made it much harder for us to see our drug use as a destructive force.

Sexual Awakenings

Drugs, however, were not my only escape. When masturbation had entered my life back around the age of nine, I had quickly learned how to put the feeling it produced to work. Like a drug,

70

its power to temporarily alleviate emotional pain caused me to turn to it obsessively. Self-pleasure became my number-one solace and source of anesthesia when I was feeling stressed, rejected or unloved.

At nine years old, I had not yet connected the sensation I felt with sexual thoughts or images, but porn soon changed all that. I became obsessed with *Playboy* during my stint in the Boy Scouts. Our local drug store stocked several books that were very risqué for the time, such as *Candy* and *Lady Chatterley's Lover*. I sneaked into the store after school on an almost daily basis and read the dirty parts. The clerk did not seem to mind. When *Penthouse* magazine came out, it became my favorite, especially the letters to the editor in which people told stories of their sexual encounters. It was also the first mainstream soft-core porn magazine that included men in the pictures, which subtly fueled my burgeoning homosexual confusion.

Over the years, masturbation and pornography became the perfect solution to my fear of rejection, or so it seemed. I could take care of my sexual needs without the risk of being turned down by real partners. The men and women in the pornographic pictures were safe. They *could not* reject me. They would always be pleased with my "performance." They never demanded anything from me—unlike some of the girls I had met along the way.

My first opportunity to have sex with a girl had come too suddenly, the night Jill had come back to my dorm room and I had been too nervous to really do anything about it. The next chance had come a short time later, with a waitress at the local Howard Johnson's. It was my first summer vacation from college, and I refused to go home to Easton. Instead, I stayed in St. Petersburg and kept working my job as a dishwasher and busboy. I had been working at the restaurant for several months when a new manager arrived on the scene—a buxom Swedish redhead. And she was not the only addition to the staff. Two sisters from

New Jersey were soon working as waitresses. Maria was nineteen and very pretty. She had the thickest Jersey accent imaginable, an aggressive attitude and big, dyed-blonde hair with a ringlet that curled in front of her right ear. Melinda was seventeen, a brunette with the same accent. She competed continuously with her better-looking sister for male attention and affection. The two of them were like something out of *American Graffiti* or *Jersey Shore*. It seemed fairly obvious from the start that these girls had, as they say, been around the block.

Maria asked me for a ride home one night and invited me in for a beer. I was suffering from a slight temperature and was not feeling especially playful. Maria tried her best, but I ended up passing out on the bed from the alcohol and the fever. She put a record on to get me in the mood—Dusty Springfield's "Son of a Preacher Man"—but the last thing I remember was hearing a frustrated sigh as she watched my eyes close in sleep. Evidently no one had ever turned Maria down before, so that was my last invitation to her house.

Not long after that, I met a girl I will call Sara. She was a classic hippie chick, very friendly, easygoing and mellow. She had slept with several of my friends and had repeatedly made it clear that she was available to me, too. Finally one night we had intercourse, and it turned out to be just about all that I had hoped for.

Sara and I kept seeing each other informally for a while. Then I became conscious of a vague discomfort lingering in the back of my mind. As wonderful an experience as my relationship with Sara turned out to be, I could not escape the feeling that something was missing. Why hadn't our pleasurable interlude filled the emotional void inside me?

I began to think that it had to do with men, not women. In the past, unexpected contact with a boy or a man had sexually electrified me. I could clearly remember the shocking erotic thrill

I felt when Josh had given me a shotgun of marijuana. And the porn that captivated me was far from limited to images of women. This left me with a devastating conclusion: Somehow I had a deep-seated craving that a woman could not completely fill. I did not want it to be true. But it was.

I can still remember the evening when I told Sara that I could not sleep with her anymore until I got this "other problem" resolved. She had been wondering why I had been avoiding her advances in recent days. It seemed only right to mollify her insecurities by telling her the truth.

The thing that frightened me most was when she reacted to the news by saying, "I knew it!"

How did she know it? I wondered. *Is there something obvious about me that telegraphs it to everyone?*

— 5 —

The BEST DAY
of MY LIFE

By my third year of college, I was nearly suffocating in feelings of insecurity and self-loathing—made worse than ever by an unmanageable drug addiction and a struggle with same-sex attraction that I did not want to have. If I had seen a psychiatrist, the diagnosis surely would have included serious clinical depression. Then, out of nowhere, along came a moment of joy that, for a short time, put me on top of the world. Once again, it was the thrill of success in a sporting event that temporarily lifted my troubled soul from the depths to the heavens.

It was baseball season, and our school was encouraging us all to participate in intramural softball games. Each dorm complex was challenged to field a competitive team. Joining such a team was something I normally would never have done, but maybe I could not say no because I loved baseball so much. Or perhaps I joined the team in a desperate attempt to pull myself out of depression and the drug stupor that dominated my days.

Whatever my motivation, before long I found myself on a baseball diamond, standing just a few steps off second base. There were not enough mitts to go around, so I had to field barehanded. It was the seventh inning. The other team had runners on first and second, so I mentally prepared for what I would do if the ball came to me. I did not want to panic. After all, the überjock of the entire college was pitching for our team. Committing an error in front of *the* alpha male during my crisis of masculinity would have finished me off psychologically.

Suddenly, the batter hit a screaming line drive directly at me. Instinct kicked in, thanks to the hundreds of games I had played at the neighborhood ball field in Easton and the countless major league games I had listened to on the radio. Well seasoned or not, I knew exactly what to do.

First, I caught the ball so soundly that it did not even sting my hands. The batter was finished. Out one!

Since I had caught a fly ball, the runners had to turn back and touch the bases they had just left, or they would be out. I quickly took two steps to my right and stepped on second base before the runner could return. Out two!

In a moment of time so brief that it could only be recorded in nanoseconds, I spun around toward first base and instantly saw that my moment of glory had come. The runner from first had led off so far that he could easily be thrown out as he scrambled to get back.

For once I did not choke. I zeroed in on the first baseman, who was as intent on catching the ball as I was on throwing it straight. It was his moment, too. I rifled it as fast as I could, and it was a perfect throw. To this day, I can hear the solid snap of the ball as it struck the first baseman's mitt dead center. Out three!

Our alpha male pitcher threw his mitt straight up in the air and shouted, *"Triple play! Foster just made a triple play!"*

The rest of the team began cheering, too. In that sublime moment, I was simply a guy succeeding as a guy and being cheered by other men. Later in my room, as I relived my moment of glory, I was moved to tears. It had been the greatest day of my life.

One of my worst days was soon to follow.

— 6 —

GOING OFF
the DEEP END

Despite the male applause I enjoyed after the ball game, on a deeper level I was still reeling from the shock of telling Sara that I was wrestling with homosexual feelings. It was unlike me to disclose the details of my inner self to anyone, much less facts that could embarrass me in the future. Was I gay? It was a secret of mine that I had vowed never to tell anyone—ever. *So why did I tell her?* I kept asking myself.

It really was not such a mystery. Sara and I had been enjoying a sexual relationship, and she was very into it. I also noticed that she seemed to have experienced a lot of rejection. Since I had long felt that same sting in my own life, I did not want to cause similar pain to anyone else, so I had to tell her. I calculated that somehow, saying I was attracted to men would save her from being hurt.

But what about me? I thought.

Uncertain how far the news would travel, and distraught that I had revealed my inner conflict, I determined that I should settle the matter once and for all. I would sleep with one guy, and that would put an end to it. Regrettably, the guys who attracted me were all straight, and there was no way I would jeopardize those friendships. Whom would I choose?

It would have to be one of the homosexuals in the theatre arts crowd. The simplest way to get it over with as quickly as possible, without any risk of failure, was to signal this guy who persistently threw looks and smiles my way. He had already been letting me know that he was interested in me. It sickened me to think of it, but it would have to be Paul.

Paul was everything I feared I was becoming. He was effeminate and cloying. He completely identified with the homosexual underworld, walking around like some Roaring Twenties diva, making a mockery of all that was male and masculine. I also felt sorry for him, which made matters worse. Offering "pity sex" was a weakness that would get me into trouble repeatedly in the future.

That weekend, I drank myself into oblivion to make things easier. Sure enough, at about 2:00 a.m., Paul sauntered into our lounge. One return look from me was all it took, and we were off to his room.

The experience was agony in every possible way. Not only was I not attracted to Paul, but something deep in my soul was being seared. I felt as though I were dying. I felt a profound sadness at the core of my being over finding myself hopelessly trapped in a role that I had not asked for and did not want to play. I was grieved because all my hopes and dreams of finding a girl to love, of having a wife and children to live for, seemed over. That night, my self-hatred exploded into an inferno.

It's God's fault, I told myself. *How many dozens of times have I cried myself to sleep, begging Him to take these attractions from me? Why does He always ignore the most sincere plead-ings of my heart!* My fiery anger at God blazed to new heights.

I never looked at or spoke to Paul after that night.

The next day, I tried to kill myself.

What do you do when you believe you can no longer be re-deemed, spiritually, sexually or otherwise? One option is to end the pain inside you as quickly as possible. I decided to scout around to all my dealer buddies, hoping to score some Seconal, the powerful barbiturate we called reds. One overdose and I would simply fall asleep, never again to wake up. That would make it easy and painless.

Unfortunately, all my friends were pot and hallucinogen deal-ers. Downers were a rare treat brought on campus by people we did not really know. So instead of Seconal, I found someone with LSD—twelve hits of it. I bought them all.

Twelve hits of LSD would normally take about six months to finish off. Each trip would last twelve to fifteen hours, and if it turned out to be a bad trip, it could take weeks to recover. The acid that was available was what we called "orange barrel" and "purple barrel," heavily cut with speed. In fact, the speed alone in those twelve hits of LSD could have killed several people if taken all at once. And who knew what the LSD itself might do?

I decided to walk out into Boca Ciega Bay, which was near my dorm, and drown myself. The LSD would give me the ca-pacity to see it through, especially if I took all twelve hits. That way, my parents and their church could make themselves believe that it had been an accidental drowning or an accidental drug overdose, whichever they preferred.

Without much hesitation, I popped them all.

I knew there would be a wait of one or two hours before the acid kicked in. During that time, while looking out over the water, I began to reminisce about my life. Thoughts of my par-ents began flooding my mind. On the one hand, I did not want to contemplate the tears my mother would shed over me. Nor could I bear the thought of what I assumed my father might say: *That boy was never quite right, you know. There was something wrong with him from the beginning. He was a bad seed, and he got what he deserved.*

Silently I began to argue with Dad: *You never loved me. Now you'll wish you had. You deserve whatever embarrassment this brings upon you.*

But something strange was happening. Two hours into my attempted suicide, neither the LSD nor the speed had kicked in. *Surely it will happen soon,* I kept thinking. In anticipation, I slowly made my way out toward the seawall. It was about 2:00 a.m. and no one was around.

I decided to put my feet into the water to get used to it. Within five minutes, I was all the way in, waist deep. Skimming my hands across the top of the bay while twisting in circles to keep warm, I looked around to make certain no one was watching. The dorm was a good fifty yards away, and not a soul was in sight. I could hear the muffled din of dorm life wafting into the air from Zeta Complex. It was ironic to feel the energy of life and the silence of death pulsing alongside one another. No one in the dorm would have imagined what I was about to do.

Now I was up to my neck in the water, vaguely wondering if a roaming shark might ruin my plans for a peaceful death. At the same time, neither the LSD nor the speed mixed with it had begun to faze me. Normally, just one tab would have smashed into me like a freight train. What was going on?

I looked up at the stars and began to shout at God. *"Why won't You HELP me? Why did You make such a beautiful world and then let it go bad? Why didn't You take away my attractions to guys when I begged You to? Why don't You LOVE me, or at least send someone who will? Why am I here? What good am I? Why don't You ANSWER me?"*

I was too afraid to tell God how much I hated Him. But I did hate Him, and I knew I was going to hell.

As frustrated and angry as I felt, however, I could not deny the exquisite beauty around me. A warm breeze had begun to ripple the water. The stars were glistening. Fleecy clouds, so white that I could see them clearly, raced across the black sky. In the distance, lights were twinkling atop the Sunshine Skyway Bridge.

By then I had lost track of the time. After what seemed like just a few more minutes, I asked myself, *What am I doing out here in the water?*

Perhaps that sudden loss of memory was the most the drugs were going to do for me, or maybe God had simply made me forget my suicidal plan. Either way, I was in the midst of a miracle. Bewildered, I found myself all alone, almost submerged in Boca Ciega Bay's waters, and for no apparent reason. Since it was not unusual for me to awaken from a drug-induced stupor and not know where I was, I simply made my way to shore.

I returned to the dorm, and as I walked into the lounge, I noticed one guy slouched on the couch, watching the *Merv Griffin Show*. Merv was interviewing a boy guru from India named Guru Maharaj Ji. I glanced at the television just long enough to notice the guru, with no idea of the role he would play in my life down the road. At the moment, I had other things on my mind.

Deeper Still

The next day, I called the counseling office at school and asked to see their primary therapist. I was told that he would not be able to meet with me for six months. With uncharacteristic persistence, I told the receptionist that I needed to see him—no one else—and that it had to be *very* soon. I thought that if I was going to go through the agony of telling another person, it could only be someone who had the expertise to actually help me. It also crossed my mind that I should threaten suicide, but I decided it was a bad idea. I did not want to be kicked out of school. I had no place else to go, and returning to my parents' domain would be the worst nightmare I could imagine.

Somehow, I managed to get an appointment scheduled for that Friday. When I came for my appointment, I thought the doctor seemed a little curt, but I cut him some slack. Perhaps his distant, aloof style was part of his professional persona.

"What can I do for you?" he asked coolly.

I had gone through this conversation dozens of times in my mind. But now I was afraid to tell him what was really bothering me. Instead, I played it safe, hoping he would ask leading questions. I did not want to volunteer too much information.

"I'm having problems with girls," I began, shocking even myself with that statement.

He nodded. "Tell me about it," he said, repeating what was, no doubt, a routine line of questioning.

"Well, I'm attracted to girls, but . . . not exclusively."

He listened, silent and still. His silence fed my insecurities, and frankly, it pushed at least part of me over the edge. I heard my tone of voice rising, along with feeling an escalating anger and frustration. "Okay, so I had sex with a guy, too. *So what?*"

It was not exactly a shouted statement, but it was definitely emphatic. By that time, the doctor seemed completely detached from the conversation.

I struggled on. "So . . . I don't want to have those attractions. I just want to be normal."

Long pause. I decided that after spilling my guts like that and exposing myself so freely, if he did not have any helpful advice for me, I would not say another word. The silence stretched out into minutes between us, exposing, more than anything else, what I felt was this so-called caregiver's apathy.

"Why don't we take it from there next week?" he finally said, scribbling a note.

I rushed out of his office, storming past his secretary without making a follow-up appointment. *What a crock*, I thought. Not only did I need to get away from the school shrink; I needed to get off campus for a while. On a whim, I decided to hitchhike to Bradenton—the town where I was born. Bradenton elicited a scattering of pleasant memories from earliest childhood, unclouded by the emotional upheaval of later years. It was only twenty miles south, and I quickly got a ride.

The driver was in his midsixties, bald, cheerful and affable. He was also nervous, as was I. It was the first time I had ever hitchhiked in my life. *Oh man, Dave*, I cautioned myself, *you've done it now. What if this guy is a murderer? He's got you!* But as we talked, he seemed harmless enough.

He was a retired teacher of some sort, and the interest he showed in what I had to say touched the part of me that hungered for acceptance, especially from a father figure. He lived in Sarasota, which was not far from Bradenton. He invited me over to his home to talk more. He lived in a dilapidated, seven-story walkup near the Ringling Bros. and Barnum & Bailey Circus headquarters. He warned me not to say anything as we hurried through the lobby and headed up the funky old elevator. It was a rather conservative place, he explained later, and he did not want rumors flying. I could not guess what the other residents might have thought, seeing a teenage hippie with hair down to his shoulders walking in with an elderly gentleman.

His room was small and narrow, with a bed and nightstand, several chairs and a table, a closet and a small bathroom. He lived on the top floor, so the ceiling sloped downward toward the window. I took a chair opposite his bed. He showed me some articles he had saved from random papers and other publications. Then he handed me a magazine that featured handsome male models. "You could be one of these boys, you know," he quietly pointed out.

How wonderful finally to meet someone who seems genuinely interested in me, I thought. As we continued talking, however, I began to notice things. He kept glancing below my belt and complimenting me on my looks. Soon it was obvious, even to me, what he really was interested in. Still, I pitied him—old and living alone as he did. I could see the desperation in his eyes, and I felt drawn to give him what he wanted. Besides, I had already done it with one guy. What did it matter if I let this old man get his thrill, too? As long as I did not have to do anything to him.

He invited me over next to him to look at something on the desk, and with great fear and trepidation, brushed the front of my pants with his hand. When I did not back away from him, he proceeded with the seduction. As things progressed, I was afraid he might have a heart attack from his excitement. Pleasure at innocence lost once again.

Afterward, he began telling me about a guy in his early thirties who regularly came over to "service" him. I had not a clue what he meant by that. Perhaps it was his way of introducing me to the idea of becoming a male prostitute. But more than anything else, I pitied him and was happy that I could fulfill a fantasy he may have had for a very long time.

As he drove me home in silence, I tried to console myself. *After all*, I thought, *I've done a good deed, haven't I? And no money exchanged hands.* It was not a very convincing argument. Deep within myself, I knew that something was seriously wrong with me. Whatever it was, I did not want to think too much about it.

Movies still captivated me, and more than ever I needed to distract myself from the confusion that roiled my mind. A new version of *Romeo and Juliet* delighted me. I saw it at least 25 times and memorized every line. It caused me to reflect on the romantic relationship with a girl that I had so longed for, but had never found. The more I watched the film, however, the more clear it became that I was sexually attracted to both lead actors—Leonard Whiting and Olivia Hussey. For the first time, I began consciously to acknowledge that reality.

Then I discovered an obscure film called *Deep End* and immediately became obsessed with it. I saw it over and over again. It spoke to my fears of women, and to my obsession with enjoying them sexually and thus conquering my homosexual feelings. It also affirmed my suspicion that many girls were teasers. The movie was about a fifteen-year-old boy who found a job at a London bathhouse and became infatuated with a woman there. She flirted with him and his fixation grew, until she finally laughed off his advances and he threw something at her, accidentally killing her in the deep end of the pool. The final scene showed him in the water with her now-dead body, hugging her in a vain effort to love her back to life.

It was a bizarre movie, but I identified on a deep level with the young boy's fantasies. He wove them around in his mind the way I did. I also identified with his sense that no one understood the profound depth and importance of his feelings. I felt a kinship with his pain as this sexually mature woman carelessly wounded him with her mocking and easy ridicule.

I went to see *Deep End* almost daily for two weeks and sat through it several times each visit. I became obsessed with the boy's obsession, which actually frightened me. Did my preoccupation with the movie indicate that I, too, was going off the deep end?

My junior year I ventured into X-rated movies. They helped me discover what stimulated me and what did not, providing additional clues to my sexual orientation. Going to those films also gave me a particular sense of delight when I thought about how much my parents would have hated them. Anger at Mom and Dad still reigned as a major factor in my life.

Then came *Summer of '42*, which had a major influence on me. Like the other films, I saw it many times. It was a wartime story about a woman in her thirties who had been left alone during her husband's deployment and a fifteen-year-old boy who fell in love with her. The two made love at the end. The cinematography was beautifully done, and I fell in love with Jennifer O'Neill. Seeing the role she played in the film awakened a dream of mine that perhaps someday, a beautiful older woman would fall in love with me and help me learn how to please her sexually. What better way to alleviate my anxieties than to have a safe tutor like that?

Movies always carried me away from my tiny, cramped world and helped me understand the bigger issues of life. The thought of acting—of living *inside* a movie—never failed to excite me. *Would being an actor offer an avenue of escape from the ugly reality that seems to follow me wherever I go?* I wondered. I knew I wanted to someday find the answer.

In fact, films had been such a formative staple in my development that I was beginning to wonder if the choices I was making were not in some way being formed by a subconscious need to live a dramatic and colorful life—as compensation for the pain of having to live life at all.

— 7 —

ALMOST DROWNING

To this day, something about ocean waters at night seems to convey peace to me. Maybe it is the vastness of the sea, and the breakers' gentle rolling in the dark as warm salt mist wafts across my face. Maybe it is the absence of artificial noise, and the sound of the water that seems almost to whisper in the dark. In St. Petersburg, the pier seemed like the best place to go to steal a moment or two of peace. That is where I often went to think, pray and even rail against God over what I had become.

As a college freshman, I had imagined that college would allow me to escape the heartbreaks of home. Instead, I found myself drowning in a sea of coping mechanisms—from drug addiction to perverted sexual desire—that were incessantly tugging at me. With each attempt to move away from my problems, I seemed to get pulled deeper into them. At least in the relative quiet of the waterfront, I could imagine that the sound of the bay was washing away layers of pain and disappointment. At least here, I could not mess up my life any more than I already had.

As I leaned against the pier railing late one night and asked God to rescue me from the hell of my life, out of the corner of my eye I became aware that some of the cars in the ceaseless caravan that drove up and down the pier were slowing as they approached my location. I began to wonder, *Is this some kind of homosexual or drug hangout? Great! I come here to seek God's help, and I'm being pursued by evil men!*

As my anger at God swelled, so did my desire to defy Him. I wanted Him to know just how much I hated Him for never answering my prayers, for never rescuing me from my distress. How many times had I come to Him, weeping and crying for His help? And now this?

Just as I turned back to face the water, a car honked directly behind me. I turned and could see the driver waving at me. It was dark, so I walked over to see if it was someone I knew.

"Hey buddy, whatcha doin'?"

"Oh, nothing much," I said a bit suspiciously. "What do you want?" *Drugs,* I thought. *Good—maybe he knows where to find some.*

"I'm new in town and thought you could show me some . . . er . . . where the action is."

Now it was clear. I was in a pickup spot for homosexuals. I decided to feign ignorance and leave it at that.

"Sorry, man. I'm new here, too," I lied and began to walk away.

"Don't you want to find out how much I'm going to give you?"

The sudden realization that he thought I was a homosexual prostitute hit me like a fist in the face. It struck a powerful blow to my self-esteem. Speechless, I walked away without a word. But as I did, a guy who had witnessed the scene from across the street caught up to me.

"Need some help?" he asked.

"No thanks."

"Been doing it long?"

I turned in anger and asked, "Been doing what?"

"Hey man, loosen up. . . . I'm your friend."

I sat down on a bench and assumed an aloof, defensive attitude.

"I'll give you a few pointers," the guy continued. "First, you gotta show 'em the merchandise. Wear white pants or something."

Still angry, but curious to hear what he was talking about, I just stared at him.

"How long you been doing it?" he asked me.

"A few years." The lies were coming more and more easily as I settled into playing the part.

"This is the place, all right. You were in my spot, but I let it go 'cause I could see you were new. Where you from?"

"L.A.," I lied again.

"Oh yeah? I hear there's a lot of action there."

"Yeah, but I like it here better . . . no smog." I was enjoying the game of deception, as well as the pretense of being something I was not—someone wild and reckless, someone with a dark, secret life, the kind they make movies about. I wanted to be in the kind of movies that James Dean or Marlon Brando would have starred in.

"Yeah, I guess. Bet the money's better in L.A."

That caught my interest. "What do you get here?" I asked.

"Oh, if you don't have to do anything yourself . . . if you know what I mean . . . it ranges anywhere from ten to thirty, depending on their financial condition."

I suddenly became repulsed by the whole conversation and wanted to get out of there. "Yeah, well, I got to split."

As I got up, a Cadillac slowly cruised by.

"Hey, there's one of my regulars. Why don't you take him? It's an easy twenty. All you got to do is sit back and relax."

I did not even have time to voice my objection.

"No, no, I insist. Take it. Go ahead. It's on me!"

In my view I was trapped, and the usual set of contradictions raged more powerfully than ever. I was feeling aroused by the danger, along with the chance to play a dark character from a movie and the opportunity to show God just how much I hated Him. Before I knew what was happening, I was in the Cadillac, being ogled by the driver. My heart was racing a million miles an hour. So was my mind. *What if he's a vice cop? What if this is a sting operation? Am I really a homosexual? What will my parents think? What does God think?*

"You know, you're really beautiful," the driver said quietly.

That took me completely by surprise. I laughed nervously and turned away to look out the window. It was the last thing I had expected him to say. Yet as confused as I was, those words were like water poured out onto the empty sponge of my soul. *Beautiful?* No one had ever said anything like that to me before. The intensity of my reaction was frightening.

"Straight?"

"Yeah."

"That's terrific."

Does he mean a guy can be straight and still do this?

The driver pulled the car over to the curb under a large banyan tree. He pulled out a fifty-dollar bill and handed it to me as he knelt in the floorboard in front of me.

Later, as the Cadillac pulled away from the pier, I stood on the walkway dazed, shaken and fifty dollars richer. I was beyond confused. What I had done was not only sinful, but I had taken money for it. Yet at the same time, that stranger had managed to make me feel like some kind of god, an object of worship, which was precisely the opposite of what I had experienced all my life. The hunger in me that longed for acceptance and approval cried out for more. I was also exhilarated by the thought of how many drugs I could buy with the money. And at the same time, I was happily thumbing my nose at both my coldhearted father and his unresponsive God.

I stayed at the pier. I felt free and flattered there. Men wanted me. They begged to have me, and, in case I doubted their sincerity, they put their hard-earned money in my hand. I became a pro, and I always seemed to stay for one more score. Why? Because I was hoping for something very special—someone who would carry me away to a life of luxury and pleasure, a place where everyone would love me, want me and be there for me.

Finally one night, a guy in his early twenties pulled up in a beat-up old car and invited me in. "How ya doin'?" he gleefully asked.

"All right. You?"

"Not bad at all, especially now." He looked me over, long and hard. "You're absolutely gorgeous!" he exclaimed.

Once again, this was new territory. Words I once had longed for were finally warming me, and it was a heady experience. I had waited so long to hear such words, and they caused powerful emotions to flood over me in waves of excitement.

"So what will you do?" he asked.

"You can go down on me, but that's it."

"Cool!" He smiled.

"What have you got?" I interjected. I coolly thumbed through one of the porn magazines that were strewn on the passenger-side floor.

"Oh, maybe ten," he said a little tentatively.

"Twenty," I responded.

"Ten is all I've got."

I felt so complimented by then that I would have done it for nothing. "One of these magazines," I told him, "and your ten bucks."

"Done." He breathed heavily. "All except for that one." He pointed to the best of the porn mags.

He pulled the car to the side of the road, again under a tree. I continued to flip through the magazine. And as the other man had done before him, this one also treated me like some kind of god—literally worshiping me. After he finished, he held my legs tight, almost whimpering, as if he never wanted to let go.

For someone desperately in need of recognition, affirmation and attention, this feeling of being all but worshiped was instantaneously addictive. I knew that I would come back to experience this feeling again—and often.

Handing me the ten bucks, the guy began complimenting me again about my looks. By that time, I had heard enough and wanted to get out of there as fast as possible. I selected one of his porn magazines and left, walking quickly back to my car, which was hidden several streets down.

That night, back at Eckerd, lying in my bed, I considered the gravity of the line I had crossed. I somehow came to the conclusion that since the line had already been crossed, I might as well continue on my course. If what I had done would send me to hell, it was too late to worry about it. I already was smelling the smoke anyway. Besides, even though the money was easy, the words of affirmation were golden. I *had* to do it again.

I hustled every weekend after that at the pier in downtown St. Petersburg. At times, some of the customers were scary. Others were delightful. To some, I gave myself away for free. I charged others as much as thirty dollars, depending on what kind of car they were driving and how revolting they seemed.

These guys gave me certain things I wanted: money to feed my drug habit, an outlet for my rage against God, praise and admiration, and sensual gratification. They were mostly older men—father figures—who always seemed pleased with me, so unlike my real father. These men affirmed me and expressed

92

their desire to be with me. They also took care of my sexual needs so that I did not have to return to the frightening world of dating and rejection.

In addition, as any prostitute will tell you, hustling can put you in a powerful position. I usually felt in complete control when I was with a client. I held the power to build him up or to destroy him. And in that brief exercise of domination, I felt I could "rescue" a soul who was dying inside from loneliness and self-hatred. I could take control of a life holding on by a thread. And I could be the defective degenerate I had always considered myself to be. It was all so sick and twisted and hopeless.

Silent Scream

My final year of college was one of frenzied self-destructiveness. My self-hatred had grown to epic proportions, matched only by my self-pity. We are all made to be loved, and for me the absence of that love was more than I could handle. Drugs had helped a little in the beginning, allowing me to escape the onslaughts of distress and despair that so often washed over me. But as my need for more and more potent drugs increased, the cycle became increasingly perilous.

One night it all overwhelmed me. I got righteously wasted and grabbed a knife, hoping that some wild impulse would enable me to end it once and for all. As I thought about what I was about to do, it occurred to me that more than wanting to die, I wanted people to care. I stumbled out into the small student lounge and collapsed into one of the plastic chairs, thinking that if I sat there with a knife, someone would either stop and ask me what was wrong or call for help. Normally at that hour, someone would walk through the lounge every five minutes on the way to his room. But no one came through after five minutes, ten minutes, and then fifteen. In absolute frustration, I began stabbing the top of my leg and ripping at my jeans with the knife.

What are You doing, God? I silently screamed. *Do You want me to die? Why aren't You sending someone to help me?*

Finally, the impulse to take my life faded and the danger passed. God answers prayers in strange ways, and sometimes He even saves our lives by using our own rage. Slinking back to my room, I dove into the bed and buried myself in pillows, covers and tears. *It'll be better tomorrow*, I promised myself. That was my last thought as I faded off to sleep.

It was a toxic brew—self-hatred, self-pity, drugs day and night and a secret life of prostitution. I had heard voices telling me to kill myself since childhood, so I knew there was something darkly spiritual mixed into the cauldron. Every once in a while, it would boil over and I would either take a risk with my life while hustling on the streets or try to end it all by more direct means.

One huge source of frustration was that I had a small set of friends who actually seemed to like me, yet I was sure that if I told them who I really was and what I was really doing in secret, they would abandon me. A lovely girl named Elaine was a constantly frustrating presence. I truly adored her and wanted very much for her to adore me in return. I knew she liked me a lot, but as had happened too often before, she had no interest in me as a boyfriend. She wanted a clean-cut Christian guy with short hair, and I was a drug-addicted, long-haired hippie freak in full-blown rebellion against God.

One night, I invited Elaine and most of my other friends to a party in my room. This kind of gathering was a bit unusual in that half of those I invited did not do drugs. Instead, we played loud music and drank. Those of us who used drugs did them prior to the party.

I had finally managed to get my hands on some barbiturates, and my plan that night was to overdose and time it so that the pills' effects would overtake me while everyone was with me. I thought maybe this would elicit a demonstration of love and concern for me that would go beyond the superficial, party-time affection that typified all my friendships. If I showed them the dangerously self-destructive side of me, maybe that would cause Elaine or some of the others to sit down with me and let me pour out my interior brokenness to them. Maybe I would discover that they truly loved me, and the pain would finally go away.

So that everyone's attention would be fixed on me, I deliberately acted animated and energetic that night, jumping up and down on my bed, impersonating a rock star while the music blasted around us. Everyone was delighted and surprised that this normally stoned and laid-back friend of theirs finally was showing some spunk and energy. Or perhaps they could see my desperation and were laughing because they did not know what else to do. For whatever reason, they seemed to be having a wonderful time—especially Elaine.

Finally, after I had exhausted myself with my histrionics, I collapsed on the bed and slowly passed out. The last thing I remember hearing was the R.A. in the hallway asking the others as they filed out of the room if I was all right. I heard someone say, "Oh yeah. He's okay."

But I was not okay! I was hurting so deeply that I could not bear it. Why hadn't anyone noticed? Why hadn't anyone really seemed to care?

As it turned out, Someone did care, Someone who had been watching over me and protecting me from death all my life. He cared very much, and I did not even know it. I woke up the next afternoon as if nothing had happened. Once again, the God I hated had neutralized the deadly effects of a drug overdose.

One Last Grasp at Hope

At the end of my college experience, I pulled myself together and adopted a new positive attitude in order to launch off on a search for fame and fortune in Hollywood.

I cannot explain how I ever did it, but in June 1973 I picked up my diploma as a graduate in the bachelor of arts program. At about that same time, I went to see Liza Minnelli in concert. For some strange reason, her voice spoke to me.

I saw her in the movie *Cabaret* and returned to the theater, as was my habit, again and again. Something about her excited me—her zest for life even in the midst of living a sad life, and her positive, "can do" spirit. These were qualities I lacked, but also knew I needed in order to survive. Liza's dramatic posing for attention mirrored my own. Then there was her embracing of people others rejected and her talent in song and dance—I loved it all. In that particular film, she embraced a man who was bisexual. I lived in fear that anyone discovering such a thing about me would find it abhorrent. The idea that somebody could love such a person in spite of his sexual confusion brought great solace to my soul.

One night Liza came to town, and I begged and pleaded with a friend to go with me to see her. I even bought his ticket so he would go. He was from Brooklyn Heights, and I knew he would absolutely love her, if he could only get over worrying about what his friends would think about his going.

96

I went with high expectations, and my friend went with low ones. But from the opening curtain, with cap tipped sideways on her head and cane in her hand, she had us both. She was astonishingly talented. She danced like there was no tomorrow; every move was brilliant. And she really knew how to strike theatrical poses and punch up just the right words in her songs. Before I knew it, my friend had disappeared from our balcony seats and sneaked down the center aisle to see her more closely. Although he never let on otherwise, he was captivated.

I was so encouraged by Liza's attitude that I decided to give life one more try—one more good shot. If I was going to live, I wanted to live life to the fullest, to make something great out of myself. So I pulled myself up by my bootstraps and decided to start all over again. I would try to find my future in Hollywood.

For a number of years, I had been keeping a journal. It helped me work through my thoughts, even though it terrified me to think that someone might find it and read it. It was worth the risk, however, because I figured that when I did succeed at suicide, or when I was killed while hustling, at least I would leave behind a way for my family and friends to understand why I had done what I had done. In my entry for October 10, 1973, I wrote,

On October 24th I will be flying to Los Angeles to seek my fortune. . . . Received my plane tickets today. I am filled with excitement! Many of my past dreams are now on the line. I feel that if I make a total concerted effort, I can really make something of myself. I dream to reach a position of great significance. At this point I don't think I can be happy unless I do.

My biggest problem will be to retain the enthusiasm and self-confidence that surrounds my mind now. I can remember many times when I've failed to achieve anything big due to losing confidence, and subsequently enthusiasm.

This is my big chance to make it and I'll have to go all out. Liza Minnelli's spirit of confidence and "never say die" gives me an example to follow. That's why I like her so much. She's got that all-out total effort kind of spirit that I definitely need to develop. I know I have it deep down inside. If it is ever going to surface, it has to now.

Hopefully a friend of the family will give me a job when I get out there. Then I'll simply have to work as hard as I can to prove myself, and advance in the TV business. My dream career has always been in films or TV, and now I have a chance.

I've known for quite some time that I could never settle for an ordinary job. I've got to have sparkle and recognition in my life. It has to be unconventional and I'm determined to make it so. Hopefully when I reread this ten years from now I'll be a very successful person.

California—just the thought of living on the Pacific Coast is exciting. The change of locale is greatly needed. I was going to live in New York City for the experience, but now with this opportunity—no way. Darryl Zanuck, watch out!

People are constantly warning me not to get my hopes up and I assure them that I have not, but I'm only fooling them. My hopes are actually at the top. I just think that if I'm to make it big, I have to think big—i.e., if I don't shoot high, I have a lesser chance of obtaining anything great. What I have to work on in that field is accepting defeat and then jumping back into the game with as much self-confidence as before.

PART THREE

HOLLYWEIRD

What happens when you forsake all to pursue sex, fame and fortune? What happens when you invest every last ounce of courage and energy into the pursuit of a career in an industry that takes no prisoners?

Believe it or not, some can weather the journey relatively unscathed. But when you are love-starved and have lived a life with precious little affirmation, and when you have created a mental library of fantasies that you have come to believe can rectify your plight, well, it is usually not pretty.

Oh yes—I met a lot of wealthy and famous people and even developed friendships and other kinds of relationships with them. And I realized much success in my pursuit of an acting career. But the harsh realities of that life simply would not sync with the small-town romantic fantasies of one very naïve young man.

As I rehearse the events of my years in Hollywood, I can scarcely believe that anyone could live through what happened to me.

— 8 —

HELLO, HOLLYWOOD

The night flight to Los Angeles ended in a magnificent display. As the plane approached my new hometown, the vast city stretched below like a sea of diamonds, sparkling with the hope and promise of the future that was pounding away in my heart. The L.A. panorama went on and on for what seemed like a quarter of an hour, and I never wanted it to end. As the wheels touched down, I felt exhilarated. I had made it to sunny California! I had made my vows to avoid both drugs and prostitution. I had promised myself that I would soon become a star and leave the past behind me. My course was set.

My old college roommate Robin met me at the gate. Now that he was in grad school, studying chemistry at USC, I noticed that he had shorter hair than before. He had the same cheerful personality, though—positive and thoroughly upbeat. I was never sure what he was really thinking behind that chirpiness. Was he really that happy all of the time? Who knew? But for now, he was just the kind of friend I needed to usher me in to my Hollywood dream.

At first we both slept in his tiny studio. It was cramped, and those first few days were a little discouraging. But soon we found a nice, California-style one-bedroom apartment in Westwood, near UCLA—one of the best neighborhoods. I was delighted, even though it meant that my bedroom was also the living room. Still, we had a pool and were within a block of the bus stop, from where I could travel either to the beach or into Hollywood. It was perfect.

Now I could start searching in earnest for jobs "in the industry," as everyone in Hollywood called show business. My situation was difficult since I could not get a regular nine-to-five job and still be available for the golden opportunities I was looking for. I also had the added disadvantage of not belonging to any of the performers' unions such as the Screen Extras Guild (SEG), the Screen Actors Guild (SAG), the American Federation of Television and Radio Artists (AFTRA) or Equity. That created a frustrating catch-22. To get an acting job, you had to belong to the Screen Actors Guild, but to join the Screen Actors Guild, you had to have an acting job.

It was tough to get my dream moving forward and off the ground. One thing was clear from the beginning: I had to start meeting people. I took the bus faithfully toward Hollywood and tried to be seen at all the right places. I hung out at the Beverly Hills Hotel and the Beverly Hills Post Office. I went to Joe Allen's restaurant, the Musso & Frank Grill and the Hollywood Brown Derby, when I could afford them.

One day, I saw an ad in the *L.A. Times* announcing that a modeling agency was looking for male models. They signed me up on sight—but there was a costly caveat. I had to have a composite done by their photographer, an 8 x 10 glossy with three or four poses that illustrated my acting "type" range. Of course, I had to pay for it, which I did. And of course, they said they would get back to me, which they did not.

Thanks to that bad investment and to the fact that I was not working, my meager cache of money soon began to dwindle. Even the bus became too expensive, so I started hitchhiking. The first two times I hitchhiked from Westwood into Hollywood, the drivers propositioned me for sex. Since I had committed myself to starting out with a clean slate and staying away from drugs, alcohol and hustling, I politely turned them down. But the more my remaining funds disappeared, the more difficult it was to say no.

For months on end I searched diligently for work, trying to meet people and keep myself clean and emotionally upbeat. I knew I had to project a personality that was energetic, optimistic and cheerful. After years of chronic depression and, more recently, weeks of throwing myself headlong into the constant effort to find work, it was amazing that I somehow was managing to keep myself together, but such is the lure of Hollywood. Still, it was just a mask, and a very thin one. My conflicted sexuality and deep insecurities lay just beneath the surface.

And I was not the only one.

People who take the Hollywood route to fame and fortune are particularly good at self-deception. They do not quite live in the real world. I began to see that I was like a lot of other people in town—we all had had unhappy or repressive childhoods and had adopted Hollywood's fantasy world as an escape mechanism. We did this because the stories on the silver screen had given us hope. The possibility of playing the role of someone else, whether on the screen or not, provided us with "freedom" to try a variety of self-expressive behaviors, some of which were prohibited by our families, childhood communities, churches and synagogues or other more conventional environments.

In the entertainment industry, it was easy to lose any sense of morality. Everything was about "making it," and that soon included my own set of values. Losing my moral compass came quickly and easily. And it was not just about sex and drugs. Our apartment in Westwood was just one bus stop away from Gelson's Market in Century City, with its rich Beverly Hills clientele. I made that my grocery store of choice, imagining that I would meet some famous or influential people there. It was discouraging to have no money in one of the wealthiest places in the world. It did not seem all that bad to steal steaks from a store that was making so much money that it would not really miss them. Several times a week, I shoplifted filet mignon steaks from Gelson's, which, of course, offered the best beef in town.

In my twisted way, I convinced myself that God was allowing me to steal food without being caught as His way of providing for me during my time of unemployment. My modus operandi was to wait until the meat section aisle was empty and then tuck a steak between my belt and stomach, with my shirt hanging over it. I did that for about a year.

Eventually, a clerk spoke to me quietly as I made my way out. "You'd better put it back or 'the man' is going to get you," he said.

I heard him loud and clear. I did what I was told, so frightened by the close call that I stopped shoplifting altogether.

The Men behind the Curtains

By that time, I was hitchhiking again. A 1950s convertible that stopped to pick me up looked classy, but once I got inside, I was taken aback. I recognized the man right away. I had watched him on TV ever since I was a little boy and had always seen him as a strong, righteous father figure. The image he presented on TV was one of kindness, gentleness and humor. He had hosted a very popular game show for years, and it surprised me to see him in person—especially under these circumstances.

The man seemed angry and spoke rudely to me. I might have thought he was drunk, except there were no other signs of intoxication. I had barely gotten in the car when he proceeded to question me about why I was hitchhiking and where I was going. I went into my innocent high-school-kid routine, and he started asking me why I was wearing white pants and what I was trying to show off by wearing them. Then he started asking more explicitly about my sexual anatomy, behavior and habits. As intimate as his questions were, he continued in a very angry and accusatory way.

Maybe he was angry with himself for being attracted to someone he thought was a young teenager—that can be humiliating to an older, egotistical person. Maybe he hated the fact that he was so weak that he could not stop himself from picking me up. He could have been angry at God, as I was, for "making me this way" or for "not healing me after I've begged You so many times."

I understood all that.

Many homosexuals are angry about their condition and angry at being under the power of attractive adolescent kids. And if they are at all spiritual, they can be angry at being such vile sinners.

Whatever this famous and even cherished man's story might have been, I did *not* want to stay in that car. I became convinced that if I went with him to a hotel or some other private destination, he might become violent. I named a nearby intersection, and when we arrived, I almost jumped out the door. I was in shock and kept feeling sorry for his wife, who was also a well-known and beloved celebrity.

Then there was the sweet character actor who picked me up twice over a one-year period. He was also a well-known face, a sort of sad clown, and his words were very gentle. I sensed that he was emotionally touched, looking at me as a young kid who had to work the streets. I do not think he was fooled by my act. In fact, I got the impression that he had been in my shoes himself in years gone by and knew the routine from both sides. On both occasions, he held my hand but never made any attempt to go further. His eyes were warm, aglow with desire and an unspoken request, but words of seduction never came out of his mouth. Alternately, he may have been afraid of getting arrested, as I looked much younger than I really was.

Hustling: For Love or Money

More than 90 percent of the men who picked me up when I hitchhiked propositioned me. Like all the others before them, they were looking to corrupt the innocence I projected. I suspected that some were trying to ingest the innocence they saw in me so as to recapture it for themselves. After a short period of reticence, I finally gave in and began honing an act that would keep me from having to touch the customers or allow them to do anything to me that might spread disease. Since I looked the part, I presented myself as a straight sixteen-year-old surfer from Malibu who was hitchhiking to the beach, but was feeling down and in need of getting high. That made me a vulnerable target in their eyes. It also won me the drugs or alcohol that I needed to continue doing what I was doing.

With those parameters in place in my mind, I was getting a quick twenty dollars for "doing nothing." And that meant I could buy drugs and food and pay the rent. At least, that is how I rationalized it to myself. The truth is, I was one messed-up dude.

Before long, getting a regular job seemed out of the question for several reasons. First was the hard fact that hustling was quick and the money too easily obtained to stop doing it. I had already crossed the line, so why not continue? Meanwhile, it was true that a career model or actor needed to be available to audition at any time, sometimes several times a day. I did not have a car to take me from one place to another, and the L.A. bus system was notoriously slow.

I decided to keep hitchhiking and turning tricks—as Steve, the teen surfer who was lost, lonely and vulnerable to being corrupted by men who considered themselves experts at it. Sometimes I would even throw "preacher's kid" into my self-description when I sensed that the act of corrupting my innocence particularly enhanced a client's pleasure.

I was not happy with myself about it—that I was back to doing something I had promised myself I would never do again. I felt trapped and ashamed. I did not want to think of myself as the type of person who would do such things and, worse yet, enjoy them, so I started hating myself again.

I might have pretended to be too innocent, naïve, vulnerable, and eventually too drunk and stoned to resist my clients' advances, but in truth, I always managed to stay in control of the situation. I knew there were men out there who loved to torture and kill kids like me, and I always wanted to be alert enough to prevent that from happening. Like it or not, somewhere in the basement of my excuse-cluttered mind, I knew I was responsible to God for my actions, and I did not expect Him to protect me from predators such as those.

As before, hopelessness gradually overshadowed my life. Again, the shame and loss of self-respect sent me searching for more frequent and intense painkilling behaviors. I tried to deaden the ache in every way possible. I did as many drugs, had as much sex and drank as much alcohol as I could. The higher I got, the easier it was to rationalize that it was not really "me" doing all this. It was that other guy—the guy in the mirror, whom I hated. In the depths of my soul, I suspected that I would never be able to stop. I had gone too far, and for someone like me, there remained only the specter of judgment. The only real unknown was when that sword was going to drop.

After my first encounter with prostitution in Hollywood, I made my way back to the apartment. I headed straight for the bathroom, locked the door and spent the next ten or fifteen minutes berating the man in the mirror: I reminded him that he was a loser and a despicable person. At one point, I looked straight into his eyes and said out loud, "You are a *prostitute!* That's what you are. A *whore.* You sell your body to the highest bidder. You're going to hell, fella. There's no turning back now. God hates you. I hate you. You're the lowest form of life on this planet!"

Many nights thereafter, I would stand along some street or boulevard with my thumb out while tears were coursing down my cheeks. As was my habit, I was silently screaming at God, begging Him to rescue me and cursing Him for not answering. I had begged Him since my early childhood to release me from this evil world, to love me and let me know that He was there. And with His silence, I seethed ever more.

How well I remembered those long, lonely days I had spent at the Avalon Theatre, watching the same movies over and over again. It was my escape from home. It was a world where I could forget the unloving reality of my family life. I also remembered those nights after the final show was over. How often I had waited, sometimes for an hour or more, for my father to arrive to pick me up. I stood in the cold, watching other, more loving parents showing up one after the other. I would mumble some embarrassed excuse when the owner of the theater asked if I was sure somebody was coming to get me. After she locked up, I would be out on the street all alone with my tears. How could my father not realize that he was broadcasting to the whole town that he did not care about me?

My Hollywood street hustling was, in some ways, a continuation of that earlier scene from childhood—standing on the street, waiting for love. It was also a way of penalizing my father for leaving me out in the cold all those years and penalizing God for not doing anything about it.

Since I felt that neither my earthly father nor my heavenly Father provided it, I had figured out a way to get the love I needed somehow, somewhere, some way. Phony as it was, at least it was something.

"So You Want to Be in Pictures?"

When my first Hollywood job finally materialized, it was an exciting opportunity. To my amazement, I was hired to model for *Teen* magazine. It was my first national modeling shoot. It was set in picturesque Malibu, where I posed alongside two gorgeous girls and a great-looking guy. I could not help thinking how very different this was from my real high school experience, where I felt like such a misfit and no one thought I was good-looking at all.

The experience also reminded me of the many heartfelt prayers I had poured out to God during my middle teen years, pleading with Him to make me good-looking so people would accept me. Now it had happened. Had God answered my prayer, or was it a coincidence? Had He waited too long? The shoot lasted until about 3:00 p.m., and then I boarded the bus and headed home. About six months later, the photo spread was published. Once it appeared, I received some letters postmarked Easton, Maryland, from some very surprised classmates who had seen me in the magazine.

Another break came along a few months later—or so it seemed at the time. I was sitting at the counter at Schwab's Drug Store, reading *Daily Variety*. Since I was a fervent believer in the show biz legend about Lana Turner being discovered at Schwab's (though she was actually spotted at the Top Hat Café on Sunset Boulevard), I made a habit of hanging out at Schwab's whenever I could, hoping lightning might strike twice.

At first, I thought maybe it had. A man in his forties strolled up to me and introduced himself. He was relatively nondescript and short, with slightly oversized front teeth. I noticed that he was making an effort to dress and act younger than he was, like many Hollywood homosexuals, whose world revolves around youth. This fellow was open and amiable—almost childlike. He claimed to be a producer. I must have seemed unconvinced, so he quickly brought over a newspaper and opened it to the movie section. There he pointed out a full-page ad for his hit movie, with his name in the credits. I still was not so sure, but his enthusiasm won me over. Several days later, I followed up on his offer for me to drop by his office at 20th Century Fox.

It was a heady feeling to give my name at the gate and be waved through once the guard found it on his list. *Just like in the movies*, I thought. Giddy, I pulled into a parking spot right next to the one reserved for Mel Brooks. I could almost feel the pulse of Hollywood history emanating from the hardwood floors and whitewashed walls as I made my way up the stairs to my new producer friend's office. *How many famous stars and producers and directors have walked the very same steps?* I wondered.

This producer shared a fairly large, impressive two-office suite with his production partner. Considering that at that very moment, they had a critically acclaimed, prestigious hit movie out, such an elegant place of business seemed appropriate. The two of them also lived together, so I assumed they were lovers. His partner appeared to be around twenty years old—not great-looking, but not bad, either. Once I met him, I realized that he really liked to talk about how attracted he was to young boys. The two of them seemed to have a typical older man/younger guy partnership of the sort that so often takes place in the gay community. I never saw either of them with underage kids, but the partner certainly enjoyed talking about the myriad schemes he used to pick them up. I would learn over the years that pedophiles were in many top positions in the film and record industries and that they were too powerful for anyone to risk doing anything about them.

The three of us chatted in their office for about twenty minutes, and then as I was leaving, they invited me to a screening at their apartment a few days later. Each time I was invited out with them after that, the older of the two tried to proposition me. I continued to assure him that I was straight and disinterested. He assured me that it was not a problem and that all I had to do was just lie there and let him take care of my sexual need. I had made a decision, however, that I would not sleep with anyone in order to succeed in show business and that my life of prostitution would be completely separate and unknown from my life as an up-and-coming actor. I was pleased and impressed that despite my refusal to sleep with him or even to let him touch me, he did not make false promises about my career. And he did indeed help me get into the Screen Extras Guild.

A Foot in the Door

Believe it or not, the Screen Extras Guild was more difficult to get into than the Screen Actors Guild because it had a limit on membership. I used the name Kyle Foster on my SEG card and got a lot of work. I cut my hair short so I could regularly work on the hit teen shows of the time—*Sons and Daughters*, *Happy Days*, *Lucas Tanner* and others—and I worked almost daily.

Getting a job consisted of being listed with Central Casting and a few smaller casting companies. I would call in each day to see if they had a job for me the following day. The phone would ring and ring—sometimes twenty to forty times. Finally an agent would answer, and I would quickly give him my name. "No work!" he would mutter. Or if he anticipated work that might still come in, he would bark, "Try later!" and hang up. In the best-case scenario, he would say, "Hold on." Then he would rifle through some papers. Finally, he would read out where I should show up tomorrow, when I should be there and what kind of clothes I should wear.

My first job was on the set of *The Front Page*, a Billy Wilder movie that starred Walter Matthau and Jack Lemmon. Then I appeared in a Ben Gazzara gangster movie, *Capone*, filmed on the Warner Brothers lot, where I was costumed in period clothes. Then came jobs on *Kojak*, *McMillan & Wife*, *Lucas Tanner*, *Happy Days*, *The Waltons* and lots of movies. One film, *The Fortune*, starred Warren Beatty and Jack Nicholson. During the shoot one day, I found myself sitting across from Warren Beatty at lunch—just him and me alone at this superlong table. Unfortunately, we extras were under strict orders not to talk to the actors unless they first spoke to us, so I did not dare to start a conversation with him. Sadly, he was in his own little world, oblivious to my presence. Close, but no cigar.

Even though being an extra was a lowly position—one that I would need to hide and later deny altogether—it did get me into the flow of show business, on the studio lots, in the commissaries and around the major actors of the day. It did nothing for my acting abilities, but it accomplished a lot for my hope, enthusiasm and vision about where I was heading.

Meanwhile, I was still hitchhiking. And hustling.

One day while I was thumbing a ride into Hollywood from Westwood, a man who worked for one of the top game show production companies in town picked me up. He paid me for a few intimate sessions over the next few weeks. In the course of our conversations, I told him about my dreams of making it in show business. Guys like him like to show off their new boy toy to their buddies anyway, so he introduced me to some of his friends in the biz.

He introduced me to Joe, a dancer who had performed with such stars as Juliet Prowse, Joey Heatherton, Debbie Reynolds and others, and to Mario, Joe's roommate and would-be promoter, agent and/or producer. Even though I was certain he had bragged about his exploits with me, I decided to let them suspect that he was making it all up. Mario took a liking to me and decided he was going to help develop my career. He and Joe were gay, but neither of them made sexual advances toward me, which I appreciated.

Mario managed to get me invited to a very private party for Rock Hudson's birthday. Hudson had almost married one of Mario's friends to hide his sexual orientation from the public, but decided at the last minute to marry Phyllis Gates instead. He thought Phyllis was better looking. Quite a few big names were at the party, like Stefanie Powers and Ross Hunter, the producer of many of Rock's films. Character actor Hugh Gillin was there. Hot young star John David Carson was there with Disney actress Kim Darby.

I did not know anyone, so I sat shyly in the corner and people-watched. It was a small party for Rock Hudson's closest friends, and when he finally arrived, he came in acting very effeminate, with his gay lover on his arm. You could have knocked me over with a feather. I had no idea he was homosexual, and to see such a masculine screen figure prance into the room like a fairy was shocking to this small-town preacher's kid.

Sometimes Joe invited his dancer friends to his home to watch old movies in a makeshift theater he had set up in the garage. One night he invited Vera-Ellen, who had danced with Danny Kaye in *White Christmas*. I was absolutely ecstatic because Vera-Ellen had been one of the women who had most attracted me when I was a boy. By then, however, she was an alcoholic and rarely uttered a coherent word. She simply sat impassively in silence, watching old movies from her glory days.

I also met Eleanor Powell at one of Joe's gathering of dancers—the greatest female dancer in movie history. She was a terrific lady, brimming with energy and excitement. She was always gracious toward me, even though I was so shy that I could barely form words when she was around. We must have watched dozens of her movies, and watched them again many times over in the next few years. One time, Eleanor even danced for us in the kitchen hallway, where there was a wood floor. She tap danced and was as fast and good as she had been in the movies. After we watched her films, she regaled us with behind-the-scenes stories about what Fred Astaire was really like, what she thought of Ann Miller—the only film dancer that rivaled her talent in the 1930s and '40s—and other similar tales. Months later, after I no longer went to Joe's gatherings, she continued to send me birthday cards. She did so for years.

I was beginning to feel at home in Hollywood after a somewhat rocky start. But as my fledgling show-biz career began to grow, so did a burgeoning sexual addiction. I found myself needing a nonstop infusion of lustful flattery and sensual gratification morning, noon and night. Not even almost daily prostitution encounters were enough to satisfy me.

— 9 —

PLAYERS, PREDATORS and PEDOPHILES

I decided to place a series of personal ads in the *L.A. Free Press*—a progressive and provocative rag that readers could obtain in curbside newspaper machines throughout the city. I started with a fairly straightforward approach: "SWM 18, looking for big brother and fun. Steve, POB 1234, LA, Ca. 90025." As time went by, my ads became more explicit, but they were always worded to attract older men who would pay generously for being with a young teen. In one ad, I even attempted to find a female sugar daddy. In another, I tried to find guys my own age who wanted to have free sex.

After several responses to my ads, I began to catch glimpses into the world of child sexual abuse and pornography. I discovered an entire subculture of middle-aged men who sell pictures of young boys—and, all too often, sell the boys themselves—among their perverse circles of friends and colleagues.

Nearly every time I met someone who had answered one of my ads, he would immediately try to impress me with his collection of teen porn, most of it comprised of photos he had taken himself. I recognized that this was done to break my resistance. These predators wanted me not only to have sex with them, but also to allow them to take similar pictures of me. After all, they assured me, if these good-looking kids—many younger than me—had agreed, why shouldn't I? For fear of ruining my acting career, however, I never allowed nude photographs.

The pederasts (lovers of teen boys) I met were surprisingly polite and considerate. Besides the hoards of them in show business, they were often executives, real-estate salesmen, ordinary blue-collar guys—even one pool cleaner. And they seemed to me like the last sort of people you would ever suspect of preying on boys.

I became part of a retinue of boys that some of these guys "saw"—a better word is *used*—on a rotating basis. They often asked us to have sex with each other while they watched; they also showed us teen pornography and provided us with drugs and alcohol. This, of course, served to break down our resistance to whatever perverse acts they wanted us to perform. They found our personal weaknesses and exploited them, creating dependencies in us and making us more amenable to whatever they wanted. These things were not only done to me (with the exception of the photographs), but I also saw them repeatedly done to others.

Everyone knows about wild and crazy parties that are generously supplied with sexy call girls for the pleasure of the guests. But in my Hollywood days, I was taken to parties—set up exclusively for the very rich—where scores of boys were supplied and made available for the adults to take home. Some of the biggest movie stars, rock stars, ballet company directors, film and television producers and directors—even heads of studios—participated. (Oh how I wish I could name names.)

One Bright Spot

With moderate success in my career on the one hand and scandalous failure in my personal life on the other, no one from my earlier years had a clue about what I was really up to. But one bright spot during this time was the abundance of letters I received from old friends and family back home. I soaked up their affirmation like a sponge.

It was incredibly important for me to know that people who had discounted me in my past were changing their minds about me now that I had achieved some success. It did my heart good to hear them acknowledge it.

In high school and college, I had been so unimpressive that I failed to impress even myself. Finally, however, I was becoming the "small town boy makes good" in the eyes of the community back home, as the letters I got showed:

Congratulations! I was shopping at Eckerd's tonight and decided to look through a Teen *magazine to see if you were in it—lo and behold . . . there's David Foster's picture splashed across the pages—I was so excited!! David, you look just GREAT!!*

It's certainly a mind blower to some far-out degree to think of little Davy Foster from Mt. Pleasant Elementary School glittering across a national magazine. . . .

Well, David, I guess you finally made it! I heard about your debut on national television from Steve. Did you know your image hit the cathode tube? They said the camera passed over you in the audience. Seen any stars yet?

Crossing the Line

Hollywood's social and show business worlds are inseparable. Everybody who wants to find success in acting, modeling, screenwriting or any other career related to the entertainment industry knows what has to be done—networking. That means trying to meet famous people, getting invited to parties involving well-connected players, being seen with the "right" people and developing name recognition.

In my case, it was not quite that simple. My ongoing sexual adventures and various addictions constantly threatened to destroy my career track. I got into a few relationships that crossed over the line. One of them was with a well-known TV director. It all began when I was working as an extra on *McMillan & Wife,* waiting for the scene I was in. A man I will call Joseph, the director of that particular episode (I was in many), was circling around as if he were trying to decide where he was going to place the camera. To my amazement, he stopped next to me and asked my name.

Directors rarely speak to extras, so I hoped he was considering me for a small speaking part—which would have guaranteed a SAG membership for me and thus would have been my ticket to real acting. At first, that is what it seemed he had in mind. After a brief conversation, he gave me his phone number and asked me to call him. "I'd like you to read for me sometime," he said.

I was ecstatic. I called the next day, and he invited me to audition at his beachfront Malibu home. My fears that he might be hitting on me were assuaged when he mentioned inviting another couple who would also be auditioning.

I arrived at his spectacular home, and he suggested that I go into a bedroom to familiarize myself with my lines so that the couple in question could read their lines undisturbed. I eagerly sat on the bed, script in hand, and began to work out the character, going over the lines again and again.

Not more than five minutes later, Joseph walked into the room and closed the door. "We can do the scene right here," he explained, "while the others use the living room." He sat next to me on the bed and began to ask about my background. Then he asked me to read the scene with him. He leaned close to me so he could see the script. I became aware that Joseph had not asked me there to read when he reached his hand under the script and touched me. I was terrified. For the first time, I became aware that I could seriously damage my career if I turned him down or even led him on and offended him later. He was high up at Universal Studios, and in those days Universal was the biggest name in television production.

This created a serious dilemma for me. Hustling was one thing—bad as it was, it was my prerogative. But being fondled by a lecherous man—and, I might add, an unattractive one who happened to hold power over me and my future—was humiliating and demeaning. I did not know what to do. I tried to pull away as subtly as I could; I tried to let him know that it was killing me to have him do what he was doing. He probably thought I was just shy and inexperienced. After all, I was a preacher's kid whom he saw as a fresh, all-American, small-town teenager. The idea of "corrupting" me was exciting him all the more.

Of course, he had no interest in my acting, so that went nowhere with him. But as much as I despised him for being a predator of young boys, he was a mild-mannered father figure whose hugs I craved. I continued to visit him at his house for the next year or two after we met. He convinced me that he had had a similar relationship with the late actor James Dean, which gave me a sense of being connected to the very actor whom I emulated.

I was young and inexperienced, and although I had had my share of experiences hustling, I did not have the same street smarts about such high-powered sexual predators. I did not know that these high-ticket users gain as much pleasure from discarding their victims as they do from defiling them. Their inflated egos cannot handle the fact that they are sexually and emotionally addicted to a child or adolescent, so they lead their young prey on with one lie after another, until they have demonstrated their superior power through deceit and conquest. The child is not a person to them; merely something they need for a moment and then discard—like toothpaste.

Another similar character was Jay (again, not his real name)—a big-name producer who was even higher up at Universal Studios. He was probably in his late thirties or early forties. I met him at a big bash attended by such luminaries as Barry Diller (then head of Paramount), Tennessee Williams and many others of similar repute.

Jay was holding court in the living room, seated alone with people grouped around him. I was on the opposite side of the room, sitting alone. He motioned for me to come over, and when I sat next to him, he asked who I was and what I did. It was especially difficult for an actor to get an interview at Universal without inside connections, so I thought this might be an opportunity for me to get my foot in the door. He seemed very nice and reasonable. As we parted, he said, "I'd like to see you again." I assumed that meant that he would consider me for future roles, so I gave him my phone number.

A few days later, Jay's live-in boyfriend, a young, handsome guy in his early twenties, called me to arrange a dinner at Ma Maison, the trendiest of restaurants in Beverly Hills. I met the two of them there, and we had a pleasant conversation. But as they plied me with drinks, I began to wonder what they had in mind. By then it was too late—I was so drunk that, throwing caution aside, I followed them home to Jay's house in the Hills. Of course, they wanted more from me than talk. Jay's boyfriend—who was considerably more attractive than Jay—made the first moves. Once I gave myself over to his seduction, Jay joined in. Drunk and slightly hopeful that this might evolve into a big break for me, I just closed my eyes so I did not have to look at Jay—the face of my compromise. It was quite possibly the most defiling moment of my young life.

To my horror, my carefully compartmentalized search for significance through stardom and sexual conquest had come unraveled—now replaced by a dark sense of shame, failure and self-hatred. I knew I was responsible for what I was doing and had no one to blame but myself.

I left as soon as I could—running, then walking down the streets of Beverly Hills in the early morning light with tears streaming down my face, wishing I could die. Men like Jay used boys and discarded them without a second thought. Did I really think I was any different from the others?

On another occasion, a friend invited me to a party at a famous playwright's mansion in Malibu. This award-winning writer—I will call him Hugh—lived in a fabulous house on a hillside overlooking the Pacific Ocean. As it turned out, Hugh was also on the boy-trading circuit, and once he got word about me, he began pursuing me with shameless desperation. He loved blond boys. And I had an unwise pity for pathetically desperate old men.

Hugh never offered me any money or favors, and I never asked for anything. But his desire was so intense that I gave myself to him rather quickly, in the limited way that I did for the men who picked me up. I did so every time I returned to his home. For obvious reasons, I was frequently on his guest list. Hugh had a superstitious belief that by satisfying his hunger with boys, he would remain forever young. He often spoke of the culture of ancient Greece, where wealthy older men kept young boys for that very reason.

As I look back at those desperate years, I realize that although it seems odd, I never considered myself homosexual. I saw myself as a vulnerable, mostly straight kid who was so messed up that he put himself in certain situations and allowed himself to be taken advantage of by sexual predators in order to obtain the touch never given him by his father. Even at this point, I had that much figured out.

While hitchhiking, as I mentioned before, I always presented myself as a straight young teen who *might* be persuaded to allow another man to touch him in sexual ways, if the man would help him out of a financial jam. This protected me from getting arrested for prostitution by undercover policemen, and it kept me from having to perform sexual acts on customers that I simply was unwilling to do. Only in my private sexual adventures did I make exceptions to that, and even there I refused to participate in the majority of the perverse activities that pervade the homosexual lifestyle.

With only two exceptions, I did not frequent gay bars. In the first place, it would blow my cover story of being a straight surfer. Second, I simply did not like the lurid perversity so prevalent there. Coming from a prostitute, that is quite an indictment of the reality of gay sex—but it is true.

On my final visit to a gay bar, however, I noticed the older homosexuals seated at the bar, completely alone, heads hung low. They had lost their youth and beauty and were having to come to terms with the fact that no one had really ever loved them. They had been loved for their youth and beauty, or perhaps for their power, influence or money. Had they truly been loved, however, they would not be sitting all alone while a party raged all around them. They would not have to pay young hustlers to give them the time of day, and perhaps some comfort. So they drank themselves into a stupor every night while all the young, beautiful and/or powerful gays danced the dance of their impending obsolescence.

I swore I would never end up like those guys.

In Hollywood, I became aware of a network sometimes called the "gay Mafia," a term that refers to homosexuals in positions of power who use their influence to manipulate countless young men and women into sexually compromising situations. I saw so many young hopefuls get involved in sexual relationships with these older men (or women), gambling that doing so would cause their careers to skyrocket. Of course, it seldom turned out that way. Some of us learned about this futile trade-off the hard way, but not one of us ever spoke up about the abusers or the abuses, for fear of ruining our "one big chance."

One of the biggest musical film producers in Hollywood was just such a man. He would lure teen boys into sexual situations by promising them screen tests. What they could not know was that there was never any film in the cameras. And after he had taken his fill of them, in order to cover his tracks, he made certain that they would be blackballed from the industry.

The irony was, of course, that I was using my body for financial purposes anyway. The difference—at least in my opinion at the time—was that I was in charge of the situation when I was prostituting myself, not some movie mogul. I could choose what I wanted to do (or did not want to do) and with whom, and therefore it was not quite so degrading.

— 10 —

HE WORKS HARD
for the MONEY

I preferred hustling on Sunset Boulevard. It was better than Santa Monica Boulevard because I considered myself superior to the "common" hustlers. Sunset was the wealthy and influential thoroughfare that proceeded westward to the more expensive sections of Beverly Hills. I thought it was where I could best ply my trade, such as it was, because it carried men who would not risk trolling for sex, but who would not mind picking up a young teen hitching home from Hollywood High School.

"Where you headed?" came the shout from the expensive, perfectly shined luxury sedan.

"Oh, no place in particular." That told the driver that I had time on my hands and was vulnerable to coercion of one sort or another.

"You in high school?"

"Yeah . . ." I knew he was trying to find out how old I was, and the younger the better. "I'm a freshman."

"So you're what? Sixteen?"

"Yeah . . . almost." That confirmed that I was youthful, pretending to be a little older than I really was.

"Just sort of wasting time, huh?"

"Yeah. Hoping to find a way to make some money. Maybe a job or something." This let him know that whatever perversion he had in mind, it would cost him.

"Well, if you've got a little time, why don't you stop by my house and have a swim?" He was closing in for the kill.

"I don't have any swimming trunks." I was helping him.

Taken in 1974 by a paying customer during the first year of my stint in Hollywood. Meet the hustler "Steve," the name I used with such customers.

"That's no problem. The pool's fenced in. You don't need one."

"Okay, I guess." I always feigned reluctance and projected wholesomeness, which made the conquest all the more exciting for the customer.

The truth is, I hated most of those guys. I hated them for pretending to love me when they only wanted sex. I hated them for using their coercive powers to seduce and defile kids like me who were vulnerable financially and in the throes of sexual confusion and self-doubt. I hated them because I needed them to fill temporarily a deep psychological void that had developed within me. I hated them because I needed the money enough to sacrifice my self-worth and dignity on the altar of their perverted lusts. And most of all, I hated them because what they were doing to me was driving me inexorably to suicide, and they did not care.

But there were some whom I did not hate. Instead, I felt sorry for them. Some of the men who picked me up did not aggressively attempt to coerce me, and often they were elderly or physically unattractive. My heart went out to them because I remembered being unattractive, too, and spending countless lonely hours in tears before a mirror. Now I had become the quintessential blond surfer, with a sleek body to match—the very object of their fantasies.

I saw the years of hurt and rejection in their eyes. At times some would even whimper as they held me, never believing in their wildest dreams that someone like me would allow them to touch him in such an intimate way. For these, I sometimes avoided the question of money or agreed to whatever small amount they suggested. I wanted to make their dreams come true. It was one of the few things I could do to feel better about myself. Such noble sentiments helped me pretend that my life was not as bad as it really was.

The hitchhiking I did was dangerous—that was obvious. This was so not only because I might be arrested or found out by my industry friends, but also because there were psychopaths riding around L.A., robbing and murdering young hitchhikers. I tried to stick to respectable spots—detouring around the known haunts of the hustler crowd.

One night, I was hitching at the corner of Sunset and Highland when a superfriendly middle-aged man picked me up. In order to give him lots of time to get around to asking for what he wanted, I told him I was going to Santa Monica. He suggested we cut through some back streets to Santa Monica Boulevard, and I agreed.

He pulled over into an unlit area between the boulevards. "How much you want for that?" he asked, pointing to my groin.

"Thirty," I replied.

"Okay, let's go," came his reply as he motioned me into the backseat.

Suddenly I felt his hands tighten around my neck. He was strangling me with all his might, screaming, "Don't fight me now! I got a gun! Don't you make me use my gun!"

His grip was fierce. His long fingernails were digging into my flesh. Blood was dripping down my chest, staining my white shirt.

The realization came quickly: *There's nothing I can do. I'll be dead within minutes.* But the fact was, I wanted to die. I was a wretched human being who deserved exactly what I was getting. I stopped struggling and resigned myself to death.

Just as I gave up, and as his fingers cut off my air supply, unexpected words burst out of my mouth: "But I'm a good person."

Everything stopped. We were both astonished because the grip he had around my neck should not have allowed me to speak. Only God could have caused those words to come out of me—words I never would have said about myself. And the effect they had on the strangler was dramatic. Something flipped a switch in his mind, compelling him to release me. Until that moment, he had thought he was getting rid of a bad person—a prostitute. Yet my words declared just the opposite and instantly quenched his psychotic rage.

"Get out of the car," he ordered, with a strange tone in his voice.

I bolted from the car and began running for all I was worth, expecting a bullet in my back at any moment. Instead, he sped off in the opposite direction, squealing his tires as he went. As I watched him drive away, I realized that God had saved my life. But I felt no gratitude. Instead, in the middle of the deserted street, I yelled out, "*God, I hate You! Why did You save my life? I deserve to die. I WANT to die! Why do You keep rescuing me?"*

There was no response. But one thing I knew: I was still alive when I should have been dead. And as bizarre as it may sound, I continued hustling, fully expecting that one day that sword of Damocles would finish the job. As far as I was concerned, hell was my destiny, and not even God could keep me from clawing my way to its depths.

Stayin' Alive

Fortunately, a wonderful married couple entered my life at about that time, and their friendship literally kept me alive. I cannot remember how I first met them. They were from Vermont and were about my age. Johnny was trying to break into cinematography, but was working as a film art director instead. He was tall, lanky and blond. Cindy was very Irish, lively and funny. She energized a room with her presence. They were a great couple, and I became fast friends with them. If I had not been able to turn to them on a regular basis, I don't know if I would be here today.

After walking and weeping and feeling like a piece of discarded trash on the heels of my near-death experience with the strangler in the car, I climbed into the old, beat-up VW that I had recently purchased and began to drive. I went racing down the hillside on the 405 Freeway from Westwood into the San Fernando Valley, so distraught that I crisscrossed all six lanes at top speed, over and over again, all the way down the steep grade. I was desperate—trying to get up the courage to simply crash into the cement barrier that divided the northbound and southbound lanes.

Instead of ending it all, however, I suddenly remembered Johnny and Cindy. Shaken and struggling with my death wish,

I drove to their house. I knew that with them I could relax, calm down and be loved—or at least be appreciated enough to stay alive. I never actually shared my deep internal grief with them, so they never knew how important they were to me. They only knew David, the actor. Never did I ever let them know my alter ego, Steve, the male prostitute.

— 11 —

READY for MY CLOSE-UP, MR. DEMILLE

While at Rock Hudson's birthday party, I met someone who put me on the right track to get my Screen Actors Guild membership, to get one of the best commercial agents in town (Don Schwartz & Associates) and to land my first acting roles. That put me on my way to "commercial" success.

Unless you are a recognizable celebrity, commercial production companies do not really care what kind of experience you have had. They simply want players who look the part and can project a vibrant personality and exude enormous energy. Commercials are high-octane vehicles—they have to be fueled by big smiles and endless vivacity.

Because landing one good national commercial can set them up financially for years, actors are likely to say whatever they need to about experience and past work to get the job. When I auditioned for a Lipton Lemon Tree soft drink commercial, for instance, the interviewer asked me if I could ride a penny-farthing. I had no idea what a penny-farthing was, but I gushed, "Absolutely! I've been riding one for years!" When I got the job, I was suddenly faced with having to learn how to ride an old-fashioned bicycle from the 1800s with one huge wheel in front and a tiny one in back. It was an *I Love Lucy* moment that first day on the set.

At the "callback" audition they had five penny-farthing bikes outside, and actors were trying to ride them, wobbling and crashing everywhere. I was able to keep my balance and look as if I knew what I was doing. Debra Winger played my girlfriend—this was before she became famous by costarring in *Urban Cowboy* with John Travolta. She was living in her car at the time of the commercial shoot, and I came very close to inviting her to stay at my apartment, but I was afraid she would make a play for me. I was too intimidated by her wild personality to feel safe with her.

Commercials are the bread and butter of any aspiring actor in Hollywood. Without them, it is practically impossible to make ends meet financially. I knew one woman who made a quarter of a million dollars a year just from commercials—and those were 1970s dollars, too. Being the perfect "mother" type, she had four or five commercials running at the same time.

I had a great time doing commercials. I was perfect for them— I had lots of small-town, wide-eyed, bouncy energy, and I possessed all-American looks. Some stage actors I knew looked down their noses at me because I had "lowered myself" to do commercials. Needless to say, they had no idea what I was really lowering myself to do.

My longest-running commercial was for Maytag dishwashers. For two days I sat around the dinner table with Grandma, Gramps and the family, eating a turkey dinner. Gramps would walk in from the kitchen and say, "Whose turn to do the dishes?"

I would reply, "Not me, Gramps!"

My little sister would say, "Let's let Maytag do it!"

Then Mom and Grandma would roll in the new dishwasher, and we would all get up and ooh and aah around it. I made thousands of dollars from that one commercial because it ran for two years.

My biggest commercial success was for McDonald's. That one also took two days to shoot. You would not think a thirty-second commercial would take that long to shoot, but that is fairly typical. I was a kid on a pogo stick in a park who gets a "Big Mac attack" and goes pogoing like mad down the street to McDonald's. It was exhausting work. Of course, at the audition I had sworn that, yes, I knew how to jump on a pogo stick. The truth was that I had never been on one in my life, but thankfully I managed to make it work.

On the second day, I had to sit in a McDonald's restaurant for hours, taking fresh bites out of a Big Mac—one after the other. I went through dozens of them. Fortunately, there was a bucket in which I could spit out a mouthful each time the camera stopped rolling, but it was rather nauseating. I was not fond of Big Macs in the first place, so after a few hours of shooting, I was more suited for a Pepto-Bismol commercial. But the show must go on, and I ended up looking delighted with each of those disgusting bites. Now *that* is acting!

A L'eggs Sport Sox commercial was a lot of fun, too. We played soccer all day at Will Rogers State Park while the crew filmed us. We had to memorize a song that we sang while we were playing soccer—something about "I love my L'eggs Sport Sox for men." To make sure the lip sync was correct, they rolled a prerecorded jingle sung by professional singers in New York. The famous cinematographer Conrad Hall did the shoot, and it was quite a thrill for me to work with him, even though it was just a commercial. Commercials are where the highbrow cinematographers actually make most of their bread and butter between film jobs.

You might think that with all this new commercial success, I was having a wonderful time, and that I had finally found happiness. There were some good times, but out of every dozen or so auditions, I would get only one or two callbacks. From those, only a handful resulted in parts. In all of 1975, I did two commercials and one movie. In 1976 I did four commercials. In 1977 I did one commercial and two movies. There were also print jobs and some photography work, but my secret life as a male hustler (and later on, a stint as a nude model for university art classes) was how I kept afloat financially.

Give My Regards to Broadway

Bill Robards was my first theatrical agent. I had only signed with him a few days earlier, when he called about a low-budget movie called *Cat Murkil and the Silks.* I was to audition for the starring role.

Hello! Never acted a day in my life and I'm about to audition for the starring role in a movie? No pressure! I thought.

It came along at a fortunate time, however. Not only was I hustling, but I was doing a lot of drugs and entertaining thoughts of suicide once again. I needed something else to focus on.

During the initial interview, I made up a story about having vast stage experience on Broadway in New York. The producer asked me to come back the next day for an audition. As I rehearsed the lines with my scene partner, I could see that it really was not going anywhere. She surprised me by suddenly stopping and blurting out, "Come on, put some passion into it! This is it! This is our only chance to get this thing. Let's do it!"

I stared at her, suddenly aware that she was absolutely right. I decided to go for broke and let my emotions take control. If I made a fool of myself, it was no big deal. I would never see these people again anyway, so I took the risk.

On the set in my first starring role, gang leader Cat Murkil, after filming a scene where I was thrown down the stairs by another gang leader. As you can see, I did my own stunts!

Acting can be therapeutic. If an actor has had an unhappy past and there are unresolved conflicts brewing inside him, he can use an acting role as an outlet to vent his true feelings and frustrations. With my wildly out-of-control personal life, I had plenty of steam. I did not, however, have the ability to come on to a girl like a stud. I had slept with only one girl my entire life, and I suffered from an acute case of insecurity when it came to women. Now this movie scene was calling for a sensual, swaggering attitude and a forceful delivery.

As the scene began, something happened that I can only describe as almost a miracle. I felt some kind of force suddenly envelop me—empowering my every word. At the same time, my body suddenly exuded confidence and swagger that came from someplace well beyond my years and experience. Maybe in some hidden part of my soul, I wanted to be that kind of man. Or maybe this was simply the way my subconscious chose to release my emotions. Whatever it was, it shocked and surprised me.

Halfway through the scene, the producer waved his hand and said, "That's enough. *That's enough!*"

I assumed that we had done a terrible job. In fact, I was feeling a bit humiliated as I headed for the door. Before I could get very far, the producer called me back and asked me to wait while he thanked the actress and told her good-bye.

No sooner had she shut the door than he turned to me rather matter-of-factly and said, "You've got the part."

The director nodded his agreement and said, "Okay, so here's the script. Learn as much of it as you can. We start filming next week, and you're in almost every scene. I'll place some press releases about you in the trades on Monday. And we'll see you in wardrobe on Wednesday, okay?"

As he went on, the frozen look of shock and disbelief on my face must have looked like a plaster cast. This was my dream of a lifetime coming true before my very eyes. How could it be happening to me—the guy who never had any of his prayers answered, the guy whom nobody loved, the guy who was so low, he could not see up?

In the film, I played a juvenile gang leader who idolizes his imprisoned brother (played by Steve Bond, more famous for playing Jimmy Lee Holt on General Hospital). My character kills a number of people in the picture during rival gang struggles, and even murders his brother's wife after attempting to rape her. At the end, a member of his own gang kills him.

A few days after I got the part, my brother John (Brother#2) called person-to-person from the East Coast, and we talked for an hour and a half. I found out a lot about what was going on back home—things my parents were keeping from me. John said Mom and Dad thought Hollywood was having a bad effect on me, and they even suspected that I was involved in homosexuality. John went on to say, "They say you've developed a foul mouth and that your soul is headed for the fiery depths of hell!"

They got that right!

That pretty much squelched my hopes for love and acceptance from my parents over my first movie. Not only would I be playing a very evil person; the script even included a nude scene.

In fact, it was a horrible script. And to make matters worse, the director did not give me one word of direction. The budget was virtually nonexistent. We went through two cinematographers, and I had an alcoholic acting coach whose only advice was, "Play the part like Dan Duryea!" No matter. I did not care—I was the *star*!

The publicity was hilarious. My little lie about having done stage acting in New York suddenly appeared in *Daily Variety* as "Broadway Legit Star, David Kyle, Heads the 'Cat' Cast." Fortunately, no one called me on it—probably because it helped what little box office there was. Plus, there probably was not a single actor in town who had not padded his résumé. Even Paul Lynde came to the wrap party that was given in my honor, so "the machine" had taken over.

The film went nowhere, of course. My aunt Joyce saw it on a double bill with *The Mini-Skirt Mob* at a drive-in in Salisbury, Maryland. The trade reviews were unexpectedly positive, though. For example, "Kyle gives a forceful portrayal as Cat Murkil." To this day, I find it hard to believe that the reviewer was not paid off.

The movie was re-released a year later as *Cruisin' High* and eventually made it around the country. But it certainly did not set my phone ringing off the hook with offers, as I had hoped it would.

Nevertheless, the dad of one of my actor friends was a VP at Fox. Using the leverage of my recent starring role, he was able to get me signed with one of the top theatrical agents in town. The problem was, now that I had starred in a movie, my new agent would send me out only for starring roles. He had to, really. Otherwise it would appear to casting directors, producers, directors and the like that my career was slipping. So even though my first role was not a big hit, it threw me into a world that was way over my head. I found myself competing against the likes of experienced stars such as John Travolta, Robby Benson and the other successful young male stars of the day.

I quickly realized that I needed some specialized training as an actor in order to live up to everyone's expectations, so I signed up with the Film Industry Workshop at CBS Studio City. There, I worked with Grant Goodeve and a number of the new young actors. But it did not go deep enough, so I signed up to get lessons from Jack Garfein of the L.A. Actors Studio. As well as having regular improvisation classes with Jack, I received great input from the likes of Harold Clurman, John Houseman and Stella Adler. It was one of the healthiest things I did while in show business.

The improv classes allowed me to act out my inner turmoil under the guise of playing a character. They were *extremely* therapeutic. Plus, it was an opportunity to be a serious actor, and perhaps one of note. I possessed all the deep inner turmoil necessary. It only needed to be shaped and guided. A great bonus were the extra classes I was able to take with the world's greatest dialect coach, Robert Easton, who had coached no less an actor than Sir Laurence Olivier. I also took dance classes from Tanya Everett, one of the best modern-dance teachers in the business. These classes were invaluable in keeping me alive because they infused me with new hope that I could have a decent future.

One evening, I decided to take in a movie at a theater in Westwood. As I stood in the endless popcorn line, I noticed that the guy in front of me was not moving forward with the others. Eventually, I decided just to move around him. Immediately, he looked up and said to me, "I'm standing here!"

I was just about to explain to the guy that since he was not moving, I had every right to go around him, when I realized, *I'm talking to Robert De Niro!*

Whoa! He was the actor I would most want to befriend, and the last guy I would want to upset. I meekly gestured to him that he was free to maintain his place in line. I was too intimidated to say anything. If I had it to do over again, though, I would say to him, "You talkin' to me?"

. . . The Harder They Fall

From 1975 to 1979, I probably had 140 theatrical interviews and 200 commercial interviews. But during that same period, I was only hired for 4 theatrical and 7 commercial jobs. The highs were rare but very high, and the lows felt like relentless rebuffs. Despite the fact that hiring in the entertainment business is, officially, a business decision and not a personal rejection, it is almost impossible not to feel unwanted and unacceptable when a job does not work out.

Add to that the shame and ever-present danger involved in my secret life, my self-loathing over having homosexual inclinations and my anger at God for not removing those desires. Then add the rising tide of my drug and alcohol use, and it is a miracle that I survived.

I must have had some acting talent, or I would never have been seen that many times by so many producers, directors and casting agents. Still, I lost several good acting roles through that time period. If I had gotten any one of them, it would have launched a national career. And it is very likely I never would have hit bottom hard enough to turn to God for help. Thank God for silver linings!

I was up for Luke Skywalker in *Star Wars*, and for Joe Hardy in *The Hardy Boys* (which I lost to Shaun Cassidy). I auditioned for the part of Nick Nolte's son in *Rich Man, Poor Man*, but one of the more lecherous men I had gotten tangled up with was also involved with the film, so I did not get that one. I also got passed over for the lead in *A Death in Canaan*, *Black Sheep Squadron*, *The Big Red One* and *The Boys in Company C*. I lost supporting roles in *Apocalypse Now*, *Jaws*, the TV series *Family*, *Little House on the Prairie*, *Happy Days*, *Dallas*, *Starsky & Hutch*, *How the West Was Won* and *The Waltons*.

There were two leading roles, however, that were more heart-breaking to lose than all the rest. *The Death of Richie* was a major film for television. It was also the first TV script I had ever read that was high quality and centered on the drama of the characters' lives. More profoundly, from my point of view, it was also very similar to my life story. I was being seen for the lead part of Richie, and I knew this was my big chance. I literally had lived this role in the real world, and the passion and anger required for the role was pent up inside me and ready to burst forth. *The Death of Richie* was the true story of a troubled teenager who hated his father and ended up killing him in one dramatic confrontational scene near the end. The only difference in my life was that I never pulled the trigger, but my hatred for my father was every bit as intense.

From the start, everyone knew I was perfect for the part. I must have gotten six callbacks, and each time, more people were present to see my audition—including the producer, director, casting agents, writer, studio execs and perhaps even the man who had been Richie. Finally, one day they all assembled for my final reading. It was a big confrontational scene with Richie's dad, and quite intense. When I left, I knew I had the part. My agent called and assured me I was the number-one candidate for the role.

It was such a slam-dunk that I already felt like celebrating. I was at home, caught up in the reverie of what was about to take place, when the phone rang. My agent, David Wilder, called to tell me that they had given the role to Robby Benson. "Look, I'm sorry about this," he said. "And you can be sure that I'll have other parts for you."

I was devastated. It was like having the Hope Diamond in your hands for a second and then watching in slow motion as it slips through your fingers and drops into the ocean.

That is the way it works in Hollywood. Production companies do not cast the person most suited to the role, or even the one with the most talent. They cast according to notoriety. In television, it is called the "TV-Q" or "TV Quotient." This refers to a "magic number" advertisers assign to actors, a quotient that informs them about how many people are likely to watch the show as a result of a particular actor being in the cast. A well-known actor—a guy like Robby Benson during my day—gets the part every time.

The same thing happened with *The Boy in the Plastic Bubble*. I thought that one was a done deal, too, since I had had all but the final, official word. All you have to do, however, is replace the name Robby Benson with the name John Travolta. John swooped in at the last minute and snatched the part right out of my hands. The only difference in this case was that playing the boy in the bubble would not have been the part of a lifetime. Playing Richie was.

I was perfect for the part of the "Bubble Boy" visually, and have always thought that I could have played it much better than Travolta did. Also, it would have significantly increased my TV-Q and would have catapulted me into roles I subsequently tried out for and did not get, some of which would have made me famous. So my sorrow over losing this role, though not as deep as my grief about losing the Richie role, was nevertheless incredibly discouraging.

God was after me. He made that clear when He saved me from being murdered, thwarted my suicide attempts and prevented me from becoming famous and highly successful. I was looking for earthly fame, but He had something far better in mind for me.

— 12 —

FRIENDS and
LOVERS

In Hollywood, it is extremely difficult to find real friends. The environment is much too predatory. Lonely as I often was, however, there were a handful of people whom I always considered true friends. They seemed to like me not for what they could get from me, but just for being who I was. While some of my motives in meeting them were not altogether noble, there still remained afterward a level of friendship that seemed to transcend the typical Hollywood scene.

For a while, I shared a house in Reseda with Derrel Maury, whom I had knocked off in *Cat Murkil and the Silks*. He had starred in the cult classic flick *Massacre at Central High*, so we were a perfect match. Together we entertained some of our peers (Robert Carradine, Lani O'Grady and others) at the old ranch house, and at one point we decided to entertain ourselves by renting out the house to a porn company for a couple days. Turned out they were Mafia types. When the shooting was over (one gay film and one straight film), the big boss, a classic Mafia guy with gold chains around his neck and a honkin' cigar squeezed between his blackened teeth, refused to pay us—and we let him get away with it!

After a year of baking in the Valley in triple-digit heat, I decided to move to Hollywood. There I met a guy I will call Jeremy while auditioning for a McDonald's commercial. He was a New York actor who found himself feeling embarrassed about being at a commercial audition. As a result, he was acting surly and disinterested when I watched him from across the room. He had recently appeared in a movie I had seen, and I had been rather taken by him then. And now, there he was in the flesh. His brooding, dark good looks were stunning.

For me, the idea of falling in love with a guy was absurd. Yet it happened on the spot, or so I felt. I never wanted to be homosexual. I did not like most homosexuals. I had never had a lover, nor did I want one. But I found Jeremy irresistible.

He left the audition before I did, but as I was driving home, I saw him walking down the sidewalk. I stopped and asked him if he wanted a ride. He hesitated at first, and then agreed to get into my little VW Beetle. He only lived half a mile away, so he invited me in for a glass of wine for my trouble. He lived in the Villa Valentino—a house that Rudolph Valentino had once owned that had later been converted into apartments.

After some small talk, I learned that Jeremy was dating a young actress I will call Wendy. *That's good news. At least he isn't gay*, I thought. *Hopefully "bi," though.*

We decided to go out to dinner. As I sat across from him in a small, candlelit Hollywood restaurant, I fell head over heels in love with him. I had no way of knowing at the time that he was experiencing the same reaction to me. He was too cautious to let me know.

We ended up sleeping together that night and every night

for months thereafter. He seemed perfect for me because he, too, was very independent and it was no big deal for us to be apart when necessary. Neither he nor I wanted others to know about our relationship, and we did not want to live together— he did not want a "lover" relationship any more than I did. I never told him about "Steve" either, and he never knew I was a hustler.

Soon after we got together, he introduced me to Wendy. She liked me a lot, she used to say, because I had never seen the TV series she was in, so she knew I was not interested in her because of her fame. She never knew about Jeremy and me, but he soon broke off his relationship with her to devote himself to me. At the same time, Wendy and I went out together as friends, and I treasured the companionship we had. For the rest of my Hollywood years and beyond, we all remained good friends.

Wendy had a beach house in Malibu, so we got together there a lot. She was great fun—somehow both shy and brash. One time she visited me in my apartment, and we talked for hours. Before leaving, she went into my bathroom and wrote in soap on the mirror, "I want your body." I discovered it after she left, but I never said a word to her about it. Assertive women were much too scary for me.

Around that time, I got a letter from a college friend, David Newman. I remembered doing lots of drugs with him in college, so the content of his letter seemed rather bizarre to me. He wrote,

> *The Christmas season has become so much more meaningful since I accepted Jesus as my Savior over two years ago. The greatest gift ever offered was that of God's precious Son, and God's loving hand is still extended to present the gift of abundant life and eternal life to all who are willing to believe and receive.*

David, if I recall correctly, you were raised in a Christian home. (Isn't your father a minister?) Well, Christianity may seem like just another religion to you, but I truly believe that Jesus is the way to God and the means by which man can more fully realize his potential.

My life has been changed so much by the love and power of God through Jesus. Please consider the claims of Christ this Christmas. He loves you, and wants to change your life. Love, joy, peace and hope are some of the wonderful things Christ wants you to have in Him.

Barely a month later, Jeremy broke up with me. Once again, I teetered on the verge of suicide. And once again, my friend Cindy saw my condition, reached out to me and offered me the affirmation and encouragement I needed. But that same week, Freddie Prinze (star of *Chico and the Man*) committed suicide, which left me even more depressed. I had met Freddie and knew the hurt he was living with.

Jeremy and I got back together, but the breakup had created a permanent barrier between us. While I still hated the idea of being a homosexual, somehow I had completely accepted the fact that I was deeply in love with him. And although I tried to hide it even from myself, I was shattered by the emotional loss when our relationship finally came to an end.

One of the places that I would run for solace was the beach. In fact, for many years I went to the beach almost daily in order to regain my sanity—usually Malibu, but often Zuma, which was my favorite. I was enamored with surfing—body or board. Not being able to afford my own board, I was not able to become proficient at surfing, but I loved the independence of it and the solitude of the sport. I loved floating in the water, communing with nature and feeling the burst of excitement upon catching a wave. The beach was a place where I could talk to God and feel close to Him. (He was nowhere to be found in Hollywood.) And the surfers were not as phony as the people in show business. They played hard and partied hard, but were real and up-front about it. As the years progressed, God used the beach to help me maintain my sanity and to keep my soul from fracturing permanently.

As I mentioned earlier, my friends Johnny and Cindy had become mainstay lifesavers for me. By now, I was spending practically every evening with them. Cindy was a ball of fun, and Johnny was a steady source of straight male bonding. They would cook gourmet meals for me, and we would stay up till all hours of the night smoking dope and laughing about our crazy encounters in show business. I still had not shared anything about "Steve" with them, for fear they would no longer be my friends, but "Steve" had his own social circle that he was involved with. He had a number of fellow hustler friends whom he met at parties centered around that world. In fact, my hustler friends were some of the most loving, dearest friends I had ever had.

— 13 —

STARDOM—TAKE TWO

In June 1977, I got a part in the NBC Movie of the Week *Murder in Peyton Place*. I played Billie Kaiserman, the D.A.'s evil son who tries to blackmail a girl with compromising pictures. The filming was done at 20th Century Fox on the *Hello, Dolly!* set. What a huge break this was for a small-town boy like me, acting on the set where Barbra Streisand had filmed one of her most famous roles.

My scenes were with Kimberly Beck—a hot young starlet. And this time, in this film, I really was out of my league. I was working for 20th Century Fox no less, and still did not feel as though I knew how to act in a movie. To make matters worse, as with when I played Cat Murkil before, the director gave me zero direction, so I had to make it up on the spot, without any idea what they wanted, how it looked or how it sounded. It was an agonizing two-day shoot, and afterward, I could not bear to watch those scenes.

After the movie was finished, the network, at least at first, refused to pick it up for airing. Of course, I asked myself, *Was*

In November 1977 on the set of my second starring role (*The Great Cash Giveaway Getaway*), with George Hamilton (seated middle) and Albert Salmi (at right). Although I never had a scene with Hamilton, he and Salmi were great fun to be with.

I really that bad? Fortunately, it aired later that year and has been rerun a number of times. I got lots of mail from back home when friends and family saw me in the movie, even though I was only in two scenes.

One day, Eve Plumb from the *Brady Bunch* and I auditioned for the lead roles in the same movie. The working title was *Grass Roots*. I was excited at the possibility of working with Eve, since we had become good friends. The production people actually had the two of us audition together. The director, Michael O'Herlihy, had not seemed that impressed with our audition, and I pretty much wrote the job off. But after a few days had passed, I got a call from my agent, David Wilder, telling me I had gotten the part. Not only that, he added, but it would include "before the title" starring credit ahead of George Hamilton, James Keach and Albert Salmi.

I was thrilled beyond belief. As a result of my recent emotional turmoil, I had begun to think more about religion and the meaning and purpose of life. Perhaps this was a sign that God was watching over me. I had reached a point where I sincerely wanted to think so.

Michael O'Herlihy was Irish and paraded around the set in a proper suit, with an ascot tie snugly tucked in around the neck. This was somewhat amusing since the temperature ran into the midnineties most days. He must have been dying underneath all his wardrobe accoutrements. I could easily relate to his desire to fulfill the romantic image of a director, and I especially loved it when he would yell, "Prrriiinnnttt!" with his Irish trill.

There was also a rather colorful public relations lady running around the set, trying to ignite and fan a spark between my leading lady and me. She wanted it to flame into a real-life romantic relationship between us so she would have a story to sell for the teen magazines, but it never happened. (My friend Eve did not get the part. Instead, Elissa Leeds of *General Hospital* fame played my girlfriend, Hallie.)

To my surprise, George Hamilton turned out to be a great guy in real life. I had had a negative image of him, but once I met him, my opinion drastically changed. Yes, he was vain about his golden tan, sitting around the set half the time with a reflector around his neck. But he was also charming, gracious and witty. He played a lot of poker with the crew and liked to flash a large roll of bills.

The man who played my father, Albert Salmi, was an actor of enormous talent whom I greatly admired. He was a genuine Broadway star and an alumnus of the Actors Studio. He had appeared in many of the early TV shows in the 1950s and '60s (*Twilight Zone, Bonanza, Gunsmoke, Wagon Train*) and could still be seen regularly as a character actor. Salmi was also friendly and gracious, even lending me money at one point when I wanted to buy cocaine. Sadly, he suffered from depression and killed his wife and himself some thirteen years later.

The most ominous presence of all were the "suits" from NBC in New York, who, while friendly on the outside, were there to judge the quality of the production. It was their job to pull the plug at any sign that the project might be unsuccessful. Officially the production company was called Penthouse Productions, but that was simply a front for NBC. At the time, the networks were not supposed to be producing their own programs.

The task of creating a believably innocent 16-year-old character was not so easy for me at the ripe old age of 27. For some reason, I still looked 16 in spite of all the drugs I had been using, but street life had taken me far away from those days of innocence. I was forced to create an Andy Hardy type character to pull it off. The executive director loved it, so I stuck with it.

It was great to be treated like a VIP again by someone other than a sex partner. It is no wonder kings risk death to keep their thrones. It is a powerful, addictive high to be thought of as Hollywood royalty—even when you know it will all vanish when the director finally yells, "That's a wrap!"

One day while on location, I wandered into a darkroom hidden inside the big rig production truck and accidentally locked myself in. No one was around to hear my shouts for help; they were all out on the set waiting for me. It was not long before they called the police for fear I had been kidnapped for ransom. When they finally found me, even then I was treated with deference and respect. When the car delivered me back to the set, the director laughed heartily to show me that I did not need to sweat the great expense I had just caused the production company. Faint praise though it was, I remember it as a deeply meaningful moment for me.

Yet despite all the star treatment, I was drawn back to the streets every night and continued to sell my body to the highest bidder, risking my entire career to feed some mysterious need that drove me to extremely dangerous behavior. Indeed, I was two very different people in one body, with two very different sets of needs. While NBC "suits" could make David feel as if he were on cloud nine, they could not give "Steve" what one john gave me the night he took me to a motel room across from Hollywood High School and asked me to hug him tightly. That was all he wanted. No sex. No nudity even. For an hour or two, just hugs.

The TV movie was aired with the title changed to *The Great Cash Giveaway Getaway*. When it was rereleased years later, it was renamed *The Magnificent Hustle*. (*There's irony!* I thought.) Even more years later, it was screened again with the original title *Grass Roots*. When filming was over, we all said good-bye amidst promises to keep in touch. We never did.

Descending into Darkness

My sex life grew ever more dangerous as I began to realize that the peace and satisfaction in life that I hoped to find as an actor was not happening. No matter how successful I might become in Hollywood, I would always be the guy who had sold himself to the highest bidder.

As my behavior grew darker, I could sense that I was no longer in control. That was never more apparent than the night I felt compelled to run through the Hollywood Hills unclothed, darting from bush to bush as the cars sped by. As I ran, I remembered a story from the Bible about a demoniac who ran through the hills unclothed, and I wondered if that same thing was happening to me.

Finally, I ran into the empty lobby of an apartment complex, hopped up on a table and looked at myself in the large mirror there. Looking back at me, from my very own eyes, were the eyes of demons. That did not surprise me at all. I walked back to my apartment, wondering how much longer I would have until the demons were able to take my life and drag me into hell. *It can't be long now*, I figured.

My confidence in myself as a man had gradually eroded over the time I spent in Hollywood. After seven years of hustling, I eventually lost all confidence that I could ever again make love to a woman. This was brought painfully to my attention thanks to a popular young actress whom I adored, but whose sexual overtures frightened me. She was lovely, and I found her very attractive. But although she was clearly interested in me, I was overwhelmed with fear after our first date and did not ask her out again.

It was ironic that in high school my problem had been rejection by girls, but now that a myriad of gorgeous females surrounded me, I was too afraid to do anything about it. My fear was not only about sexual performance; I was also unwilling to take the risk that these women would turn against me once they discovered my secrets. I had become used to the predictability of other men and the simplicity of those encounters. I had also slowly programmed my sexual response system over the years to respond only to males. I had convinced myself that a relationship with a female would be difficult and perhaps impossible.

On the other hand, I had not wholeheartedly entered into the homosexual world. I continued to avoid gay bars and bathhouses. Those places were obscene in my eyes, mostly because of the exploitation of young kids that went on there. But I also was repulsed by sleazy perversion that typified that subculture. And, strange as it may seem, despite sleeping with over a thousand males by then, I still did not consider myself a homosexual, so I certainly did not want other people thinking I was one.

I had also become aware of another fact. As an innocent young boy, I had looked up to movie stars as an ancient mortal would have looked up to the gods of Mount Olympus, gazing at them in all their glory. Once I had climbed the mountain, however, I discovered not only that Hollywood's players were mere mortals and not gods, but that they were, in fact, mortals with serious problems. There was not one boyhood hero or heroine who, once I had actually met the person, had not tumbled gracelessly from his or her pedestal.

The original intention of my Hollywood dream had been fairly simple. I wanted to become a success so that all the people who had once rejected me would love me—or would at least accept me and acknowledge my worth. But as I became better acquainted with the excesses of sin, corruption and perversion that embodied the real Hollywood, I understood that even if I could impress those people back home, it would be meaningless. Even if I had won the movie role of a lifetime, it would have given me only the *appearance* of success and importance, while leaving untouched the ugliness that hid behind it. No wonder so many movie stars commit suicide. Ironically, there is no more perfect metaphor for Hollywood than a Hollywood set—beautiful on the face of it, but completely barren and empty behind the façade.

I had to do something more than just win the acceptance of my parents, siblings and childhood friends. I had to win my own acceptance. The problem was, I knew that I was unworthy of acceptance. I was a prostitute. I had been one for years, which in my view was enough to make me forever worthless. I was also still a drug addict, as were almost all my friends. And my dreams and image of Hollywood had been irreparably shattered. Any hope that life or meaning or eternal purpose and fulfillment could be found there had become laughable.

Ironically, it was not that I had yet become a has-been. *Teen Bag* magazine was touting me as a new, upcoming star. They published a full-page picture of me with the caption, "Can You Love Him?" How appropriate! I was a new face that would surely capture the hearts of filmgoers if I got the right parts. The magazine listed my acting credits, some true, some not so true. It even reported Glynnis O'Connor (star of the popular *Sons*

* New Faces! *

CAN
YOU
LOVE
HIM?

Meet David Kyle. He's already done a TV movie of the week and a film and his friends all hope he'll make it . . . How about you?

■ Every now and then TEEN BAG will focus on a newcomer, a new face, that it thinks will capture your hearts if he gets the right roles . . . this time it's David Kyle.
   Currently he's studying at Jack Garlein's ACTORS & DIRECTORS LAB. But that's only the half of it. He's studied French and Oxford English dialects with Robert Easton. He's studied film and TV craft at The Film Industry Workshop in CBS Studio Center. Before that he was into drama and theatre at Eckerd Center Theatre in Florida.
   His talents were great and in Florida he played roles like Romeo of "Romeo & Juliet." Ronnie in "House of Blue Leaves" and the lead role in "Blue Denim. He was also James in the "Miracle Worker."
   He's 5'9" tall, has blond hair and blue eyes, weighing in at 140 pounds. Glynnis O'Connor and other young stars say he's a fella who'll go far—with the right breaks.
   These days he's added sports and fencing to his daily regime, taking modern dance with Tanya Everett. You can write David % Lew Sherrell Ltd., 7060—Hollywood Blvd., Los Angeles, California 90028.

This page from *Teen Bag* magazine in 1978 told it like it was—I was looking for love from anyone and everyone and would do almost anything to get it.

& Daughters TV program) and other young females as breathlessly avowing that with the right breaks, I would definitely reach stardom.

I was also getting fan mail. For a while, I reveled in the attention. I tried to believe the lie that I was worth something because starry-eyed, prepubescent girls somewhere in America were swooning over my photograph. But reality always has a way of catching up with us, and before long, the facts of my life settled over me again like so much dirty, greasy smog. I was like a roach at the bottom of a trash can, scurrying around looking for a way out. Life had to have more meaning than selling my body and soul to lonely, sexually confused men or even to the idol factories of Hollywood.

I had been getting pretty beaten up on the streets. The latest murder attempt was by a man who took me to a darkened warehouse and had me stand on a conference table while he shone spotlights on me. He then disappeared up into the rafters somewhere—I figured either to videotape me or to shoot me while videotaping me. A notorious serial killer of young blond boys was roaming L.A. at the time, and he liked to torture his victims, cut them up and deposit the parts in trash cans around Hollywood. Something told me this was the guy.

Yet *not* to my surprise, I did not care. I wanted to die and needed someone else to end my life for me. As I stood there waiting for the arrow through the heart, or whatever he might choose to do, the atmosphere in the warehouse suddenly shifted, as if supernatural beings had arrived and chased out the demonic powers that had been orchestrating the moment. In that instant, I knew I was not going to die, and sure enough, the man immediately appeared and ordered me to get in the car. He drove me back to where he had found me and let me out. Once again, I was left wondering why some unseen force had run interference on my willing march into hell.

I agreed to do one of my last acting jobs as a favor for some friends. Tommy Wallace had created a script with another writer, John Carpenter—a horror flick called *Halloween*. Another friend, Craig Stearns, was the art director for the film. Although I say that since it was a small part, I got involved as a favor to them, they may have seen it as doing a favor for me since my career seemed stuck in neutral. Even though I had starred in a TV movie just seven months before, as they say in the business, "You're only as good as your last film."

At the time, no one guessed that this was going to be a big hit film, one that would revive the lost genre of horror films. And no one knew that Jamie Lee Curtis was going to be such a big star. It seemed to us more like a low-budget drive-in movie, which is why I considered it a favor on my part to be in it.

I had a small role in the first scene of the film. I was practically the only guy in the movie who did not get murdered. My role was to make out with a girl on the couch in the living room, while her little six-year-old brother watched from outside the house. Then we went upstairs to have sex. At that point, the little brother entered the back of the house and got a knife. This was all done from the boy's point of view. It was shot with a then-new invention called a Steadicam and was filmed in one long 20-minute shot with no edits, a groundbreaking scene at the time.

After I came downstairs and left the house, the kid went upstairs and killed his sister. It took two days to shoot that scene;

mostly due to the elaborate way they were filming it. That left the cast sitting around in the trailer most of the time, playing cards, talking and getting a little bit drunk.

I still get residuals for the many TV airings of *Halloween*. It is ironic that the smallest part I ever played was in the only picture that continues to endure.

PART FOUR

SPIRITUAL DECEPTION

It was a night that was impossible to forget. Sitting alone on my bed, legs crossed in the lotus position and hands formed in the Gyan Mudra position, I began to meditate on "Holy Light." By now, I was quite proficient in this technique and could quickly bring to my awareness the light that shone within. It was my favorite of the four meditation techniques revealed to me by the guru because it was the most "supernatural" in its effect. I loved to bathe in the light and meditate on the belief that it was the pure essence of God Himself. I had also been taught that it was my purest essence as well, and that the ultimate goal of meditation was to become so one with the light that I would lose my identity and merge into it, thus gaining the consciousness that I was one with it.

Of course, on this night I did not expect anything different from the normal blissful experience that I had grown used to having during the meditation, but was I ever in for a shock. About forty minutes into the meditation, I suddenly moved from observer to subject. In other words, I suddenly merged into the light and became one with it. My individual identity ceased and became one with the light.

On the one hand, it was a bit frightening to lose my individual identity. Yet on the other hand, the experience felt like one of complete bliss and peace. Without warning or expectation, I had achieved "nirvana" and suddenly seemed to be experiencing the incredible God-consciousness that gurus spend their entire lives pursuing.

— 14 —

LIVIN' in the GURU . . . U.S.A.

My close relationship with the man I am calling Hugh, the well-known Malibu playwright, went on for years. He continued his obsession with me, and for a long time I needed his approval as a father figure. I also treasured the recognition of seeing—and being seen by—the coterie of genuinely talented people who surrounded him.

When July 1979 came around, on the day before my 28th birthday, I called him and asked if I could spend the night on his pool deck. My hunger for love was insatiable, and my thirst for spirituality was intensifying. Someone had told me that the "spiritual energies" on that particular day were powerful because of the full moon and some kind of a "spiritual convergence." In my emotional misery, I was trying explore the depths of life since the heights had proven so disappointing. At first, Hugh said no because he had other plans. But uncharacteristically, I insisted.

While I was there, a Malibu surfer named Don came over to visit. He was a young kid, and I assumed he was another of Hugh's boy lovers. He was nice, enthusiastic and upbeat—a refreshing change from the jaded Hollywood crowd. At one point, he and Hugh were leaving to go see a video about an Indian guru, Maharaj Ji. As an afterthought, Don invited me along. I told him, "I don't want to go see no tape about no guru!"

Then Hugh mentioned that they were going to Timothy Gallwey's house. That caught my attention. Timothy Gallwey was the author of one of the biggest-selling books at the time, called *The Inner Game of Tennis*. I had not even begun to stop chasing the great and the near great, so I went along. *Maybe,* I thought, *somebody will make a movie out of Gallwey's book. If I get to know him now, I'll be in a better position to get a part in it later.*

The author's home was in the exclusive Point Dume area north of Malibu, near Zuma Beach. Tim Gallwey had a sunken living room covered in polar bear rugs and a wife who looked as if she had just stepped out of *Vogue*. Tim was clearly part of the elite Malibu jet-setting world, so I enthusiastically listened to everything he had to say. He talked about his book and his house for a while. Then gradually, he changed the subject to the purpose of life and how important it is to find it.

I was immediately enthralled. I had hungered for acceptance, and my dreams of fulfilling that need had been crushed. By now I knew I needed something more—something substantial to satiate the yearning that burned inside me. Here I was, listening to a man with money, fame, a beautiful wife and a fabulous house, who was confidently telling me how he had found purpose in life. His words were mesmerizing.

Gallwey spoke for about 45 minutes. Then he masterfully eased the direction of his talk toward Guru Maharaj Ji. All

I could remember about Maharaj Ji was that he had been a pudgy little kid who had immigrated to the United States from India in the early 1970s, when he was 12. By the time I was at the Gallweys' home, the guru was 21. Eastern mysticism was a hot subject, so he had been on all the talk shows. I had seen him on the *Merv Griffin Show* that day I had been in the college lounge after trying to commit suicide, and then again on the cover of *Life* magazine.

Gallwey continued to hold us spellbound, relating how Maharaj Ji offered practical experience to people instead of just another set of religious concepts. His words were meaningless as far as leading people to the one true God, but they struck just the right chords in my mind and heart at that time. Then Timothy put in the videotape. For another twenty minutes, we heard from Guru Maharaj Ji himself.

I was not 100 percent sure about the guru, but Gallwey convinced me that there really could be life after Hollywood.

God and the Guru

Love and acceptance. Acceptance and love. Those three little words, and the emptiness in my soul that hungered for their satisfaction, had become something of a mantra for me. By the time I first heard about Maharaj Ji, I had given up all hope of finding any sort of emotional fulfillment in Hollywood. But now a new possibility had emerged, and I felt a ripple of hope that there was something for me in this young guru's mystical teachings.

It was clear by then that the entertainment business simply could not satisfy my deepest needs. Instead, little by little, my focus was shifting from dreams of stardom to an exploration of the supernatural. Surely the Cosmos—as I had begun to call whatever power existed beyond the material word—could offer meaning and purpose. And if my life became meaningful to the Ultimate Power, surely my need for love and acceptance would be met as well.

At that point, the Protestant denomination I had grown up in was of no interest to me. In my view, Christianity was a plastic religion populated by people who only pretended to have faith. I still respected Jesus, or at least the idea of Him. But my antagonism toward God had increased through the years, and my defenses against Him were rock hard and unyielding. I hated the "imaginary" deity of stuffy, uncaring church people. I had had enough of Him and His followers. But it was beginning to dawn on me that there might just be another deity out there—someone or something that could actually have benevolent thoughts and plans for me. The idea of an impersonal Higher Power appealed to me. I envisioned such a pure energy force redeeming my past and transforming all the evil I had ever done into something meaningful.

After the first meeting at Gallwey's home, I had been skeptical despite his brilliance. But in the days that followed, his words haunted me. I was invited to another similar event and eagerly went along. This second meeting was called a *satsang*, a Sanskrit word that identifies a gathering for the purpose of seeking Truth, the Ultimate Being, or God.

We found ourselves in Malibu once again, and this time we all removed our shoes before entering the house. As I looked around, the crowd of chic, wealthy searchers impressed me. Their warmth and sincerity melted more of my skepticism. *This isn't a bunch of poor, uneducated people grasping at straws*, I thought. Instead, they seemed highly educated and financially sound. One by one, various men and women described how uncertain they had been about Maharaj Ji at first, and how wonderful life had become after they had finally opened their hearts to the love he offered.

Tim Gallwey spoke again. Once more I was enthralled with his enthusiasm. He spoke confidently and rapidly of receiving "Knowledge"—with a capital *K*—that becomes available to us when enlightened teachers help us connect our consciousness with the Energy Force we call God. He explained that this Energy Force flows through each of us and is part of us. He called it the Divine within.

After the meeting, I gave a ride to two young guys who lived in one of Maharaj Ji's ashrams. *Ashram* is another Sanskrit word that literally means "to work." An ashram is generally a residence for followers of an Eastern guru. Ashrams are common among Hindus, and Maharaj Ji, as I came to learn, borrowed liberally from Hinduism and other Eastern religions, as well as from Christianity. He was from India, but had been raised in a Catholic school there.

I was attracted to one of the guys and thought I would try to develop a friendship—maybe even more—with him. I also wanted to see what level of poverty they had to live with in the ashram. When we arrived, I was amazed to find myself inside a beautiful modern house overlooking the Pacific Ocean. It was right below Maharaj Ji's own lavish home, which crowned a nearby hill in Trancas Beach.

I questioned the two disciples about the ashram's prosperous look. I had assumed that austerity would be a necessary part of its existence. They told me that abject poverty was a religious concept Maharaj Ji simply did not embrace. Instead, he drove a Rolls-Royce and taught that possessing material things is not a sin. "Only the attachment to material things is wrong," one of the guys explained.

I decided to suspend judgment on that one for the moment.

In becoming involved with the guru, I also failed to notice that I was repeating the same fantasy I had cherished before, when I thought Hollywood was my ticket out of the mess I had made of my life. This time, I thought my ticket was the guru. By the time he entered the scene, my life was in shambles, just as it had been when I left college. My alcohol and drug use was rampant. My dependence on hustling for both income and sexual gratification was increasingly dangerous. I knew I had to make some changes.

My new friends suggested that I travel to Miami the following week to see Maharaj Ji in person. Was he a charismatic teacher of wisdom or a charlatan? I needed to find out.

At first, I was under the impression that I would be traveling to Miami to have a *private* meeting with Maharaj Ji. However, I was disabused of that notion the minute I entered the convention center. The presence of somewhere around ten thousand frenetic *premies*—"lovers of truth" in Sanskrit—was overwhelming. What energy! What excitement! Immediately, I was glad I had come.

Hopeful as I was, however, I was still looking for signs of weirdness. Were the participants dressed in strange garb? Did they appear brainwashed or on drugs? Were they true believers, or was a shadow of doubt hovering over the room? To my relief, everyone looked absolutely normal.

Before long there was buzz and excitement, and suddenly Maharaj Ji walked onto the stage. In an electrifying moment, the venue exploded into a kind of glee approaching delirium. Arms were raised in exaltation. Cheers and squeals filled the air. This was the last thing I had expected. Until then, I had only seen relatively serene lecture videos. There was more going on here than uplifting teaching, more than the appearance of a "good" man. I watched in amazement.

This is new, I thought. *This is different. This is exciting. Even if he turns out to be a fraud, this is one bizarre trip that I've never taken before.*

I had no idea that the ten thousand people in the Miami

Convention Center actually believed that their guru was God Himself.

There are only two reasons people act this way, I counseled myself. *They are either brainwashed, or they're responding to something genuine, something transformational and fulfilling.*

No one seemed brainwashed, so I opened up my spirit to welcome Maharaj Ji in.

After his intriguing lecture, Maharaj Ji sat on that Miami stage for several hours, moving nothing except his head while the faithful paraded in front of him, kissing his feet. As they walked away from him after doing so, there was such an obvious look of bliss on their faces that I decided to try it myself to see if there was something supernatural going on. As I bent down to kiss his feet, I tried to pour out to him every bit of love that I could muster.

As I walked away, I felt only a subtle vibration and a vague sense of peace. Left and right, others were losing consciousness all around me. That puzzled me. What about me? I could not have known—would not have wanted to know—that the one true God was subtly leading me to Himself along the only path I was willing to follow.

I returned to L.A. and dove into the Bible for several weeks. Thanks to my limited biblical knowledge, I was easily convinced that Maharaj Ji was, indeed, God in the flesh. Helping me along, of course, were members of his cult, who offered a random collection of convoluted Scriptures the guru used to convince people of his authenticity.

I attended satsang almost every night after the Miami trip. I eagerly listened to the premies talk at length about their love for Maharaj Ji and what he had done in their lives. They repeatedly spoke about the meaning and purpose he had brought to the world.

I was captivated by the notion that, for some strange reason, God had decided to allow me to become a part of something ultimate and cosmic. I thought it was worth a shot, in any case. If there were any chance that this guru was God and that my wretched life could be redeemed through my involvement with him, I was going for it with everything in me. I suspended my acting and hustling pursuits to devote every waking hour to following Maharaj Ji.

New Twist: A Family in Prayer

What I did not know and really could not have imagined was that other forces—powerful forces—were at work on my behalf. Of all people, my parents were pouring out their love for me in a most unexpected way.

During the late 1970s, my parents had encountered the charismatic renewal in the Presbyterian Church and had experienced a dramatic turnaround in their lives. As they described it, "Our faith became deeper and more substantive and God more real in our lives." They believed that the Holy Spirit had come into them in a new way, and their faith had become something tangible and vital, as opposed to something academic and peripheral to everyday life.

I did not realize exactly what had happened to my parents. Instead, in my letters, I tried to convince them that they needed Guru Maharaj Ji. Unbeknownst to me, however, Mom and Dad's belief in the authority of the Bible had dramatically increased. Their network of friends had blossomed beyond the nominal "mainline" Presbyterian crowd to include serious believers and prayer warriors who were serving God all over the world. And they were all praying for me.

When I wrote to my parents about the guru, my words deeply troubled them, more intensely than I might have imagined. They knew very well that I was deceived, and they feared that I would be lost to the true God forever. The letters I wrote to them were sobering, showing how dangerously deceived and lost I really was. In a letter dated September 6, 1979, I wrote,

> *Maharaj Ji is the Lord—please believe it! He has heard my cries for help and has come to make me a devotee of him.*

Later I wrote,

> *The only clue we have to finding God is through our hearts, because that is where truth lies. There we can find Him.*
>
> *My recognition of who Maharaj Ji is was immediate. My heart told me right away. It was my mind that kept me from true devotion for all this time.*
>
> *Stop listening to your minds and you will see that he is the Lord—you will see with your heart—not your mind.*

Only in my letters did I try to convert my parents. I was afraid to talk to them on the phone or in person about the guru. In my memory, they had always denigrated my hopes and dreams, criticized my interests or tried to talk me out of them. That is why I had never shared with them my dreams for Hollywood. And now what was happening between me and my guru was way too precious to argue with them about. I was unwilling to receive their criticism in any form other than a letter that could easily be thrown away.

Meanwhile, I was tireless in my efforts to convince them of my newfound faith. Many of my letters to my parents were ten to fifteen pages long. Only my concern for their salvation prodded me to reveal slowly and gently to them that God was on the planet. As it turned out, they already knew more about God's presence among us than I did. Still I wrote,

> *Your mind, your ego, your imagination is deceiving you into thinking that Maharaj Ji is not the Holy Spirit. That*

is its job, its purpose. Feel from the heart—that is where truth lies, not in the mind.

Later, after a supernatural experience, I wrote to them,

I'm no longer the impetuous little kid that you remember who ran off and dove into things without thinking. Remember, I've been living in the unreal world of Los Angeles for six years now—have a college degree—and can safely say that I'm no fool. I have checked out every angle on this thing.

Last Saturday I received "Knowledge." There is now no longer anything of this world that can touch me as long as I use the tools of "Knowledge" given to me by God. It is absolutely forbidden by God for one who has received this precious "Knowledge" to reveal it to anyone. Only God Himself can do that and only through Guru Maharaj Ji.

When "Knowledge" was revealed to me, I saw just who Maharaj Ji was. The first thing I saw was light—incredible light, that which would power 10,000 suns. I saw this inside of me. In fact, I can close my eyes right now and see it shining. It is the very essence of God. It is God. It is Jesus. It is Maharaj Ji. They are all one.

Also I was revealed the music of God. I could, and can, hear celestial music inside myself.

In addition, I was given the taste of nectar, which is God. And I was revealed the Holy Name—that unspeakable name that is God. Maharaj Ji tells us that unless we are constantly in the remembrance of Holy Name, when the time comes for the passing from this life, we will not be saved. So we must constantly be in God consciousness to be saved because our time will come like a thief in the night. And so my effort must constantly be there. Having

"Knowledge" revealed to me alone will not save me. It is because of my true effort through "Knowledge" that I will be saved.

An Exquisite Experience

One of the factors that contributed to my deception was the supernatural element empowering the guru. I had not experienced anything like it in a direct way since my twelfth year, when I had sensed Jesus' presence in my father's church during "O Holy Night." I was unfamiliar with the spirit realm and even more unaware of Satan's power to deceive. Like so many others, I naïvely assumed that if something was supernatural, it had to be from God.

When I found myself weeping uncontrollably during the guru's teachings, for example, I assumed that God was responding to my unspoken inner request for mercy and reconciliation, and that He was doing something beyond my understanding. Indeed, in spite of all the fallacies involved, I had begun to believe that God—notwithstanding the virulent hatred I had had of Him most of my life, and despite my personal wickedness—was still willing to forgive me and have me as one of His children. To have this hope revived after I had utterly forsaken it for so many years stimulated a rising tide of emotion. And although I was feeling these emotions under false pretenses, my impression was true. God really was wooing me to Himself.

All the while, I was intent on confirming that Guru Maharaj Ji was an incarnation of God Himself. That was a key element in his teaching—that in every generation there is an incarnation of God on this earth, called a "Perfect Master." And since Maharaj Ji had arrived to usher in the final age of mankind, he had come with more power than anyone else before him. I had long carried within my heart the belief that my generation was the final age of humanity, so I was eager to believe the guru's claims. I just needed supernatural proof.

One night I knelt on the floor, surrounded by dozens of other premies who were likewise bowing to the floor in worship of Guru Maharaj Ji. We were doing *pranam*, which means bowing down—literally facedown, prostrate. And my prayer was sincere. I told God that I believed in His Son Jesus, and I asked Him to forgive me, save me and show me if Maharaj Ji was really Him or not.

All at once, I felt that a door to my heart had been opened like a camera aperture, and an enormous torrent of pure energy had rushed into my heart through the opening. Liquid love was being poured through me with such force that it seemed as if I were lying at the bottom of Niagara Falls, with the full force of the water rushing toward me. I felt both exhilarated and terrified at the same time.

Curiously, however, the torrent poured into an invisible, other-dimensional place in my heart rather than hitting me physically. It sounded simultaneously like a mighty rushing wind, millions of voices and a blast from a hurricane-force storm. It was unquestionably the most exquisite experience of my lifetime, as well as the most intensely frightening and powerful feeling I had ever known. It was pure, furious love. I knew that it would kill me if it continued, so in my spirit I shouted, *STOP!* It instantly stopped.

My first thought was, *Wow! God! You do exist!*

My next thought was, *But was that meant to show me that the guru really is You, or that You are something completely different? Was it a response to my willingness to follow Maharaj Ji, or a response to my trust in Jesus Christ?*

I still was not so sure about the guru. But one thing I *was* sure of—after years of denial—was that God was powerful and that He loved me very much. The partition between God and me had been consumed by His love for me. The angry barrier between us was no longer there. I would never, *ever* be able to doubt God's power or His love again.

At the same time, I was increasingly unsure that Guru Maharaj Ji was who he claimed to be. After the spiritual Niagara had nearly drowned me, I looked around to see if anyone else in the room had felt the same thing. Those around me were serenely bowed in veneration, clearly clueless about what I had just experienced. I was dying to tell them, but at the same time I realized that there was no way I was going to get anyone to believe what had just happened.

But maybe Tim Gallwey will get it, I thought. I walked out the front door and sat on the low brick wall that bordered the walkway, waiting for him to emerge. Almost on cue, with most of the people still inside, Tim emerged from the house. He walked toward me and asked me how I was doing.

"I have to tell you what just happened to me!" I exclaimed fervently, trying my best not to sound like a complete fanatic.

"Please, do tell me," he calmly replied, cool as ever.

I tried to find the words I needed to describe the experience. "Okay . . . while we were doing *pranam* just now, it was as if a door in my chest opened up and a rushing force of energy poured into my heart! What was that?"

Knowing of my Christian upbringing, Tim replied, "That was the river of living water. In the book of John, Jesus promised to give it to everyone who was thirsty. You have been thirsty, haven't you?"

"Well, yeah!" I replied.

"And you have been wondering whether or not Maharaj Ji is God, haven't you?"

"Yeah, I have."

"God has chosen this way to answer your prayers. He has shown you that Guru Maharaj Ji offers you the experience of

God that you've been looking for. It is through him that you will receive the eternal life you've been seeking. Maharaj Ji has filled you with the living water of Jesus Christ; he has filled you with his living water—the water that he gave to Jesus to pour out on all who would follow the one true God."

I went home that night and looked up all the Scriptures that spoke of the river of living water that Jesus Christ had promised. That was all I needed. Within weeks, I had sold everything I owned, given the proceeds to the guru and moved into his ashram in Brentwood. From that point on, as far as I was concerned, Guru Maharaj Ji was God the Father Himself, and I was the guru's—lock, stock and barrel.

"In Your Mind or in Your Heart?"

One of the reasons I was vulnerable to supernatural phenomena was because of Maharaj Ji's earliest conditioning of the premies. He insisted that questioning and doubting him was wrong; it was a sure sign that you were "in your mind" rather than "in your heart." As devotees, we were conditioned not to think, but simply to feel. Eventually, we lost the ability to discern counterfeit feelings from authentic experiences. And before long, we willingly opened our minds to demonic influences.

It was shocking that I was so willing to blindly follow a spiritual leader based on the disengagement of the mind. As a romantic, I found the idea that truth can only be perceived by the heart attractive. It might have been different if someone had shown me Jesus' words from Mark 7:21–23, "For from within, out of the heart of man, come evil thoughts, sexual immorality, theft, murder, adultery, coveting, wickedness, deceit, sensuality, envy, slander, pride, foolishness. All these evil things come from within, and they defile a person." Or Jeremiah's declaration in Jeremiah 17:9, "The heart is deceitful above all things, and desperately sick; who can understand it?"

Another element that assisted in our conditioning was the diet we were required to follow. We were strict and total vegetarians, meaning no meat and no fish or eggs, or anything that contained those things, including cake mixes (which contain eggs) and other packaged goods. It was difficult, however, to figure out how to adhere to such a diet, and many premies became anemic and hypoglycemic from getting too little protein and too many carbohydrates.

My parents were, of course, gripped with fear during that time period. It was obvious to them that I was being deceived. When I wrote to them about seeing light emanating from Guru Maharaj Ji, they responding by pointing out that the Bible clearly says in 2 Corinthians 11:13–15,

> For such men are false apostles, deceitful workmen, disguising themselves as apostles of Christ. And no wonder, for even Satan disguises himself as an angel of light. So it is no surprise if his servants, also, disguise themselves as servants of righteousness. Their end will correspond to their deeds.

I did not know enough about the Bible to understand that when Jesus said in John 8:12 and John 9:5, "I am the light of the world," He was providing a metaphor to help explain His message. He did not mean that He was literally a light inside that could be accessed by meditation.

Mom and Dad wrote letter after letter to me, trying to convince me that Jesus was the only way. I responded with letter after letter to them, assuring them that they only had part of the picture and that Guru Maharaj Ji had the rest. I spun every Scripture I could find, making venerable passages of God's Word sound like they referred to Maharaj Ji. I fed my family massive doses of reinterpreted and misdirected quotes. Meanwhile, my childhood belief in the spiritual bankruptcy of my parents became a shield against much of what they wrote.

What I did not know was that my parents had organized prayer meetings in their church family, specifically praying that God would bring me out of the cult. It amazed me when I finally heard about the long hours of tears and suffering they had undergone on my behalf. It was a heartbreaking time for them. On one occasion, my mother was lying on the beach, crying out to God for my soul. Suddenly, she heard a voice from heaven saying, "Trust Me!" and in a brief vision she saw me preaching from a pulpit. She thought she had been trusting God, but when she saw the vision, she knew that she had been trying to force God into doing something He already wanted to do. It was at that point that she truly released me into His hands.

Because I was unaware of the change that had taken place in my parents' hearts, I treated their claims of concern for me with sarcasm and disbelief—as if they were too little, too late. I did not realize that one day, I would look back on this time with deep gratitude and love for what they had done.

The Guru's Big Mistake

Maharaj Ji usually was careful to speak respectfully of Jesus. After all, in his bodily form he was supposedly a reincarnation of Jesus, Buddha, Krishna and all the "Perfect Masters" who had come before him—or so he led us to believe. In the process, he cleverly twisted and turned around what Jesus said to fit whatever the cult was teaching. This was relatively easy to do since the people in the cult who had Christian backgrounds only had a surface knowledge of the Bible anyway. No one had been a Bible scholar, for example, or even a Bible college student, as far as I knew. We were all simply disaffected "Christians" from nominal backgrounds. And we shared one reason or another for not wanting the traditional interpretation of the Bible to be true. A lot of Jews were also in the cult, looking for their Messiah.

Then one day, Maharaj Ji denied what Jesus Christ said He came to do. On Christmas Day, 1979, he said that the only reason Christ died on the cross was to get people's attention. When Maharaj Ji said those words, something inside me felt as though it were jumping to its feet and crying, "NO!" I could feel the physical reverberations of the cry echoing across the expanse of space and time.

How completely unexpected this was. I remember wondering what that cry was all about, what spirit had done it and what it meant with regard to my weakening belief that Maharaj Ji was God. Because of my "river of living water" experience, I had come to believe that God resided within me, and this "voice" confirmed to me that I was right. Now I had to decide if the spirit that cried "NO!" was the real Jesus, the Holy Spirit or some deceiving entity trying to confuse me and rob me of the true reincarnation of Jesus—Maharaj Ji. It certainly got my attention, sending me on a further search for answers.

Due to my consistent and absolute devotion to Maharaj Ji, in less than a year I was placed in a position of secrecy and trust within the cult. That trust meant I had access to information that was damaging to the group. I was now working in the main office in L.A. and had occasion to see what was going on behind the scenes. Some of it was not pretty.

I will never forget the day I sat in the office with the girl who did the books. I heard her ask her supervisor which set of books a particular source of income belonged in—the set shown to the IRS or the set that revealed the cult's real income. I asked her about it, and she made a joke about how we had to keep two sets of books in order to avoid trouble from the government.

On another occasion, I was present at a group meeting of leaders where they gloated over a coup they had just pulled off over the local PTA. The cult owned an old movie theater where they showed family-style movies to the public on weekends. I had served as an usher and ticket taker on many occasions. After a while, we found out that neighborhood parents had banded together to keep their kids from going to the theater because it was being run by the cult. They did not want their money supporting the guru, and they did not want their children seduced into the cult by the devotees who ran the theater.

In response, several cult members decided to dress up in business attire and attend the local PTA meeting. They would go in pretending to be businessmen who had just bought the theater from the cult. At the meeting, they assured the parents that it was now safe to send their kids to the movies there. This scam worked like a charm.

These two incidents caused me great distress. Why would Maharaj Ji have to cheat the government and lie to parents over money concerns? Wasn't he God? If so, he could create any kind of income he needed. Additionally, if he really was God, why would he lie? Shouldn't he be perfect and therefore incapable of lying?

I still remembered the moment when he had alluded to Christ's death on the cross as though it had been some kind of publicity stunt. Above all things, that had been the guru's biggest mistake. A conflict arose inside me, with Maharaj Ji on one side and logic and respect for Jesus on the other.

Meanwhile, my parents continued praying for me, and they were not the only ones. I had taken a job to get out of debt, and a born-again Christian co-worker named Jeff had been confronting me every day about my involvement in the group. He had repeatedly angered me with his insistence that I was following a false prophet, and he had been leaving Scriptures on my desk daily. Like my parents, he just would not give up.

— 15 —

COMING OUT

The things going on in the unseen world of prayerful intercession for my deliverance were beginning to take effect. Gradually, my confidence in Maharaj Ji was eroding. One issue that grated on me was his repeated reference to John the Baptist as "the man who wrote the gospel of John." Normally, a nominal Christian like me would never have noticed this error; it was only by God's grace that I did. The guru said it only three or four times, but every once in a while, in the middle of giving satsang (sharing his thoughts at a satsang meeting), he would refer to John the Baptist in this erroneous way.

It was so obviously wrong that at first I assumed he was joking with us. In fact, whenever Maharaj Ji said or did something that seemed inconsistent with the cult's teachings, the leaders would always dismiss it as "Maharaj Ji playing with our minds." If something seemed questionable and someone brought it up, the leaders would accuse the person of "being in your mind." We were supposed to operate in the continual supernatural consciousness of Maharaj Ji, which was just the opposite of trying to think things through rationally. It was a clever ruse that cut off contradictions, complaints and the questioning of leadership.

As little as I knew about the Bible, I did know that John the Baptist could not have written the gospel of John because Herod had beheaded him long before many of the events described in it took place. *If Guru Maharaj Ji is God*, I asked myself, *then how could he be so wrong about this? In fact, how could he be wrong about anything?*

I began to consider something new and shocking: Was the real God causing Maharaj Ji to make these statements so I could see that he was actually a fraud?

I did not know that in addition to the regular prayer meeting my parents were organizing for me, Jeff from the office had persuaded his Bible study buddies to pray for my deliverance. Jeff regularly attended a Bible study led by a graduate of Dallas Theological Seminary—a biblically rigorous and faithful school. The people attending the Bible study were all part of John MacArthur's Grace Community Church in Panorama City, California—also a bastion of biblical fidelity. Around thirty of them met at the leader's house, and after the study, they shared prayer requests, with at least one person praying for each request. When it came to Jeff's turn, he would report incidents that had happened at work and ask for prayer for me. He also sought the necessary wisdom and guidance to refute my claims.

Jeff and I shared a two-room office space, with a copier in a third room. He was a total nerd—thick glasses, the whole bit. I have always liked nerds, so I liked Jeff from the start. We worked together as office assistants, making copies of contracts, along with opening, sorting and delivering mail. At some point in the day, when there was a lull, Jeff would come into my room with his Bible. *Oh no, here it comes again*, I would silently groan.

Jeff would try to show me a passage in the Bible that spoke to the issue of false prophets and messiahs, and I would quickly dismiss his claims with well-honed cult rhetoric. Before it was over, I might swear at him or treat him disrespectfully. Still, Jeff would soon be back in the room, sharing another passage of Scripture with me, even though I had been completely dismissive and insulting just minutes before.

After this went on for months, I realized that Jeff's affection for me was unconditional, and that no matter how badly I treated him, he continued to care about me and my future. That was disarming. It was also attractive. I hated to admit it, but it was something I had been looking for my whole life.

The irony was that one of the primary reasons I increasingly abused Jeff was because he was beginning to make sense. I was gradually facing the possibility that I might have been wrong all along. Potentially, that meant I was facing a humiliating retraction of the guru's claims, which intensified my anger and anxiety. To Jeff, it appeared as though I was drifting further away from the truth. In fact, I was getting closer to believing his words with every passing day.

In May 1980, I decided to stop meditating for a while. I needed to clear my mind of doubts about the guru. I had secretly begun to read my Bible again—a practice frowned upon in the ashram—so I read it late at night under my blanket, or while my roommate was at work. One day while I was reading, the words shot out at me, almost as if they had leapt from the page, and I suddenly had an understanding of Scripture that I had never had before. It was as if a spiritual veil was lifted. Instantly, I was able to understand scriptural warnings about people like Maharaj Ji and to discern his methods of deception. Second Corinthians 11:14–15 screamed at me once again: "Even Satan disguises himself as an angel of light. So it is no surprise if his servants, also, disguise themselves as servants of righteousness. . . ."

I had also become quite fond of the gospel of John because it was mystical and therefore was a better fit with my homemade brew of religious philosophy. These verses leapt out at me:

> Again Jesus spoke to them, saying, "I am the light of the world. Whoever follows me will not walk in darkness, but will have the light of life."
>
> John 8:12

> Jesus said to him, "I am the way, and the truth, and the life. No one comes to the Father except through Me."
>
> John 14:6

> I told you that you would die in your sins; if you do not believe that I am [the one I claim to be], you will indeed die in your sins.
>
> John 8:24 NIV1984

> And Jesus answered them, "See that no one leads you astray. For many will come in my name, saying, 'I am the Christ,' and they will lead many astray. . . . Then if anyone says to you, 'Look, here is the Christ!' or 'There he is!' do not believe it. For false christs and false prophets will arise and perform great signs and wonders, so as to lead astray, if possible, even the elect. See, I have told you beforehand."
>
> Matthew 24:4–5, 23–25

> All Scripture is breathed out by God and profitable for teaching, for reproof, for correction, and for training in righteousness.
>
> 2 Timothy 3:16

That last one particularly impacted me because it went directly against the cult's claims that Scripture was unnecessary and was not the direct Word of God to us, as Maharaj Ji claimed to be.

When we meditated in our rooms at night, we used a stick to prop up a sheet or blanket over our heads, making a sort of personal little tent. My roommate was on a mattress just a few feet away, and we were supposed to be meditating at the same time. I would have a small Bible and a flashlight under my tent with me, however, so I could read the Bible instead of meditating. After my roommate had gone to sleep, I would lie down, pull the blanket up over my head, and pretend to sleep, but continue to read underneath the blanket with a flashlight.

One night my roommate caught me reading the Bible. "Why are you doing that?" he asked.

"I'm just confirming Maharaj Ji's teachings by comparing them to it."

"That's not right! You're just 'in your mind.' Otherwise, you wouldn't have to confirm anything Maharaj Ji says."

By then I was pretty sure that if Maharaj Ji really was God, the Bible would only confirm what he taught. So why the pressure not to read it? It was all beginning to seem rather suspicious.

Still, I was afraid to do anything. I had worked hard to attain the position of trust the cult had put me in. To make matters worse, the penalty for rejecting the Perfect Master of the Universe was eternal damnation. Needless to say, I had to be absolutely sure of what I was doing before I left. At the same time, months and months of conditioning could not be shaken off in a moment. I had invested so much devotion and dedication to Maharaj Ji that to even consider that he was not who he claimed to be frightened me. Nonetheless, I had to find out the absolute truth. I had to be completely certain.

In my earnest search through the pages of the Bible, I discovered a wonderful promise in Jeremiah 29:13: "You will seek me and find me, when you seek me with all your heart." Could it be true? To find out, I decided to take God at His word, travel to Israel and make a personal pilgrimage in search of Him. I sensed that getting away from the cult for a little while would allow me to think things through without distraction. I wanted to reconsider everything. And I needed breathing room—space from those who so adamantly rejected the Bible and discouraged my intellectual concerns. I had been in the guru's world long enough. Now I needed to spend some time in the world Jesus knew.

— 16 —

The PROMISED LAND

When I had flown before, I had often watched the clouds passing majestically below the aircraft. This time I fixed my eyes on the Mediterranean Sea, and once I could see a land-mass slowly becoming visible on the horizon, a thrilling surge ran through me. I was about to set foot in the land of Israel, the Holy Land, the place of Jesus' birth, ministry, death and resurrection.

It was hardly a short flight—seventeen hours—and most of it I had spent sleeping. But as the destination approached, I watched in growing excitement. Could this journey finally lead me to the Truth?

My devotion to Guru Maharaj Ji was still strong, but my doubts had grown. In spite of the constant pressure to base my faith in the guru on feelings and not on logic or rational thinking, I had found that impossible. I knew I had to have assurance on an intellectual level, not just warm emotions in my heart. If the guru was God incarnate, as he claimed, I would gladly follow him, but I had to know it, not just feel it.

When I joined the cult, I had given up all my possessions except for a TWA credit card—an odd thing to keep at the time. But when I inquired about flying to Israel, I found that a round-trip ticket to Tel Aviv was exactly the same dollar amount as the credit limit on my card. Did that mean God's hand was directing me? I was becoming more and more convinced of it.

Because Guru Maharaj Ji had a convention scheduled in Rome and the flight to Tel Aviv stopped in Rome first, my departure did not arouse suspicion. As far as other cult members knew, I was going to the convention in Rome, as many of them were. Unbeknownst to them, I would not join them there. I was bound for the Holy Land.

I can still remember my surge of excitement as the airplane made its descent into Ben Gurion Airport. My euphoria temporarily dissolved as we left the plane, however. It was 1980, and the Israel Defense Forces were on high alert. Security officers flanked the door of the aircraft with drawn pistols, and at the bottom of the stairs they stood on guard with Uzi automatic weapons. Momentarily I was afraid, but before long my fear was transformed into a sense of security.

We took a bus from the airport into Tel Aviv. Along the way, I saw scores of jeeps that were crammed with alert soldiers who were keeping an eye on everything and everybody. They seemed polite and even friendly, but it was clear that they could mow us down on the spot, if necessary.

In Tel Aviv I took a room at the Moss Hotel, just a block from the shores of the Mediterranean Sea. As excited as I was to be in the Holy Land, the trip had exhausted me. Collapsing on the bed, I could hear young Israelis in the street below talking loudly to each other in their rapid-fire Hebrew. A half-moon hung above the Mediterranean, and as I stretched out and drifted off into much-needed sleep, somewhere in the distance I could hear singing.

The next day I began a bus tour, which seemed like the best way to see Israel, considering how little money I had. It was a student tour arranged by UCLA. I wanted it that way. No Christians trying to convert me—just my searching heart and the God who had said He would reveal Himself to me. We traveled south, through Southern Judean farmland. From time to time, we saw Bedouin Arabs garbed in flowing robes and headgear, watching over their black tents and flocks of sheep. Alongside a few grazing camels, I spotted a spectacular burst of color—a field of Israeli sunflowers. Already, I was learning more than I had expected.

As we made our way past an Israeli military base—neat rows of tents and jeeps, with the blue-and-white Star of David flag of Israel snapping in the wind high above—our guide pointed out where the PLO had kidnapped and murdered an Israeli boy just a few days earlier. It had happened in an ordinary intersection, an incongruous setting for such a dramatic incident.

Slowly the terrain changed to desert, and before long we approached Be'er Sheva. I remembered the name from a Sunday school lesson I had heard as a child. It was the place where Abraham had made a peace agreement with the Philistine king Abimelech. The Hebrew name Be'er Sheva literally means "Well Seven." Abraham had dug a well, and Abimelech's warriors had seized it. Later, both groups had taken an oath of peace and Abraham had offered seven ewe lambs to Abimelech to seal their agreement.

As our bus roared through that desert town, a young Israeli boy carrying his schoolbooks and wearing a yarmulke waved heartily, as if to greet us. He was about twelve years old, and his simple gesture made me feel welcome. I turned to watch him as we drove away. He continued walking along the street, and all at once, I remembered the boy our tour guide had mentioned who had been kidnapped and killed in a nearby town. *Was he a boy much like this one?* I wondered. *Did the boy whom the terrorists murdered have a happy personality, too?* I thought of his age and how little of the world he had probably seen. *But never mind his age—why does Satan so zealously attack the innocent?* I questioned. *And what about me?*

As I reflected on these things, I began to understand that perhaps God had not caused the pain and rejection in my past. All along I had blamed Him, cursed Him, defied Him and disobeyed Him. Yet He had relentlessly pursued me with love, even when I least deserved it. Maybe it was God's enemy—and mine—who had done me so much harm.

We stopped at the ruins of Avdat, a town dating back to Jesus' day. I knew it was the location where the producers of the film *Jesus Christ Superstar* had done some of their filming. We were able to explore the ruins and observe an ongoing archeological dig. Our guide informed us that Avdat had been an ancient Nabatean city, a trading crossroads for caravans coming from Africa and Arabia on their way to Judea and Rome. It had also been a Roman outpost in the third century and a magnificent city in the sixth. Later, as Byzantine power declined in the seventh century, Moslems had destroyed Avdat.

For some reason, the site made me think of my parents' long-standing religious traditions. Their beliefs and behaviors had been constructed in bygone days, and although they had never questioned their own upbringing, my childhood had been rife with heartache and bitterness because of their unbending views. Now here was a city, long deserted and in crumbled ruins, that reminded me of my parents' traditions. Like them, it had not been able to survive the changing eras and thus had ended in calamity.

Does this mean that my life will remain in ruins, too? I wondered. *Can my relationship with my parents change? What would rebuilding a relationship with Mom and Dad require of me?*

On the second day, we drove the length of the Sinai Peninsula to Sha'arm El Sheik. The Sinai had previously belonged to Egypt, but Israel had conquered and taken possession of it during the Six-Day War in 1967. Israel was gradually returning it to Egypt as agreed upon by peace treaties, but in the meantime, Israelis and other tourists enjoyed its many attractions.

The coastline became more and more spectacular the farther we went. Saudi Arabia now lay on the opposite shore. Along the way, we got to see the wasteland that Moses and the children of Israel traversed for forty years. Wandering around in such a wilderness for that prolonged period seemed unimaginable. Then I remembered the reason for their plight: sin and disbelief. God had caused them to wander until the entire generation who distrusted God had died, except for Caleb and Joshua.

Sounds familiar, I thought. I had also rejected God, and had wandered in an emotional desert, hungering and thirsting for love and acceptance. *Is God beginning to remove the obstacles—my own version of the golden calf—that have kept me away from Him for so long?* I asked myself.

Sunday night we spent at Arad, and at 3:30 Monday morning we awakened and got underway early so we could watch the sunrise from the Judean fortress of Masada. The sun was a beautiful shade of orange, rising from behind the Jordanian mountains over the Dead Sea. As the day brightened, we slowly made our way up the steep "snake pass" to the top of Masada. The climb was well worth the trek. The view was breathtaking.

Our Jewish guide gave us a stirring account of the fortress's history. When a Roman legion had surrounded and laid siege to it, the fortress's leader, Elazar ben Yair, had convinced the people that capture was not an option—knowing that capture meant slavery for the men and sexual abuse for the women and children. As a community, the Jews chose suicide rather than slavery. When the Romans finally mounted the ramp they had constructed, they found the rebels dead. Our guide emphasized that today's Israelis look upon Masada as a powerfully symbolic site. They vow that it will never fall again, just as the land of Israel will never surrender to its Arab enemies.

I was awestruck at the courage those Jewish heroes of Masada had displayed in the face of such a hopeless situation. Then it occurred to me—hadn't Jesus said something to His disciples about being willing to die? I had seen enough of my own captivity to drugs, sex and star-chasing to realize that dying to myself and choosing freedom was a worthy alternative—but one I had yet to pursue.

After a swim in the healing waters of the Dead Sea, we stopped for the night. The next day we would head north, to the Golan Heights, and then, at last, to Galilee.

In the Footsteps of Jesus

Days later, as we rounded a mountain pass, the Sea of Galilee suddenly appeared far below. For a few moments, I found myself on the verge of tears. We stopped along the lakeside, at a spot where Jesus supposedly told His disciples of His impending death. Was I actually standing on the same ground where Jesus stood? It was a phenomenal possibility—awe-inspiring, to put it mildly.

Our guide was not Christian, and at times his disinterest and even slightly mocking tone disappointed me. But as the bus drove down the Galilean road, I thought about how I, too, had dismissed Christianity with equal disdain. I had somehow managed to hold a negative view of Christianity as a religion of fakes and hypocrites, while I lived a life of utter depravity. Yet Christianity was, in essence, the faith of those who were *trying* to live in accordance with God's law and Christ's message, while counting on His grace and mercy. Very few fully succeeded. In fact, Jesus Himself was the only one in history who had actually lived a life of perfect righteousness.

We drove by the Mount of Beatitudes to visit Peter's house in Capernaum, which is adjacent to a synagogue where Jesus taught. Later, the rest of the group went swimming in the Sea of Galilee, but I stayed on shore. I found a secluded spot and sat with my arms wrapped around my knees, staring across the lake. It was my hope that Jesus would come walking across the water to tell me whether Maharaj Ji was really divine or not.

I wanted an answer, but all I could hear were the waves lapping against the shores, the wind rustling in the trees, a few birds singing nearby and the tour group laughing and splashing in the water. I closed my eyes and tried to feel Jesus' presence. I tried to focus, sending my desire for an answer to Him through the force of my concentration, but all I could feel was the warm wind moving across my back and hair. Though disappointed that Jesus did not show up the way I imagined, I realized that I could not command a miracle from God. I could only ask and be grateful if one were to come.

The next day we entered Jerusalem by the Jaffa Gate and walked amidst the colorful merchandise along David Street, a very narrow pathway with wall-to-wall shops. As we arrived at the Church of the Holy Sepulchre, my emotions welled up at the significance of where I was. I felt an encounter with the Living God was surely near. Inside, I visited the various Greek Orthodox, Armenian and Roman Catholic altars, including the slab of stone they say Christ had been laid on after His crucifixion. Upstairs were two main altars—one at the spot where Christ had been nailed to the cross and another at the spot where the cross had stood when He was crucified.

Despite my anger about the merchandizing of these holy sites, I felt a deep sense of reverence at that second altar, and I reached out with my spirit to try to touch Him in His pain. Later on, I

Standing in the Red Sea at Elat, during my escape from the L.A. ashram to Israel in 1980. This was just a few days before my encounter with God in Jerusalem—an encounter that would change my life forever.

looked at the stones that surrounded me in the church—some fine marble, some common—announcing to the world that the Son of Man who once had died was no longer in the tomb. All my life, I had found the seemingly phony ritualism all around me offensive. It occurred to me that I had allowed the phony trappings that surrounded Christianity to keep me from the very real Savior. My self-righteous preoccupation with judging the false had itself kept Him hidden from my sight. I wanted that to end.

The next morning, with a sense of exhilaration I set out to visit the Mount of Olives. At the top of the hill, I looked across a broad panorama of the Old City—the Dome of the Rock, the many mosques, the church spires and the restoration that was still taking place in the Jewish Quarter.

My tour had ended the day before, so I tried to stay close to an English-speaking guide and his group so I could learn the history of what I was seeing. Fortunately, no one seemed to notice that I was not a paid member of that tour. I followed the group down to a church built on the site where Christ supposedly wept over Jerusalem before making His entrance into the city, and I took a self-timed picture of myself with the city behind me. The tour guide then stopped to read the passages

With the Temple Mount behind me, I am seated on the Mount of Olives at the very spot where it is believed Jesus wept over Jerusalem. It was here that I heard the voice of God speaking the Word of God into my spirit.

from Luke's gospel describing the long-ago scene. As he read the words from his Bible, I was startled to hear Jesus saying them in my spirit as well. I did not see that coming! Instantly, I realized that the Bible was *literally* the Word of God—words spoken by an eternal God and therefore words that are eternally being spoken.

This was a paradigm-shattering moment for me. I reasoned that if every word in the Bible is truly God-breathed, as it says in 2 Timothy 3:16, and is spoken from God and carried along by the Holy Spirit, as 2 Peter 1:21 claims, then knowing God and knowing His will could be infinitely more plain and simple than I had ever imagined. When Jesus cited Deuteronomy 8:3, He summed up the whole matter: "It is written: Man shall not live by bread alone, but by every word that comes from the mouth of God" (Matthew 4:4).

If I can learn God's Word well, I concluded from my thoughts, *I'll have an objective way to test the voices, experiences and teachings of those who claimed to speak for God.* This was indeed big news, and I was left wondering, *Why has no one ever told me this before?*

I followed the group down to the Garden of Gethsemane. What a beautiful sight it was. Some of the huge, weathered olive trees were thought to be two thousand years old. Were they the very ones Jesus had walked among? It seemed as though they had been well tended for centuries, and they were a pleasant change from the mostly barren Mount of Olives, which serves as a vast cemetery.

A Gethsemane Encounter

The Church of All Nations was built in the Garden of Gethsemane, around a white section of rock believed to be the place where Jesus prayed on the night He was betrayed and arrested. The rock rises up through the floor of the church so that visitors can kneel and pray at its edge. As the tour guide read the very prayer that Christ prayed—probably close to that very same spot—I was profoundly moved.

By now, a real battle between my devotion to Guru Maharaj Ji and my belief in Jesus was being waged inside me. The guru spoke respectfully of Jesus most of the time, but he insisted that Jesus was simply another embodiment of God. The guru, on the other hand, was supposedly the ultimate manifestation.

I had been taught as a child that Jesus claimed to be the only way to God. Who was right? Was the guru right, and was organized Christianity simply getting Jesus' message wrong? Did Jesus really mean that He alone was the way to the Father? If so, did that mean the guru was a fraud?

I had always respected Jesus, but I was not completely sure that He was what Christianity taught He was. My knuckles whitened as I grasped my hands firmly together in front of me. I reminded Jesus that I believed in Him. I told Him once again that I was sorry for my sins and reminded Him that I had come all the way to Israel to make sure that by following Maharaj Ji, I was indeed following Him.

I had hoped for some miraculous sign, but by then, I had come to realize that since Satan could appear as an angel of light, he could just as easily masquerade as Jesus. He could have come walking toward me on the Sea of Galilee, and I would have been misled. I suddenly understood that finding the answer to my question would take more than a miracle. But what could that something be?

As I knelt in prayer, straining with hope that God would give me the answer, I said, "God, You can do miracles, and Satan can do miracles. How am I supposed to know who is truly from God?"

I was surprised that a reply came so quickly into my mind—a thought so abstract that it could never have been my own: *Who proved His love for you?*

At first, the thought did not make sense to me. As I struggled to understand it, the image of Christ's scourging and torturous crucifixion flashed through my brain. In fact, I had just visited the very places where those things had taken place. Yes, Jesus had demonstrated His love for me in a practical way by enduring that long, agonizing death to pay for my sins.

Then I began to consider Maharaj Ji. He had certainly made me *feel* loved at times. But as I tried to remember practical demonstrations of Maharaj Ji's love, nothing came to mind. In fact, the only thing he ever did in practical terms was take from us. He took our time, our money, our belongings, our service and even our minds.

The guru took. Jesus, the Savior, gave.

It was so simple. And so marvelous. Why hadn't I thought of it before? Jesus alone had demonstrated in a practical way, and had thereby proven, His love for me. And He had risen from the dead to prove that He was powerful enough to save me.

I rose up from that rock feeling featherlight, as if the heaviness of the world had been lifted from my shoulders. A veil of deception had been removed from my mind. I had received my answer at last, and the answer was Jesus.

Joyous and free, I hurried back toward my hotel, reveling in the peace and love I was feeling. I finally had a certainty about who God was—from the lips of God Himself and from the confirming historical record of the demonstration of Jesus' love on the cross during His sojourn on the earth. He was a God who took on human flesh and died a torturous death in order to take upon Himself the punishment of those who were at enmity with Him. It was mind-blowing!

Homeward Bound

Once I returned to Los Angeles, I was not sure what to do next. First of all, I was completely broke. Although I did not have the money to move anywhere else, I certainly could not stay in the ashram. I decided not to do anything for a while, acting as if nothing had happened, until I could figure out a strategy. Already, however, I was preparing a lengthy letter to all the guru's premies. The finished letter was ten pages long, typed front and back, single-spaced. In no uncertain terms, I spelled out how and why I knew that Maharaj Ji was a phony. As I read and reread it, I thought it was a masterpiece.

In the meantime, I decided it would be wise to appear at satsang, in case I had fallen under suspicion. As far as everybody knew, I had just returned from a blissful trip to see Maharaj Ji in Rome. Just a week after my return, I made my way with great trepidation into the Loyola Theatre in Westchester (near LAX airport). It was a large, old-fashioned movie house with red-carpeted aisles and stuffed red velvet seats that folded backward. An actual stage still graced the front of the auditorium, and the movie screen was hidden behind red velvet curtains. A lone microphone stood on the left side of the stage, awaiting testimonials.

Fear fluttered inside me. I knew intuitively that someone would ask me to give satsang. There was no way I could speak that night. For one thing, I was incapable of articulating what had happened to me. Knowing what I did about the cult, I actually feared being physically attacked and bodily thrown out if I stood before the audience and announced that the guru was a fraud. Yet at the same time, I knew that eventually I had to tell them. They were all being deceived, and I wanted to let them know it. Some of the cult members really mattered to me.

I had intentionally arrived late and had slipped silently into the very back of the mezzanine section, clinging to the hope that I would not be noticed. Someone was watching for me, however. I had been seated only about twenty minutes when the young woman at the microphone called for me to come forward. I slid more deeply into my chair, hoping to look unwell. I had noticed before that occasionally, someone did not respond to the request to speak. Thankfully, after an agonizing minute or two, she called on someone else.

Later that night at our ashram, a few of the guys began to question me about my trip. Why hadn't I gone to see Guru Maharaj Ji in Rome like I said I would? Why had I gone to Israel, of all places? Did I think it was permissible for an ashram premie to simply go off on a vacation trip? Weren't we supposed to be working hard together?

I tried to explain my concerns, first to the guys and later to my roommate. I was as honest as possible about my doubts, but as it turned out, my sincerity did not help me much. The trip to Israel, combined with my growing skepticism about Maharaj Ji, were bright red flags in the face of the cult's leadership. My days at the ashram clearly were numbered.

Fortunately, my friend Shirley agreed to take me in. She was a lesbian psychologist who shared a house with a homosexual ballet dancer. They had been my friends for years, and they graciously made their basement apartment available for my use during this crisis.

It was not long until I needed it. Sooner than I expected, the ashram informed me that because I no longer fully believed in Guru Maharaj Ji, I would have to leave. The cult's spokespeople were unbending, unkind and impatient. I told them that I would be out within a few days. It was sobering that these so-called brothers, who allegedly loved me devotedly, had no problem whatsoever kicking me out into the street without a word of consideration for my well-being.

I moved into Shirley's basement, feeling confident that God was with me and that He and I could handle anything. But doubts soon gathered. Shirley was into some sort of angel worship, and as I was kneeling beside my bed each night, I would hear her angel-worship music moaning through my ceiling—an eerie, mournful sound. "Lord," I prayed silently, "are You *sure* You want me here? After all, they're homosexuals *and* angel worshipers! Shouldn't I be in a healthier climate?"

One day I decided to walk the two blocks down to Hollywood Presbyterian Church, thinking to myself, *Even though they're almost certainly a bunch of hypocrites, I can still worship God there.* To my utter surprise, the church was spilling over with born-again believers who really seemed to care about me. I had never run into that before and was quite taken by it. Paul Cedar was the associate pastor, and he was preaching all that month. To my astonishment, each Sunday his sermon answered the primary question that I had put before God that very week. It was a marvelous example of the Lord's detailed concern for me. He was there, and He was listening.

A week after being ejected from the ashram, I stood outside the old satsang hall and distributed my letter to the premies. At first they probably assumed that I wanted to repent. But instead of going in, I stood outside and handed my ten-page document to every person who passed. Within a few minutes, one of the leaders came out and asked me to come inside so they could talk to me about the statements I had made.

Now more than ever, I mistrusted them and refused to go with them. They ordered me off the property under threat of arrest. I refused, pointing out that I was standing on a public sidewalk. They stood next to me, warning people not to accept or read my paper. I pretended to leave, but instead went to the parking lot and starting putting my letter under windshield wipers. The cultists eventually spotted me and starting ripping the papers off the cars. I responded by slipping copies through partially opened windows. Finally, the disgusted cultists left, and I learned later that they had urgently warned the guru's following not to read a word of what I had written. I fervently hoped that this ban would stimulate interest all the more. Once I had handed out every last copy of the letter, I left and never returned.

The next morning at my office, Jeff was ecstatic. For the entire day, his big smile never seemed to fade. And it was not a gloating smile, either. He was overflowing with sheer love and joy for me. He listened carefully to my story, and he promised to share the details with everyone who had prayed for me.

I had sent my parents a postcard from Israel, so they were more or less aware that something good was going on. Since that day at the beach, God had given my mother an assurance that I would leave the cult. Now, with all these changes behind me, I decided it was time to go see my parents. But I gave them no warning and arrived entirely unannounced.

I got to their house just as Mom was leaving for church. Dad had gone on ahead. As I walked up the driveway, Mom could tell right away that something had changed. As she studied my face, she could clearly see that the old David had died and a new one had been born. I told her a short version of my visit to Israel. I explained how my thinking had changed on the trip, and then I presented her with an olivewood Last Supper sculpture I had bought in Jerusalem.

After this brief exchange, I rode with Mom to White Clay Creek Presbyterian Church in Newark, Delaware. Mom found Dad and told him someone was outside, wanting to see him. Just as he walked out of the building, I headed up the steps.

"Hello, I'm Phil Foster." Dad introduced himself to me, extending his hand. He did not even recognize me.

I had not been home in years, and I suspect that my countenance was radically different from the last time my father had seen me. Previously, I had been angry and sullen. This time, I had the Holy Spirit within me.

"Hello," I said quietly, "I'm your son David."

Dad looked both stunned and extremely embarrassed. I moved past his extended hand, and for the first time since I was a small child, I gave my dad a real, honest-to-goodness hug. Sadly, he stood stiffly against my attempt. Perhaps I had caught him too much by surprise, and he did not know how to respond. Or perhaps he held more against me than I thought.

We made our way into the building together. During the service, I was surprised by a time of testimony that was shoehorned between the offering and the sermon. When my father asked the congregation of several hundred if anyone had a prayer request or a praise report, I knew it was only right that I tell the congregation—many of whom had been praying for me for years—what had happened to me. I rose, and in appropriate nonemotional Presbyterian fashion, I reported that the Lord had saved me during my recent trip to Israel and that I wanted to thank everyone for praying for me. Presbyterians or not, I am certain that I heard more than a few sniffles among the congregants during the minutes following my testimony.

In one important way, I was home.

But in another, my journey had just begun. Within a few hours, I was back on a plane to L.A.

PART FIVE

LEARNING to WALK

The Vineyard Christian Fellowship in Anaheim, California—John Wimber's church—was a spiritual oasis that tied together the reality of heaven with the everyday world of our supernatural God. While attending there, I still wrestled with my past. I felt I needed direction for my Christian walk, so I made an appointment to see a pastor. I walked into his office and greeted him, but I did not tell him too much at first. I thought perhaps the Spirit would reveal something to him about me so I could be sure that God was speaking through him.

Shame must have been written all over my face, because the pastor studied me for a moment and then asked, "Tell me, David— what has been your greatest sin?"

You don't want to know about my sins, buddy, I thought as flashbacks of my unholy history flickered across my memory. But then, just as quickly, God surprised me. A sudden realization dawned on me that my greatest sin was not some perverted sexual deed, or a mind-bending drug trip, or a theft or another grave offense of thought, word or deed. All at once I understood that one specific moment in my life had been the culminating act of rebellion against authority. It had set in motion almost two decades of intense pleasure-seeking and self-destructive behavior. And it had all emanated from a direct and defiant rejection of the father whom God had given me.

Everything that followed that single defiant act had been a variation on the theme of dishonoring and disowning my father and the God he represented. It had been a spiritual flash point, causing me to conclude that I was condemned for all eternity. That assumption of condemnation became, in turn, my subconscious rationalization for seizing as much pleasure as possible on my way to hell.

I took a deep breath, looked into the pastor's eyes and quietly confessed, "I committed the greatest sin of my life at twelve years old, when I pushed my father down the stairs."

Thankfully, the pastor's face remained impassive. He simply suggested that we wait on God in prayer while staying with that memory. Watching me closely, he must have noticed when the color suddenly drained from my face. He asked, "Is God showing you anything?"

At first I hesitated, unsure about whether he would understand. "Yes," I finally responded. "I see myself standing on the center stair in our house. It's a wide spot because the stairs take a 90-degree turn at that point. My father is standing there with me."

The pastor nodded his head. "And what else do you see?" he asked.

Suddenly, I saw Jesus standing on the stairs with us. He was radiating a light so brilliant that I could not make out the features of His face. He was clothed in absolute holiness and purity. Seeing Him there and realizing that He had watched me push my father down the stairs, I was filled with unbearable shame, and a flood of tears suddenly gushed forth.

Then, just as suddenly, Jesus put one arm around me and placed His other arm around my father. He hugged us both tightly. I was completely unprepared for that loving embrace. I was expecting chastisement and judgment, yet instead, I was receiving love and grace. More tears poured down my face as I recognized what was happening. I felt a deep infusion of healing from the Lord as He replaced my shame with His love.

Jesus had met me and forgiven me at the point of my greatest sin. But that was not all. Since He had forgiven my worst sin, it was now clear to me that He had forgiven the many other sins as well—behaviors that had sprung up like poisonous weeds, sprouting from that one deep root of bitter rebellion against my dad. There had been so, so many sins. Yet now I understood that there was no more room for guilt or shame. I was free!

— 17 —

RENEWING the MIND

Long before I was able to find release from the deep sin of dishonoring and hating my father, and long before discovering the wonderful spiritual haven offered by the Vineyard Christian Fellowship, I had started walking in my new faith. And I began like a toddler taking his first steps—unsteady and unsure of where I was headed and how I was going to get there. I knew that I wanted to keep walking with Jesus, but which pathway I should take was a mystery. And, for obvious reasons, the fear of falling never left my mind.

The transformation that took place after my trip to Israel was dramatic, miraculous and fraught with upheaval. I had so much to learn, and all within the boundaries of a new relationship with God. I had to embrace His biblical principles while responding to His voice, and I needed to learn from those who knew Him much better than I did. I was filled with joy by the new beginning He had given me, yet I could not help but wonder how someone who had passed through the kind of darkness I had encountered over many years—in college, in Hollywood and in Maharaj Ji's cult—could ever fit into a genuine Christian environment.

I was still battling with the past, and with the fear that if the people at my church—I was attending Hollywood Presbyterian Church at first—knew what I had been and had done, they would never want to know me, much less be my friends. I could not get this worry out of my mind. Once again, I made my way to the church in search of answers. This time I sat down with one of Hollywood Presbyterian's associate pastors. I decided to blast him with the brutal truth of my hopeless sexual addiction and get the rejection over with as quickly as possible.

"I've been sleeping with three to four people a night for ten years," I blurted out, "and I know you're going to tell me to stop, but I can't just stop!"

Without skipping a beat, the associate pastor replied, "I'm not going to ask you to stop."

I stared at him in disbelief. *He must be one of those liberals I've been hearing about!* I told myself.

But that was not the case at all. He went on to explain that, with my cooperation, Jesus was going to empower the transformation and change me from the inside out.

"For you to recognize your inability to fight the devil and overcome the desires of your flesh is actually a good thing," he continued, "as long as you continue to trust Jesus to keep you from falling."

I was a brand-new believer. No one had gotten to me yet to tell me what Jesus could *not* do, so I took this godly man at his word. I walked away from his office with the simple but powerful idea that as long as I sought Jesus wholeheartedly and obeyed what He said, He was going to take care of the battle with demonic powers and my wicked ways for me.

And He did. That day marked the end of my participation in homosexual behavior, the use of pornography and more than a decade of drug and alcohol abuse. From that day on, I knew that as long as I wanted freedom from such things, God would provide the power for me to overcome the temptations. The tasks ahead of me involved learning how to remain willing to be free, and how to appropriate God's power at the point of temptation.

One night, I was kneeling at my bed, complaining that I was unable to drive down Hollywood Boulevard without stopping at the porn racks there. The Lord's voice immediately spoke to my spirit: "So don't drive down Hollywood Boulevard!" It was kind of a "duh" moment, but I was too overwhelmed by my own sinful drives to see even the obvious.

Considering all I had been through, you might be asking, "How did you know it was the voice of God?"

Believe me, I recognized it immediately. It was the same voice that had spoken to me in the Garden of Gethsemane. Additionally, I was now born again and could recognize His voice according to His promise in John 10:3–5:

> The sheep hear his voice, and he calls his own sheep by name and leads them out. When he has brought out all his own, he goes before them, and the sheep follow him, for they know his voice. A stranger they will not follow, but they will flee from him, for they do not know the voice of strangers.

On another occasion, I was lamenting the unbearable compulsions that were ripping and tearing at my soul. The Lord spoke to me and said, "Call each demon by name—by what they are tempting you to do—and cast them out in My name!"

I obeyed: "I cast you out, demon of pornography," I began, "*in Jesus' name.*"

I continued on through lust and about twelve others in all—and they left. And with them went the overwhelming compulsions to do those things. While temptations to pursue past sins have returned periodically over the years, their enormous power over me has never returned. From that night on, I have had the strength and authority to choose. God always has my back, as long as I choose Him rather than my own idolatrous desires—which is an uncomplicated truth with straightforward results.

Perhaps most important of all, however, I learned that falling in love with Jesus at deeper and deeper levels was the key to my sexual healing. True intimacy with Him made possible my spiritual transformation. The love and focus that I placed on Him undermined certain deeply entrenched influences that were yet to be consciously uncovered and removed. Though I had many years of healing ahead of me, from the beginning of my new life, it was the grace and love of God that taught me to say no to ungodliness—just like it says in Titus 2:11–14 (NIV1984):

> For the grace of God that brings salvation has appeared to all men. It teaches us to say "No" to ungodliness and worldly passions, and to live self-controlled, upright and godly lives in this present age, while we wait for the blessed hope—the glorious appearing of our great God and Savior, Jesus Christ, who gave himself for us to redeem us from all wickedness and to purify for himself a people that are his very own, eager to do what is good.

A New Man among Men

My family knew that I longed to grow in grace and be more formally educated in God's Word. During a visit with them, Dad took me to Princeton Theological Seminary—his alma mater and also his father's—so I could interview for the school's fall seminary classes.

I did not want another guru coming along and fooling me again, but I did not exactly want to go to Princeton, either. I had heard that the seminary was theologically liberal in its views, and I certainly was not interested in hearing why the Bible *was not* God's Word. I already knew by divine revelation that it was. Nonetheless, I wanted to honor my father—he was a diehard Princeton man who wanted the family legacy to continue—so we drove to the beautiful campus together.

The interview, which I had dreaded, turned out to be quite comical. My radical Christian conversion in Israel was still vividly on my mind. It had filled me with passion and fire for the Lord, and with unrestrained enthusiasm, I poured out the story of my conversion to the woman in the admissions office.

There was a pause after I finished, and then she shook her head. With some measure of regret in her expression, she said, "You wouldn't do well here."

I heaved an inner sigh of relief and thanked the Lord for His way of escape.

Meanwhile, one of the pastors at Hollywood Presbyterian had recommended a seminary near Chicago. I believed God wanted me to enroll there instead. I applied, was interviewed, and the door to Trinity Evangelical Divinity School (TEDS) swung wide open.

Standing in sub-zero weather in front of the administration building at Trinity Evangelical Divinity School in Deerfield, Illinois, in 1980, my first year of seminary, feeling very blessed and loved by God.

Just weeks later, by faith and with no money, I began attending Trinity in Deerfield, Illinois, just north of Chicago. I was 29 and immensely grateful to be there. I had entered another world and was starting my life all over again. I slept on the couch of the student lounge for a week, until a room opened up for me. It was a private room—just what I was praying for. I did not want the temptation of a good-looking roommate, but more to the point, I needed privacy to work through the innumerable issues I was facing, both small and great.

Night after night, I poured out my brokenness to God. I begged Him to heal me, transform me and help me understand things so that I could walk free from all the sin and bondage that had dominated my life up until then. I figured that outside that dorm room, there would not be a soul on that entire campus who could possibly understand me, fathom what I had been through or support me as I climbed out of the depths of sin I had lived in for so long. So it was just God and me, wrestling next to the bed.

I found the campus chapel services especially healing. They were almost always packed out. There I stood, shoulder-to-shoulder with hundreds of like-minded men, singing the great hymns of the faith. At times, I wept copious tears of thanksgiving for the healing I was receiving by the Spirit of God. He worked in my soul through their voices and the glorious lyrics of every hymn. I was a man among men for the first time—holy men who did not want to use me. I certainly could tell the difference—these men loved God with all their hearts, souls, minds and strength.

After the powerful praises ceased, some humble yet mighty man of God would then ascend to the podium—men like J. I. Packer and John Stott. Once again I found myself weeping. How could God be merciful enough to place me in such a place of grace and truth? Why would He trust me with such a privilege after all I had done?

Wonder of Wonders, Miracle of Miracles!

During those early days at seminary, my sweet, humble grand-mother graciously gave me her life savings to pay for my first quarter's tuition. She wrote in a note,

> *We were so happy yesterday after reading your letter to the congregation at the Presbyterian Church in Newark. We were all in tears with joy after reading the beautiful words. God has endowed you with the ability to put forth His message. You are surely one of His chosen ones to carry His word forth to the world.*
>
> *Love, Bessie Carey*

As inspiring as it was, this was not an easy time in terms of energy and focus. I had to work nights at UPS in order to prepare for the second quarter's expenses and beyond. It was hard work, driving late at night in the sub-freezing winter of Chicago. I quickly realized that I would never learn anything with such an insanely demanding schedule. I did one of those crazy things new believers do—I prayed in all sincerity that God would send a millionaire to pay for my seminary education.

Over Christmas, driving over the Sunshine Skyway with my father on our way to my hometown of Bradenton, Florida, the Lord suddenly spoke to me. Out of the blue came the unsolicited thought, *The owner of Tropicana Orange Juice must be a millionaire.*

I did not even know if the man was a believer. But acting in sheer faith, I tracked down his address and wrote him a letter, describing my salvation experience in Israel, my admission into seminary and my subsequent need for financial help. As it turned out, Anthony Rossi was not only a millionaire; he was a strong Christian. Even more amazing, he had a private foundation that sent people through seminary who could not otherwise afford to go.

Miraculously, a month later I was granted a full three-year scholarship by Mr. Rossi's foundation to pay for my master of divinity degree. The grant covered all my costs—books, room and board, tuition, even toothpaste and flights home for Christmas.

And God was not through yet.

At about the same time, Dad called to let me know that a member of his church wanted to pay my way through seminary. The Bible promises that the Lord "is able to do far more abundantly than all that we ask or think, according to the power at work within us" (Ephesians 3:20), and there could not have been a better example of this promise being kept. God had sent not one millionaire, but two! Since millionaire #2's offer came after Mr. Rossi's, she decided to pay off all my college loans. Unbelievably, my education was entirely debt free.

Although Princeton Theological Seminary had a more elite reputation, Trinity Evangelical Divinity School was one of the most academically demanding seminaries in the world. Consequently, I was in over my head from day one. More than once, I heard about some student transferring into TEDS from Princeton and, all too soon, returning to Princeton because TEDS was so difficult. We had not yet studied the concept of bargaining with God, but I cut a deal with Him anyway. Here is what I told Him: "I'll make sure You are the priority in everything I do. I'll attend chapel every day, and I'll study very hard. But You'll have to supernaturally enable me to pass, because I don't think I can do this on my own."

God seemed to agree. Learning Greek and Hebrew were particularly difficult for me. But I studied hard, knowing that I did not understand either subject well enough to pass. "Lord, either put the questions that I know the answers to on the test," I told Him, "or just provide the answers to my mind supernaturally as

I need them." To my utter delight, I experienced Him answering both requests many times.

At the same time, my professors would plunge into deep theological truths and cite dozens of Scriptures during my other classes. They did not read the passages, but simply noted chapter and verse, assuming we all knew the Bible by memory. Having just emerged from a cult, having been both a prostitute and a Hollywood actor, and having spent the last twelve years zonked out on massive doses of drugs and alcohol, I did not know even one passage by its biblical address. I felt lucky to remember my own name. But I did not want anybody to know that, so I kept silent and carefully wrote down every reference so I could look it up later.

I remember hearing John 3:16 cited so many times in one classroom that I was frustrated and decided to raise my hand to ask what the text said. Thankfully, God came to my rescue. Just as my hand started to move upward, a strong impulse *not* to raise my hand overshadowed me. Once I discovered what the verse was, I realized that it was a good thing I had not asked. "For God so loved the world that He gave His only begotten Son, that whoever believes in Him should not perish but have everlasting life" (NKJV). Even I recognized that one once I heard it!

God continued to treat me as His beloved son. I had never been better than a B or C student; I had never even liked school. But seminary was a different story. Something I can only describe as a supernatural passion for the Word of God overtook me, and I could not learn enough. Consequently, I went from being a B or C student to an A or B student. In fact, it was during seminary that I made the first straight As of my life. For me, that was as miraculous as the parting of the Red Sea!

In a very real and moving way, I felt as if I were living the answer to Tevye's dream in *Fiddler on the Roof*, when he sang about wanting to spend several hours every day with the learned men, discussing the holy books. I could not have imagined a greater present from the Lord. Indeed, I had to agree with Tevye that it was the sweetest thing of all.

But what a radical shift it was. It is impossible to describe the change—going from partying with fellow prostitutes to "sharing" with a tribe of holy people. And by that I do not mean they were self-righteous. They were, in my eyes, simply pure of heart and good to the core. I often invited various people to coffee so I could find out just exactly what their parents had done to enable them to be so holy. I wanted to know so that if I ever got married, I could do the same thing for my children.

New Life, New Challenges

At the same time, of course, no one knew my real story. They assumed I was as holy as they were, and at times I felt as if I were playing the role of a secret agent. I never spoke of my sexual exploits. However, word of my experience in a cult spread rapidly across campus. Within a few months, I found myself on the local speaking circuit, lecturing about cults to churches and civic organizations all around Chicagoland. It did not take long for God to aim me in the general direction that He wanted me to go, toward a career that would involve writing and speaking.

A Presbyterian church in Lake Forest—the town upon which the movie *Ordinary People* was based—invited me to serve informally as an intern working with the youth group. I accepted, partially in an attempt to please my father by starting out in a Presbyterian church, since I had disappointed him by not going to Princeton. It was an extremely wealthy church community, and the kids grew up way too fast as a result of the neglect of their parents. The biblical teaching was liberal, so I considered my calling there as being that of a missionary of sorts. I hoped to be able to rescue kids who were about to fall into some of my own earlier behaviors.

Still, it was shocking. Suffice it to say that the youth pastor was from the most liberal seminary in the United Presbyterian Church (UPC), and he ran the youth group like a country club. Whatever the kids wanted was just fine with him. Getting drunk in the church while at youth group and leaving beer cans lying around? No problem. Having sex while on youth retreats? That was fine, too.

One night, I received a distress call from one of the teen girls in the group. She begged me to meet her at McDonald's so that she could tell me everything. When I arrived, I noticed that she was decked out to the nines, and I feared that she might be about to run away with some guy. It did not take her long to get to the point, however. She was in love with *me*. She wanted to run away and get married. And she was not going to take no for an answer.

Apart from the emotional recoil I was feeling, visions of lawsuits immediately danced in my head. I racked my brain, trying to figure out how to extricate myself from this potentially dangerous situation. I knew I had to be careful because she was clearly unstable. What if my rejection resulted in a suicide attempt?

"You know," I began, "I like you a lot, too . . . but I'm gay."

That revelation quickly quenched the fire, and we parted ways amicably. It never occurred to me, however, that she would tell everyone in the church what I had said!

Several weeks later, there was a lunch at the youth pastor's house. Parents and their teenagers were all standing around chatting. All at once, the youth pastor's four-year-old son planted himself in front of me. In a loud voice, he announced to the crowd, "He's gay!"

Standing on an outcropping of rock during my 1982 mission trip to Nigeria. I served under the Sudan Interior Mission and the Evangelical Church of West Africa during my "rocky" time there.

Of course, the youth pastor thought his cute little guy was hilarious. And as far as he was concerned, there was absolutely no problem with my being gay or with his son humiliating me in front of everyone. But I decided to resign my post. I assumed, probably rightly, that any further effectiveness I might have had leading those youth to a godly life was over and done.

After completing my second year in seminary, I traveled to Nigeria to take part in a short-term missions project. By that time, I felt convinced that God had called me to the mission field to follow in the footsteps of great heroes of old like William Carey or Hudson Taylor. Surely that was the "great thing" for which God had saved me.

It had not been all that long since I had lived the life of a Hollywood actor, and I was still driven by grandiose visions that only happened in the movies. Still, the missions project was an exciting opportunity to enter the field under the aegis of the Sudan Interior Mission (SIM), founded in 1893 to reach the people of sub-Saharan Africa. Naturally, I got myself a proper safari hat and shirt and took off for the wild unknowns of deepest, darkest Africa.

I was in for a rude awakening. First of all, Nigeria did not need me. They needed Greek scholars to teach in their seminaries—and that did not describe me. Second, it was extremely dangerous there for Western missionaries. The city of Kano, where our team made its entry, was a stronghold of militant

Islam. Churches in the north of Nigeria were regularly burned, and people were massacred. Even though SIM was headquartered in Jos, near the center of the nation, roving bands of gangs were still on the move along the fringes, attacking Western compounds and hacking the inhabitants to death with machetes. I spent many a sleepless night listening for the sound of large, sharp blades slicing through the brush outside our locked-down mission compound.

One Sunday, we traveled to a church in Bauchi State where I was to preach. It had recently been attacked by Muslims, and I wrestled with myself, well aware that I had little or nothing to say to people who were living so much more sacrificially than I was. I told myself more than once that they should be teaching me.

God surprised me, though. In an entry from my journal, I described the scene:

> As I stood to preach, I silently prayed that the Lord would take away my fear and help me communicate effectively to the congregation. It was miraculous how my fear vanished after just the first few words. God is truly faithful in all respects. I even felt the power of the Holy Spirit give me boldness and ease with speaking loudly and forcefully. It was exciting to feel the Spirit overcome all of my natural inadequacies. It was also amazing to see a clear verification of God's leading in the sermon I preached. Much of it had to do with the "blessing" of being persecuted for the sake of Jesus Christ. The fact that the very people present had, just the day before, undergone persecution from Muslims was no coincidence at all. God was answering prayer. I cannot think of anything more exciting!

On the other hand, there was the Nigerian food. My delicate digestive system could not handle it, so I lived on a diet of dark chocolate bars for two months. In summary, I ended up writhing on the floor in agony, suffering from a stomach ulcer.

Still, it was not all for naught. I wrote in another journal entry,

I had been assigned the job of teaching Nigerian Sunday school teachers about Christian education. It was a terrifying assignment, as I had never taught Sunday school and had never taken a course in Christian education. What was God thinking?

So, using quickly purchased textbooks on the subject, I fashioned a series of lessons, prayed a great deal and stepped up to the podium with great fear and trepidation. To my utter amazement, while I was teaching God began to place thoughts and ideas into my mind, and as I spoke them, I felt the power of God going out with the words. It was as if the words were being lubricated by the Spirit as they were being spoken.

Then, during question time at the end of each session, God supernaturally gave me the answers to questions that I did not know the answers to—and as I gave these answers, I experienced the same spiritual dimension to the utterances. This was the first time that I actually experienced the truth of the biblical promise that God would give us the words to speak when we spoke in His name.

I have assumed, however, that this Spirit-backing would not have come if I had not prayed for God's help out of my weakness and natural inability, if I had shrunk back from attempting what God called me to do due to the apparent impossibility of the request, and if I had not first been faithful to do all that I could to prepare for the sessions.

In another section of my journal, I wrote:

I feel that the Lord is stretching me in many ways. I hope that I'll never again be the same unfriendly American that I have been in the past. The Nigerians have taught me a great deal about the value of human friendships and a people-oriented society. They've taught me to give more and be less selfish. They've taught me great lessons about being genuine and consistent and unprejudiced. . . .

It is so wonderful to be teaching along and to have the Holy Spirit put words and concepts right into my mouth. I could really feel His presence and provision as I taught. Even the question-and-answer period was blessed by the Spirit's work. He gave me quick, clear and good answers to every question that arose. It is very exciting to have this happen to me.

While in Nigeria, another blessing took place—although a blessing in disguise. This unexpected event provided an opportunity for healing old wounds. I received a letter from my parents that included an article from the Wilmington, Delaware, newspaper near where my father pastored. The writer, a former high school classmate of mine, had interviewed me a few months before. Then he had written an article about my unhappy childhood, but he had done so and published the article without including any of the positive statements I had made about my father. Sorry and saddened, I wrote to both my father and the newspaper, trying to explain the one-sided inaccuracies of the article and how terrible I felt as a result. I also wrote in my journal,

It is amazing how God has used this incident to make me grow. It has made me realize truly for the first time that I cannot blame my parents for my wicked and unhappy life. As I was suddenly thrust into the position of defending my parents after the onslaught of this article, I discovered that the case I came up with in their defense was far better than the case I had unconsciously held against them in my heart. I really am completely at fault for the sad way my life went. It was my own sinfulness and selfish nature that resulted in such a messed-up life. God holds us responsible for our actions even when circumstances appear to leave us no other logical choice. People today are obsessed with vindicating themselves by blaming forces beyond their control—like fate, or parents or society, when in fact, they are only dodging the recognition of their own guilt in the matter. I only regret that I learned this lesson at the expense of my father's devastated heart. Please, dear Lord, heal the wound and forgive me!

Before leaving Nigeria, we really did have a Hollywood-style adventure at the Yankari Game Reserve. It began happily enough. Our group went on a safari into the bush, where we saw a myriad of exotic animals, including elephants, hippos, monitor lizards, warthogs, wildebeests and spectacularly colored birds. That was just what we had hoped for. But then, after being swarmed by tsetse flies, we were pursued in a high-speed chase for nearly twenty miles by drunken bandits clearly intent on theft and murder. Knowing this sort of thing often happened in the area did not make us feel any better. After a terrifying half hour or so, we made it to safety. By then, the exotic patina of our African safari had tarnished considerably.

July 10, 1981, brought my thirtieth birthday. In my view, it was another miracle—perhaps one of the greatest I had experienced. From childhood, powerful compulsions to end my life had tempted me to jump off high buildings and bridges. My first suicide attempt at age 9 had been followed by several more during college, so I had been surprised to make it to 21—and not altogether pleased.

Then, during my twenties in Hollywood, there had been three murder attempts against me. In varying ways, the hand of God thwarted each attempt on my life. I mentioned two of them already, the strangler in the car and the odd guy who took me to the darkened warehouse. The third happened the week after I returned from Israel. I had decided to return to the disco that I had frequented for so many years, only this time just to dance—not to find someone to sleep with. While I was hitchhiking back to the ashram at 2:00 a.m., three guys picked me up and tried to rob and kill me. The guy next to me in the backseat began wailing on me with his fist while grabbing for the gold chain around my neck. But God made a way of escape, because we soon came to a red light in heavy traffic and I was able to bail out of the car. As I ran away, God spoke strongly to me that I was playing with fire and that I had to leave all vestiges of my former life behind in order to walk with Him.

After a grand obsession with death, celebrating thirty years of life was nothing short of astounding. Needless to say, this was especially true following our harrowing escape from the Nigerian bandits.

Even more astonishing, from my point of view, was finding myself in a seminary and serving as a missionary on my thirtieth birthday. How unlikely and unforeseen was that? By now, I thought God surely had something important for me to do. I spent the day silently pondering these things and wondering what my calling from Him might be. One thing was clear, however. I would not be serving Him in Africa.

To celebrate my birthday, my missionary friends took me on a wonderful outing to Kafanchan Falls in Kaduna State. The countryside was absolutely gorgeous. The hills were covered in lush, green vegetation, with rocky outcroppings. Later, my friends treated me to a homemade birthday cake with real icing and candles. Because the ingredients were so costly in Nigeria (especially the eggs), it was an incredibly thoughtful, time-consuming and expensive treat. What a great birthday it was! I wrote in my journal,

> I think the Lord is leading me into a greater desire to seek for righteousness constantly—not to separate the secular from the sacred—but to always seek for Him. It is a development I've prayed hard for and still do. How I wish I could give my all to Him constantly!

The Valley of the Shadow

After saying farewell to my new friends in Nigeria, I decided to explore Europe on the way back to the United States. I bought a Europass, determined to take the train to as many countries as possible in three weeks' time. After a whirlwind trip through Holland, England, Scotland, France and Italy, I had an unforeseen time of intimacy with the Lord while touring the Interlaken area of Switzerland. After hiking to the headwaters of Giessbach Falls, I wrote in my journal,

> The view of the lake became more spectacular as I climbed. The sun broke through the clouds and it felt like paradise. As I walked, I repeated the 23rd Psalm to myself and was filled with the wonder and glory of the Lord. His creation is too beautiful for words, and I was moved to tears of gratitude. His guidance and protection, newly recalled, gave me a deep and warm sense of His love. That was a moment to remember forever.

Once I returned to seminary, it was not long before the "shadow of death" so beautifully depicted in Psalm 23 fell across our family. It was not unexpected. My father had had several heart attacks over the years, but this time, in November 1982, it was fatal. I rushed back to Florida to be with my family. My father had been serving at Pasadena Presbyterian Church in St. Petersburg as a pastor to senior citizens when he went home to be with the Lord.

Quite miraculously, since my salvation experience in Israel, my father had gone from the man I most hated to the man I most loved. Much of that change of heart had to do with my salvation, although as I would later discover, I still had some forgiving to do. But there had been a dramatic change in my father, too. As I mentioned before, he and my mother had gone to a convention of charismatic Presbyterians and had been utterly transformed by the baptism of the Holy Spirit.

The change in Dad had been particularly profound and apparent. My childhood perception of him was of a cold and distant stranger—one who would not and probably could not love me. But after Dad's spiritual transformation, he softened. I experienced him as a warmhearted friend, one who seemed genuinely happy to be with me.

I also noticed that Dad had a different spirit toward the simplest things in life. He had somehow gained the heart of a servant. He had always, for example, washed the dishes after every meal. But now he took on this everyday task joyfully and without any recrimination—even when I did not volunteer to help. Meanwhile, he and Mom had become as affectionate with each other as two puppy dogs. The quarrelsome spirit in their home had become only a memory.

I arrived at the funeral home, where my brothers immediately met me and led me into the viewing room. They stood there with me—one on each arm and the third nearby. As I approached the casket, my eye caught site of a Masonic ring on Dad's finger. Somehow the sight of that symbol knocked me backward so powerfully that my brothers had to catch me.

Everyone present assumed it was the shock of seeing the most powerful man in my life no longer alive. But it was more. It was all that history—all the tears, the raging arguments, the emptiness and despair at feeling rejected by him as a child. I felt a burden of guilt because I had never made a formal apology for my rebellion against him. And there was grief, too, that I had never received my identity as a son from him—a hope that was now lost forever.

But it was also the ring. By then, I had been speaking on cults on a regular basis and knew the occultic history that undergirded Masonry. The demonic powers were, no doubt, trying to intimidate me and make me think they had won. But they had not. My dad was as born again as could be by then. He was in the arms of his heavenly Father.

And I knew then and there that if I was ever to find my masculine soul and become secure in my male identity, it was to that same heavenly Father that I would have to go.

NAVIGATING RELIGION

In my father's memory, at least in part, I placed myself under the care of the Presbytery of Northern Illinois of the Presbyterian Church in America (PCA). Even though they were more legalistically conservative than I thought was necessary, I loved their uncompromising stand on the inerrancy of Scripture. It was a decision that would bring me a great deal of heartbreak in the months ahead, however.

But first came a New Year's Eve surprise out of left field. I was in Florida for the Christmas holiday when I got an urgent phone call asking me to fly to Michigan to help two girls entangled in a cult. I had been doing that kind of work behind the scenes during the last year, serving as a biblical consultant for a Midwestern deprogramming team. Now they had an emergency on their hands. The parents of the two girls were wealthy and influential, and they were more than willing to pay for my flight. Would I please come and help while they had the girls at home for Christmas?

Normally, I prayed and asked God if He wanted me to get involved in jobs like that, but this time, I just went. Bad decision! What I did not realize was that the FBI had been staking out the parents' house for days—one of the girls had led them to believe that she and her sister were being held for ransom. I was walking into an FBI sting operation.

Oblivious to all of that, I entered the house carrying two suitcases filled with Bibles and Bible commentaries. The FBI agents surrounding the building assumed that I was bringing in weapons. They had been surveilling the family's home for days with listening devices. Once I arrived, they would spring their trap.

The parents and the deprogramming team asked me to go down to the basement to talk to the younger girl about how the Bible differed from what her cult leader had been teaching her. After an hour or so, she was coming around very nicely. Then suddenly, a loud commotion broke out upstairs. I assumed it was her cult members attempting to rescue her, so I barricaded the door and leaned against it.

When I heard the sound of heavy boots charging down the basement stairs, I knew I was in for the fight of my life. Removing my glasses so that they would not get driven into my eyes by possible blows, I returned to the door to reinforce my position.

"FBI—open the door!" a male voice commanded as they pounded against it, trying to break it down. There must have been five or six of them.

FBI? Right. Like I'm going to fall for that one! I thought as I continued pressing against the door.

Suddenly, they stopped pounding and shouting. Just then, the Lord spoke to me clearly and with great urgency: *"Open the door!"*

It sounded crazy, but by then I knew the Lord's voice when I heard it. I opened it, braced for the blows that would surely follow. And what to my wondering eyes did appear? Half a dozen FBI agents armed with shotguns and pistols—all aimed at me. They had been seconds away from blowing the door away in a hail of bullets. All I could see were FBI hats and jackets, and the weapons. And like a dumb hick with no sense at all, I exclaimed, "Why, you *are* the FBI!"

There was a beat while they assessed whether I was being smart or stupid. They quickly decided on stupid and burst out laughing.

The FBI dropped all charges when they saw what was actually going on. The state's district attorney was running for office, however, and he knew a great campaign opportunity when he saw one. He charged my colleagues and me with felony kidnapping and threw us in the county jail for three days. At the same time, because the parents were superwealthy and famous, the story was front-page news the following day, even appearing on the *CBS Evening News with Walter Cronkite*.

We did not know that, of course. There was no newspaper delivery in our jail cell. As I sat in that holding cell for three days with the rest of the deprogramming team, I came up with a surefire strategy: I would simply let this blow over and not tell a soul. After all, I was in my last year of seminary! I was a good person; I had not done anything wrong.

Since it was New Year's Eve, the cell, which was designed for a maximum of fifteen inmates, was crammed with at least thirty. It was, to say the least, frightening. Two dozen thugs were strutting around bragging about what they had done, trying to establish their place in the pecking order. I noticed one guy sitting by himself—a murderer who did not need to prove anything. I figured nobody would cause him any trouble, so I sat down right next to him. It was a chancy move, but it worked.

My biggest question at the time was, "God, have I done something wrong here, or am I suffering for my faith?" It was not lost on me that, like Jonah in the whale, I remained in that place for three days and three nights.

The D.A. decided to charge everyone but me. I guess he figured it would not be so easy to convict a seminary student who had shown up to the scene of the crime with two suitcases full of Bibles and Bible commentaries. At the end of our third day in jail, they let us all out at once. To my horror, CBS, NBC, ABC and a phalanx of assorted reporters, lights and video cameras met us at the prison door. Like some kind of dubious celebrities, we were whisked away in a private limousine by the parents' bigwig lawyers. They took us to a safe house for debriefing. A posse of lawyers followed in close pursuit.

Taken by my mother on campus just after my graduation from seminary in June of 1983. Words cannot express the gratitude that I felt toward God at this moment, the gratefulness for the persevering prayers of my dear mother when I was totally lost and the exciting adventure with God that I anticipated was still to come.

When I finally arrived back at my seminary dorm room, I was met with a dozen notes taped to my door, all of which said, "See the dean!"

My name and that of the seminary had appeared in many of the front-page newspaper articles, so the school had been getting calls from all over the world. I am sure people were wondering what kind of divinity school they were running, with kidnappers as students.

The dean's name was Art Volkman, and I will never forget his words to me. After hearing my sorry tale and my tearful apologies for ruining the reputation of the seminary I loved, he looked at me and said, "We're going to support you 100 percent!"

I was ecstatic, and overwhelmed with gratitude. As I left the room, Art decided to try some comic relief and asked, "How did you ever get in here, anyway?"

"The grace of God," I replied.

Six months later, I was awarded a master of divinity degree from the most wonderful seminary in the world.

Success and Disappointment

Since I was convinced by then that my future did not include being a missionary, I had seriously begun to consider becoming a pastor. There were pros and cons—one of the cons being my childhood struggle with life as a preacher's kid. On the other hand, the idea of serving as a pastor seemed like a perfect circle of redemption for me. God had clearly paved the way for me to receive an M.Div., which is usually looked on as a pastoral degree.

Meanwhile, attending seminary had revealed to me some areas of dissention that divide the Christian world, particularly among Protestants. One big divide, of course, was infant baptism. As I saw it, given the presuppositions of each argument, both had merit, and there was not enough textual evidence in Scripture to dogmatically pronounce a verdict. There was a lot of pressure at seminary, however (mostly from other students), to join sides on issues like this.

The Calvinist-Arminian debate was another point of conflict. To adopt any one of these systems of theology required ignoring all the sound hermeneutical principles on the other side. This was most evident in the cessationist versus charismatic debate, where in order to get it to fit their system of theology, the cessationists were forced to brutally twist into a pretzel the 1 Corinthians 13 passage that tells us that when the perfect comes, the imperfect—prophecy, tongues and the like—will cease (see verses 8–10).

The conversations were interesting, but I knew that I had not been saved from so many dangers to join somebody's theological club. I was there to discover God's truth, even when reason forced two seemingly opposing truths to be held in dynamic tension. Above all else, I was saved to follow the Lord, who delivered His truth to us through His Holy Spirit. So from the very beginning, I promised God that I was not going to adopt man-made systematic theologies. I was going to find out what the text of Scripture said and believe all of it.

The excitement of my last year in seminary increased as I candidated with several denominations for a pastoral position of one kind or another. My refusal to adopt man-made systems of theology made it difficult to settle on any specific denomination or even on the vast majority of independent Bible churches. But I never gave up hope that one of them would accept me, even if I did not toe their every theological line.

My single status was perhaps a larger drawback. Most churches wanted a "twofer"—a pastor, youth pastor or whatever, *plus* his wife, who would be expected to do any number of important tasks in the church for free. I will never forget one denominational representative who looked at me sadly and said, "Call us when you get married." In light of this concern, most of the senior men and women at the seminary were scrambling to find "the right one" and get married that same year. The air was filled with frantic hormonal tones of fear and consternation. After all, in the rush, what if somebody picked the wrong mate and got stuck with him or her for life? This was no small threat.

In honor of my father, I first tried being a candidate in the Presbyterian Church USA (PCUSA). Although it was rapidly sliding into liberalism, I believed that God wanted witnesses to the truth—leaders who would minister to those who did not want to abandon Christian orthodoxy. I also assumed that because my father had been both a pastor in the PCUSA and an evangelical, it would be fairly easy for me to get in. This was not the case.

One interview followed another, and my conservative stance (particularly on abortion and the authority of God's Word) blocked me at every turn. Unbeknownst to the membership at large, conservative candidates were being weeded out at the presbytery level. It quickly became clear to me that a slide into full-blown liberalism was inevitable for that denomination.

My next try was with the Presbyterian Church in America (PCA), a more conservative denomination that was one of the fastest growing in the nation. I went "under care" of the presbytery in my area and served in a church near the seminary for about nine months as I prepared for the licensing and ordination gauntlet.

The licensure exam came first. It was known as the most rigorous exam of any denomination, and it certainly met those expectations. Nonetheless, I squeaked by and headed for the presbytery meeting, where it was expected that I would preach a sermon before the elders. Then they would question me on doctrine, and I would be voted in.

On the way to the meeting, however, someone in the car asked me about my views on the gifts of the Holy Spirit. I had studied the issue at length, of course, but was most persuaded by my father's transformation after getting baptized by the Holy Spirit. I confided that personal example, not foreseeing that my questioner would double-cross me and ask the same question from the floor of presbytery. (It was common knowledge that the denomination frowned upon the exercise of spiritual gifts.)

I preached what I thought was a fairly decent sermon, but then the grilling began. Most of the presbytery members were from Dr. Bruce Dunn's congregation—a church that had just undergone a major split over the charismatic issue—so they were none too happy with my position. Nonetheless, I stood my ground. "Bottom line," I said, "my father was saved and radically transformed by the baptism of the Holy Spirit, and I do not believe that if Satan were behind the gifts, he would be in the business of doing work like that."

I had to leave the sanctuary while the vote was taken. The first ballot was a tie. On the second ballot, I was denied licensure unless I would go under the tutelage of an anti-charismatic teacher. The plan was that once I changed my opinion, my license would be made permanent.

I was unable to comply because I was soon to move to Charleston, West Virginia, to live with my brother John and his wife while I looked for work. But in any case, I would not have changed my beliefs in order to secure a position.

So it was that I was not accepted for licensing in the Presbyterian Church, liberal or conservative. And in the process, all the father-wound rejection issues I had ever known were ripped open afresh in my heart—only this time by an entire roomful of pastor-fathers. In the years to come, I would come to recognize this experience as God's blessing, but at the time, I was completely devastated.

Downhearted, with no money and no future plans, I dragged myself to Charleston to stay with my brother and his wife. Charleston turned out to be a way station, however. After a few months, I came to see that my quiet personality was not suited to the shout-from-the-pulpit style of preaching in that part of the world, and I moved to Florida to be near my mother, who was still a new widow.

Those early months of 1984 were dark and difficult for me. The dramatic highs of my supernatural conversion experience and theological training at one of the finest seminaries in the world had been followed by the lowest of lows—my failure to find acceptance by pastors who shared my spiritual birthright. Once again, I had that old feeling of being "not good enough," and of being excluded by those who bore a symbolic resemblance to the Presbyterian pastor-father who—in my perception—had rejected me as a child.

Not wasting a teachable moment, the Lord spoke to me clearly one night that He wanted me to be a man of truth. He wanted me to tell the truth at all times—even in those situations when a little white lie could potentially save another person's feelings (such as when your mother asks how you like her new hairdo). Interestingly enough, after committing to obey His request, I discovered that the Holy Spirit always had something brilliant to suggest that I say during such moments that was not only true, but that also avoided offense. It was by then a familiar "divine" modus operandi: genuine commitment to obedience required first, the capacity to obey imparted second.

What I did not realize at the time, but would see great fruit from later, was that my commitment to being a man of truth pulled the rug out from under the edifice of sex addiction that I had built over so many years. The truth was, if I could no longer lie, then I no longer had the cloak of secrecy necessary for a sex addict, whose deeds are so embarrassing that public disclosure is too fearsome a prospect.

But there was a deeper purpose still. One night as I was wrestling with the recent rejections by clerical father figures and feeling just a little abandoned by God in the process, an internal river of anger toward God began to rise to the surface. Of course, it was ridiculous that someone who had been granted such mercy from God could be angry with Him. Nevertheless, there it was. All through seminary, I had tried to deny it and shove it down, but as a man of truth, I now had to admit that I was still very angry with God over the events of my life.

Bracing for the worst, I let it fly. In a torrent of white-hot honesty, I let God know how much I hated Him for all the painful things I had experienced in my life. Exposed and unguarded before God for perhaps the first time, I fully expected a harsh reply, or at best the same sort of lengthy sermon that Job had received. Instead, I was stunned as God hit me with a wave of love. I could literally feel the wave wash over me, and I was for quite some time rendered speechless.

Finally, I mustered, "I just told You how much I hated You. Why did You hit me with a wave of love?"

His reply: "You've finally been honest with Me. Now I can help you."

In some cosmically mysterious way, in spite of my insufferable ignorance and disrespect, the greater good was the honesty. God could handle the anger, but He would do nothing without the honesty. That was a tremendous breakthrough moment for me that bore fruit for decades to come.

For a while I drove a cab. Then I worked as a substitute schoolteacher for a few months while trying to figure it all out. Why would God train me to minister and then not give me a place in which to do so? I just could not make sense of it. One day, remembering that my father had been a church planter, I came upon a likely solution—perhaps I should plant a church! That effort—beginning with a Bible study in my apartment—carried on for a while, but it also came to a crashing halt when a pastor and his wife accused me of doing the work of the devil. It might have had something to do with the fact that their youth leader, unbidden by me, had left their church to join me in the church plant. But I did not want to take any chances that I might be doing the devil's work, so I gave it up.

Then a new door opened. I received an invitation from a media ministry out West to come to work for them and their nationwide radio show. The celebrity host had written a Christian book on cults—a topic I knew more than a little about. So off I went.

At first I was delighted with my new job. I loved having the Rocky Mountains as a backdrop, and the weather suited me. But the new boss who was over me was another matter. Extremely difficult to work with, he had a rather Napoleonic personality verging on the paranoiac. I soon realized that the employees were spying on each other and reporting their findings to him. He treated his wife like a dog. And as time went on, I observed that he regularly engaged in questionable fund-raising tactics.

Despite the employee spying and other dramas, I worked hard. It was not long before I was given a raise and promoted to vice president of the radio network, which included numerous stations that carried the ministry's daily radio program. By then, I was participating in all the top meetings with programmers and fund-raising gurus. And I did not like what I was seeing. My years in the cult and my more recent efforts to find intimacy with the Lord had sharpened my discernment skills. I will never forget the day when, in a meeting with my boss and one of the top fund-raising consultants in the Christian world, a demonic spirit swept into the room. At first, I did not recognize it as a demon. It gave me an exquisite feeling of ecstasy and power. It was so powerful, in fact, that it appeared to immediately take over everyone and every activity in the room.

While I was reveling in the delightful feeling of authority and prestige that I was filled with, the Holy Spirit clearly informed me that this was a diabolical sensation. It was the same demonic principality of power that supernaturally intoxicates the boardrooms of Congress, the White House and big business and that can cause them to serve the kingdom of darkness rather than the Kingdom of God. In a flash, I realized why government and businesses are so corrupt. If not for the Holy Spirit's whisper to me, that influence would have corrupted me as well, because it felt so good and made everything seem so right.

The business of the meeting soon revealed that the lust for power and money I had felt was, in fact, driving the ministry. Dishonest tactics were being used to collect funds. I knew I had to resign. I did not want to be a party to deception—and worse, to using the Gospel to pull it off. I started asking God to lead me to my next adventure.

But the Lord was not quite finished with me there. Before I left, I had a marvelous revelation from Him. There were about twenty employees in the office, most of whom I did not know. To my shame, as vice president I had been too busy and too "important" to get to know them. On that day, a secretary walked past me. She was someone whom I had not cared to know. But as she passed by, the supernatural love of God for her poured out from heaven into my heart. I suddenly loved her with the same pure love that the Father had for her.

It instantly became obvious that I had never loved anyone before—not really. I did not know how to love someone. Oh, I had had my romances, flirtations and infatuations—more than I could count—but they had always been self-serving and self-centered. Now I felt pure and selfless love pouring through me. It was frightening, because I knew that if I opened my mouth, I would say something stupid like, "I love you more than all the suns and stars in the heavens put together!" I kept my mouth shut and kept walking.

As I walked away, the Lord said to me, "No one has ever loved her before."

I was stunned and deeply moved, but still, I kept moving. Why was I so afraid to love another human being?

One thing was perfectly clear: God was willing to love people through me in ways I was incapable of on my own. By then, I was aware that intimacy with God is the prime directive of life. John 17:3 says, "This is eternal life: that they may know you, the only true God, and Jesus Christ whom you have sent" (NIV1984). Only through a profoundly vulnerable relationship with the Lord would I ever be able to truly love anybody else.

— 19 —

LEARNING
to LOVE GOD

With no job prospects in sight after leaving my position at the radio network, I decided to fly to Dallas to attend a James Robison conference, hoping the Lord would speak to me there. I respected Robison and also liked one of his guest speakers, John Wimber, whom I had seen on *The 700 Club*. I appreciated the fact that although Wimber was charismatic, he did not shout and scream and gyrate to manipulate the crowd. He did not punch people in the stomach to get them to fall down "under the power of the Spirit" or twist their arms to raise money.

The convention center was huge, so I went early and found myself a place in the fifth row. I was a good seventy feet away from the speaker's podium. The floor of the convention center was concrete, and the chairs, at least in my section, were metal—an important detail regarding what happened next.

John Wimber walked up to the microphone in his customary Hawaiian shirt and sandals. He was utterly unpretentious.

He paused for a moment, and then in a gentle, calm voice, he simply said, "Come, Holy Spirit." And he waited.

We had just finished a time of worship and praise and were still standing. Within seconds I heard people all around me crashing through the metal chairs onto the concrete floor. No one had touched them. They had simply fallen over backward onto the floor. From what I could tell, they were unhurt, despite the metal and concrete.

I was concerned and amazed at the same time. After some of my experiences with Maharaj Ji, it was reasonable for me to ask myself, *Is this God or Satan?* There was no question about the supernatural nature of what was happening, so I determined that I would find out which it was. Right then and there, I made a decision—I was moving to southern California to thoroughly check out Mr. Wimber and his traveling miracle show.

A few weeks later, I loaded up a U-Haul trailer and took off for California. This time neither Hollywood nor Malibu was in my plans. I was going to settle down in the low-profile community of Garden Grove, in an apartment just two miles from Disneyland.

John Wimber's Vineyard was the real attraction. The music was magnificent, and I found great joy in being among some three thousand worshipers every Sunday morning and evening, with hands lifted high, singing love songs for forty minutes non-stop to our Father God. It was an amazing experience to lose myself in worship and weep copious tears without attracting unwelcome attention. It was impossible to feel self-conscious when everyone's heart was set on God and God alone. I also was delighted to see that the worship leader, Eddie Espinosa, wept along with us, even though he had sung the same songs hundreds of times. And I was moved by the fact that we were singing love songs directly to God Himself. It almost felt as if He were physically there, receiving our petitions and praise. These people were head over heels in love with the Lord and unashamed to show it. What a refreshing freedom that brought to my soul.

Even more freedom became mine after the counseling session I described earlier with the pastor at the Vineyard, where I told him about my "great sin" of pushing my father down the stairs of our home. So much healing came when Jesus showed me that He was with us in that moment and that He forgave me for it.

At just the right moment during my time at the Vineyard, a new opportunity to serve the Lord came my way. The California prayer center for *The 700 Club* TV broadcast from CBN was located in nearby Orange, California, and I began volunteering as a phone counselor there. I was quickly hired as the "floor pastor" of the center. My task was to rewrite the training program for the phone counselors, instruct everyone in its use and help oversee the prayer counselor activities on the floor.

One huge issue I dealt with was that the counselors were spending far too much time on the phone with callers, and as a result were about to bankrupt the program. The holder of an 800 number had to pay the long-distance charges for the time the callers spent using the number, so the lengthy calls were racking up hefty long-distance charges for the ministry. Orders had come down from Ben Kinchlow that we needed to reduce the time spent with each caller to an average of seven minutes.

Needless to say, this caused quite an uproar, especially among the veteran counselors who were used to spending as much as an hour or two with a caller when they deemed it necessary. "Certainly the suicide callers need all the time we can give them," they argued.

I asked the Lord what to do. I did not have much choice—we had to reduce the average call time or lose the program altogether. In prayer one night, the Lord gave me the most brilliant of answers. We should ask each caller two questions. First, "What exactly would you like God to do for you today?" And second, "Are you willing to do whatever it takes to be healed or set free?"

The first question challenged people to get to the point without extraneous conversation. It also helped them focus in on a specific concern to bring before the Lord. That way, it would be obvious when He answered—which would build the caller's faith, and at the same time, give Jesus more glory.

The second question sifted out the "social" callers—people calling just to talk or complain, or people who simply did not want to get better. Sometimes people asked for prayer but did not really want an answer because they received too many "rewards" from being broken or hurt. If God healed them or rectified their situation, they would no longer be the center of attention. Others simply were not willing to do the work of being obedient and making the lifestyle changes necessary to see prayer answered. These are timeless issues ministries deal with, but the two questions the Lord gave me worked so well for us that within just a few weeks, the average call was reduced to seven minutes.

Meanwhile, I decided to attend a men's fellowship gathering at the Vineyard. I hated such groups because most of them were dysfunctional gatherings where men would try their best to match up to the broken American version of masculinity. I honestly would not have gone if I had not felt a strong urging from the Lord. After the presentation, five hundred of us divided into small groups for prayer. As that time came to a close, the pastor asked us to give each other a hug.

Hug each other? I thought. I was Scottish Presbyterian, and we did not hug! Worse by far, however, was that I did not know how to hug a guy nonsexually. What if I hugged him too tightly or for too long? He might assume I was gay and reject me. I was still keeping my sexually broken past hidden away, and all my buried fears bubbled to the surface. Despite my initial foray into "full disclosure" with the pastor at Hollywood Presbyterian some years before, I had learned that most believers were not as wise and gracious as he had been. The very reason that I was not telling people about my sexual background was because I knew they would reject me, keep me at arm's length, or worse, gossip about me and laugh at me. It was the old "if they really knew me, they would reject me" syndrome—one of the most powerful instruments of torture in Satan's domain.

In this case, God gave me no time to escape. A big, burly Paul Bunyan kind of guy turned around and buried me in a bear hug. As soon as he did, I had a surreal experience of him disappearing and God the Father hugging me, purely and tightly, in a way that signaled His delight in me as His son. The restoration that took place in those few seconds, completely unbeknownst to the man hugging me, remains one of the most powerfully healing moments of my life.

At every Vineyard event I attended, I was always first in line for prayer at the altar. I knew by then that healing for my sexual issues took place whenever God poured out His Spirit. On one occasion, we lined up in front of John Wimber for prayer. And as he laid his hands on my head, I noticed that they were rapidly vibrating in a way that I could not see until he actually touched me. And the moment he did, I felt a powerful surge of energy pour out of his hands and into my body. My legs weakened, and I knew I was about to fall backward.

After some of my earlier experiences with Maharaj Ji's cult, I was unwilling to receive anything that was not from God, so I locked my legs while saying to myself, *The spirit of the prophet is subject to the prophet* (see 1 Corinthians 14:32).

I knew that God would not be coercive and would not force me down without my permission, and I was right. The second I locked my legs, the flow of power evaporated. Then I knew it was the person of the Holy Spirit at work, so I prayed for Him to return to minister to me. Just as suddenly, the power of God returned and I did, indeed, fall backward onto the floor—"slain in the Spirit," as they say.

I remained in that prone position for about twenty minutes. I knew that if I really tried to get up, the Spirit would allow me to, but I was much more interested in receiving whatever healing or anointing He was providing for me. After about ten minutes, I asked, "Lord, what are You doing to me? I know You're operating on me in some deep way, but I don't understand what You're doing. . . ."

His reply was, "I'm not going to explain this one. I'm just healing you."

Afterward, I gave that experience a great deal of subsequent thought and came to believe that I had been sexually abused as a child. As I mentioned at the beginning, at around the age of nine I went from being relatively normal to being suicidal and sexually obsessive. Such changes in a child in such a short period of time often signal sexual abuse. Perhaps God healed me that way because it would have been too difficult for my psyche to go through a revelation of the abuse or the revelation of who it was that abused me. I never was sure, though, because the Lord never told me.

At the Vineyard, we were all learning to put the gifts of the Spirit to work in the lives of others as we ministered to them. One day, I was praying in a group for a man who had confessed to having difficulty being sexually intimate with his wife. He was going on and on about the broken relationship he had with his father. Just then, the Lord spoke clearly to me: "It's his mother!"

I could not just come out and say that, so I quietly suggested, "Tell us about your mother."

After a moment of shock, the troubled man began weeping and wailing. He had known all along that it was his mother (she had actually molested him), but he had been too embarrassed to admit it. When I said those words, he recognized that God was there to heal him. His past was so profoundly shaming and debilitating that a divine healing was his only hope. With the sign that God was present to heal him, he had hope once again.

My years at the Vineyard-Anaheim were special. My living expenses and *The 700 Club*'s salary simply did not match, though, so I had to resign. I had to make more money somehow. Despite the fact that I would be returning to the scene of several personal crimes, I took a job as a tour escort with American Tours International and moved back to Hollywood to be closer to work. Was I gambling with a relapse into my old habits? I did not think so, but time would tell.

In the process, God spoke to my spirit, telling me that my life was going to be like Abraham's—I would be moving from one place to another, without an apparent purpose, but always being guided by God for His purposes. How true that was! Right then, a message I had heard in seminary was replaying in my mind: "God will eventually take you back to the place of your greatest defeat in order to bring the greatest victory out of your life." Abraham had done admirably, but I was not so sure about me. Would I be able to withstand all the demonic powers that knew me well in Hollywood, Beverly Hills, Malibu and all my other former haunts? I was about to find out.

One of the first things I did was visit all the notorious haunts of my former life and declare the victory of God at each site. As I made this private pilgrimage, I can assure you that there was no power of the enemy left to draw me in, the way he had done before. The whole thing was a marvelous and tangible demonstration to me (and perhaps to the spirit world) that God is the omnipotent Lord and that none can stand against His sovereign purposes.

Before long, I was leading two- and three-week bus tours for vacationers from other English-speaking countries, mostly

Aussies, Kiwis and Brits. We headed out from LAX airport to destinations both in California and throughout the Western states and Canadian provinces. It turned out to be an exciting, energizing job. Nature is a setting in which I have always found it easiest to connect with God, and through this job, He was providing time for me to walk with Him in that special way. I found Yosemite Valley the most beautiful place on earth and was privileged to be there just about every other week. I day-dreamed about being allowed to pastor the small church in the Valley, and I always tried to get my guests to attend services there on Sundays.

There were no tours in winter or early spring, so I had plenty of time to work on a screenplay that had been rolling around in my head. I stayed around Los Angeles during the touring off-season, doing some work as an extra and running the board at a new Christian radio station called KKLA. But it was not long before the Lord let me know that I would be moving again.

Intimacy with God

My walk out of sexual brokenness had reached its seventh year, and for the first time I dared to think that I was healed enough to be married. My damaged and poorly formed heterosexuality had emerged once again as my true identity. Homosexual temptations came and went, but they no longer held the same power over me as before. Those attractions represented my past brokenness. They could be resurrected if I were not careful, but I really was over and done with them. They no longer moved me to act, any more than did the periodic temptations to look at porn, smoke dope or get involved with any number of other former masters that I no longer obeyed.

I was beginning to recognize the pattern God was using to bring me out of deep bondage. First, He neutralized the demonic powers that had held sway over me through my many years of sinful actions. As I repented for each ungodly behavior, renounced the sins involved and had the demonic strongholds cast out by the power of the Holy Spirit, those spiritual forces ceased to coerce and control me. When they tried to take back their ground, I had the authority Christ conferred on all believers to send them away: "Behold, I have given you authority to tread on serpents and scorpions, and over all the power of the enemy, and nothing shall hurt you" (Luke 10:19).

God was, in the meantime, renewing my mind: "Do not be conformed to this world, but be transformed by the renewal of your mind, that by testing you may discern what is the will of God, what is good and acceptable and perfect" (Romans 12:2).

He was also teaching me how to take charge of my thoughts: "For the weapons of our warfare are not of the flesh but have divine power to destroy strongholds. We destroy arguments and every lofty opinion raised against the knowledge of God, and take every thought captive to obey Christ" (2 Corinthians 10:4–5).

Jesus had provided me with a way of escape: "No temptation has overtaken you that is not common to man. God is faithful, and he will not let you be tempted beyond your ability, but with the temptation he will also provide the way of escape, that you may be able to endure it" (1 Corinthians 10:13).

I had come to understand that God would rescue me from sin every single time that I really wanted Him to. Nevertheless, I soon was to learn that a critical component of the manifestation of God's promises was that I believe them—not just intellectually, but out of a firm conviction of the heart.

One night, I was singing love songs to the Lord, and He interrupted me to ask, "David, do you believe 2 Corinthians 3:18?"

Summarized, it says that as we gaze upon the glory of the Lord, we are transformed into His image. Feeling quite smug about my belief in the Scriptures, I replied, "Yes, Lord. I believe that You inspired every word of the Bible and that it is infallibly true!"

"No, you don't," He responded.

By then I knew that God knew every inch of my mind and heart, so I said, "Show me how I don't, Lord."

He replied, "Return to praising Me, but as you do, assume that the promise of that Scripture is literally true and is actually taking place."

I began praising Him again, but this time I assumed that a literal transformation into His image was taking place in that very moment, whether I felt it or not. As I did that, I suddenly realized that the virtue I was praising Him for was being created in me. In other words, as I praised Him for His love, that love was being built into me. As I praised Him for His wisdom, that wisdom was actually and really being imparted to me.

It was amazing how dramatically my healing process picked up after learning and putting into practice that lesson on faith. It is a vital truth that is complementary to another found in Mark 11:24, where Jesus says, "Therefore I tell you, whatever you ask in prayer, believe that you have received it, and it will be yours."

On another night, God gave me a picture of what was going on in the realm of the Spirit with regard to temptations. I saw the Holy Spirit standing at the door of my heart. He was big and strong and fearsome, like a bouncer at the door of a bar. When temptations tried to enter, if, with all my heart, I wanted them kept away, the Holy Spirit cast them aside. But if I wanted to entertain a temptation for a while, the Spirit would step aside and let it in. Once it invaded, if I came to my senses and wanted the temptation gone—again, with all my heart—the Spirit cast the demon out. For Him it was like swatting a fly—only one swat was needed.

The Lord later revealed through another minivision that He would respond immediately to my requests for help, but only when I was finally ready to be rid of a habitual temptation—once and for all.

At the same time, He made it clear that He was not interested solely in dealing with my sins. He also began revealing to me—and to those who were ministering to me—specific areas of hurt, anger and unforgiveness that needed to be dealt with and forsaken. One by one, He showed me the root sources of my dysfunctional beliefs or behaviors. Then He showed me how to find healing.

I had lived a lifetime weighted down by a lack of affirmation, which caused me to believe I was both unloved and unlovable. This had been a huge obstacle for me, driving me to seek pleasure to anesthetize my pain. In fact, my obsession with being unloved had brought with it a sense of entitlement—"I deserve at least *some* happiness. . . ." That thinking made it possible for me to rationalize sinful, pain-blocking remedies. Through prayer, Scripture reading, worship and the ministry of other believers, Jesus began to profoundly confirm His love for me. As His affirmation poured into my spirit, the desire for false pleasure-patches or false sources of comfort diminished.

The Vineyard was a perfect setting for this healing process. The worship songs we sang spoke to God directly and were rich in Scriptures, through which He spoke directly to all of us. As I opened my heart to God during worship, He was able to come in and heal the wounds of my life, laying a solid foundation of love and affirmation. This left no ground for my sinful pursuits.

One evening at home, I was worshiping the Lord and suddenly found myself talking to Him as though I were a seven-year-old. At first I felt frightened and stopped myself. But immediately, the still, small voice of the Holy Spirit urged me to continue. The Lord said to me, "Don't stop talking to Me the way you are. I'm taking you back to the place in your childhood where your emotional growth stopped, and I'm restarting your growth from that point so it will be seamless and natural."

The detailed wisdom, concern and care of the Lord astonished me. Again and again, He reminded me that intimacy with Him was essential to my healing, hope and continued health. It was also necessary to remain in an intimate walk with Him if I wanted to receive the outcomes He had promised in Scripture. They were awesome promises, which I continue to hold close to my heart:

> You will seek me and find me when you seek me with all your heart. I will be found by you, declares the LORD.
>
> Jeremiah 29:13–14

> Blessed are those who hunger and thirst for righteousness, for they shall be satisfied.
>
> Matthew 5:6

> Walk by the Spirit, and you will not gratify the desires of the flesh.
>
> Galatians 5:16

> His divine power has granted to us all things that pertain to life and godliness, through the knowledge of him who called us to his own glory and excellence.
>
> 2 Peter 1:3

> I have set the LORD always before me; because He is at my right hand, I shall not be shaken.
>
> Psalm 16:8

> For if you live according to the flesh you will die, but if by the Spirit you put to death the deeds of the body, you will live. For all who are led by the Spirit of God are sons of God.
>
> Romans 8:13–14

PART SIX

MASTERING LIFE

Many times during my walk with the Lord, doubts and fears about God's love for me have come flooding in. *He saved me as an example to others of His grace and mercy, but not because He loves me the way He loves Billy Graham or the apostle John or others*, I would think. I was happy with being saved, but always thought of myself as too tainted to be fully loved by Him.

One day, as He often did, the Lord used a movie to show me that I was wrong, speaking to me through one of the movie's characters. In the movie *Dances with Wolves* there was an Indian called Wind in His Hair, who at one point vehemently opposed the adoption of Kevin Costner's character, Dances with Wolves, into his tribe. But then, from a mountaintop where everyone could see and hear him, Wind in His Hair humbled himself completely and shouted out his love and loyalty to the man he had once hated, who at that point was riding his horse in the valley below. Over and over again, Wind in His Hair cried, "Dances with Wolves, I am Wind in His Hair! Do you see that I am your friend? Can you see that you will always be my friend?" With lance raised, he yelled it again and again—embarrassingly, shamelessly, wonderfully—for the entire tribe to witness!

As he shouted those words in the film, suddenly it was God Himself crying out to me shamelessly, wonderfully, that He loved me as much as He loved anyone else in the universe—completely, totally and unconditionally—and that He would always love me. I can barely even write these words for the tears pouring from my eyes.

— 20 —

The WILDERNESS
YEARS

had always dreamed of the day when I would marry. As a hopeless romantic, I grew up memorizing every song that Lerner
and Loewe, Rodgers and Hart, Rodgers and Hammerstein, the
Beatles and all the other great composers of love songs had written. I was in love with love, yet I seemed personally incapable of
loving. With this in mind, I put the question of marriage before
the Lord on a regular basis. Although I would soon be forty,
I took note that some of my favorite people had not married
until forty—Jimmy Stewart and Martin Luther among them.
Maybe I still had a chance.

I told the Lord I was willing to remain single if that was His
call for me. But I was concerned that people would not believe
He had brought such amazing levels of healing into my life unless I married. Putting that concern before Him one night in
prayer, I was quite surprised when He answered, "Let Me take
care of that!"

I waited and waited, and I prayed and prayed. Then one night I had a dream/vision during which I was in heaven attending a wedding. I could not see much of anything except that a wedding was going on. Then, all at once, I realized that I was the one getting married. A few minutes later, I realized that I was marrying God.

That woke me up.

Was this a clear answer to my prayer—that I should consider myself married to God? If so, was He asking me to make a lifetime decision? I certainly needed confirmation from the Lord that the dream had been from Him. What about the lifetime I had spent dreaming of marrying the love of my life and having a child? Again I asked, and I waited. For a long time, He was silent.

Several months later, as I was absently looking through a catalog, a photograph caught my eye. It was a picture of a gold ring inscribed in Hebrew, "I am my beloved's and my beloved is mine"—a beautiful phrase from the Song of Solomon. I ignored it and kept turning pages. Then the Lord answered my prayer for confirmation. He spoke clearly to my spirit, "Buy that ring. It is our wedding ring."

I returned to the photograph of the ring and studied it more carefully. I realized that in Hebrew, the word *beloved* is "David."

I felt that I was hearing from the Lord, but I also knew that He was inviting me, not commanding me. The choice was mine, and His blessing would remain on me—no matter what I chose to do. Some years later, after I had searched the Scriptures thoroughly and had reached a conclusion on the issue, I gave a lecture called "How to Know if You Are Called to Remain Single." These were my main points, based on my own study of the Scriptures:

1. God will heal you before He calls you, so you will never have to worry that you imagined the call out of unhealed brokenness.

2. God does not impose the call. He does not drag you kicking and screaming. He works within your heart and your mind so that you gratefully understand the call as a great gift and embrace it as the honor that it is.

3. God works a physical miracle in your body so that you can physically and emotionally endure the particular nature of the call to singleness.

4. God gives you a supernatural revelation where you become wed to Him and thereby receive into yourself the completion of His image, normally achieved in holy matrimony with a spouse.

5. God provides multiple confirmations of the call.

6. God provides a grace to withstand the pressure of well-intentioned friends and church leaders who do not understand this call on your life.

7. God gives you the ability to distinguish a temporary call to singleness from a permanent one. The nature of my call—to a ministry that requires seventy- to eighty-hour work weeks—was also a confirming sign to me.

Even though I finally developed a certainty about God's call to marry Him alone, I always remained open to God showing me that I was mistaken. As time has passed, however, my understanding of my call has only been confirmed.

There is no question but that this call to singleness is an awesome call, but for me, it also brought with it a heartbreaking aspect. My hopes of a Hollywood version of "living happily ever after with the girl of my dreams" were shattered. In the days and months that followed my acceptance of the call, I entered into what many great Christian saints of the past have referred to as "the dark night of the soul."

I had not even begun to fathom how deep my desire for a wife and family had been. It had not been clear until that door was closed. Yes, I had shut it myself because I believed that whatever God offered me would be infinitely better. But still the grief came, and it was overwhelming.

For a time, I could not bear to watch love stories or listen to love songs without weeping. That was further complicated by feelings of guilt. I did not want God to think my love for Him was lessened in some way because of my sorrow. He graciously assured me that grieving over what had been sacrificed was a healthy thing and was something to be embraced. Otherwise, how could I be free to be fully His? So I wept—deeply and often. (Now and then, I still do.)

Wilderness Ahead

There was, however, an even greater trial in this time of my dark night. Since the moment of my salvation in the Garden of Gethsemane, I had been possessed with a fervent desire to serve the Lord in some gloriously sacrificial way. Somehow those expectations had thus far gone unrequited. I had ministered here and there, speaking or giving my testimony. But there had been no formal recognition of my call and no place of service that spoke to who I would be and what I would do for the Lord for the rest of my life.

What I had not realized until then was that my motives for serving God were impure. In a sense, I was trying to pay God back for saving me. I was trying to earn and keep His love and approval. I was also trying to win the respect of the world so the embarrassment of my past would be forgotten. And I was still trying to become some sort of a star in order to obtain the affirmation that I never got in childhood, or in Hollywood. I had never quite grasped that the source of love and affirmation I needed could be found in God alone—and that it was free.

Ironically, the sources that I looked to for affirmation—pastors, denominational leaders, mission agency leaders and other stand-ins for my pastor father—had not affirmed me in my call to ministry. This only served to reignite the feelings of rejection that I had carried around for a lifetime.

Why was God doing this to me? Did He not understand that I wanted to serve Him with all my heart, and that such repeated rejections only sharpened the pain from my past? After all, I had been trained for ministry by one of the finest seminaries in the entire world, and I was more than ready to go "do the stuff," as John Wimber used to say.

One night, I poured out my heart to God, telling Him that I could not take it anymore. Since He had placed this powerful call on my life, He needed to give it an outlet or just take me home. My heart was weighed down with heaviness, as if an elephant were sitting on it. I cried out, "Lord, I'm literally dying inside."

In His still, small voice, He gently replied, *"That's what's supposed to be happening."*

As soon as He said it, I knew that it was not only true—it was *wonderfully* true. As if I were looking in a mirror for the first time, I saw that I was full of myself—*my* ardor, *my* training, *my* need to be affirmed. Yes, I needed to die. Otherwise, my service for the Kingdom would be polluted with self rather than being a selfless overflowing of my love for Him.

The Lord was teaching me lesson after lesson about relying on Him, trusting and waiting on His timing, remaining in intimate fellowship with Him and believing that He had good plans for my future. These were far from easy lessons to learn, however, and the "education" had to be more than just intellectual. So my dark night went on for many more years. I would rather not discourage you by telling you how many.

But there were also incredible compensations. One time, the Lord asked me to begin reading the crucifixion accounts in the gospels as my nightly meditation. I thought it a worthy assignment and diligently obeyed for several weeks. Then one night as I was pondering the death of Christ on the cross, the heart of the Father suddenly swept into my heart, and I could feel the pain that He felt as He watched His precious Son being tortured and put to death. It was unbearable, the grief that swept over my soul. I had never considered the pain of the Father before because the Son's pain had always been the heart of the story. But indeed, the Father's grief was off the charts during His Son's sacrifice. It was an incredible honor to be allowed to experience just the tiniest bit of it, even though it left me devastated.

From that moment on, my heart was branded with this knowledge. The choice between sin and obedience was far easier. I suddenly knew the Father at a level unimagined before. He was not the cold, stern taskmaster of my imagination, but One who feels pain in ways not unlike our own. This unexpected revelation changed my motivation for being faithful to Him. Obedience became an act of love rather than an obligation to fulfill. What Harold St. John once wrote is very true: "The Cross of Christ means nothing until it takes your breath away!"

It was clear to me that I was being formed for a future task. One night in the late 1980s, I wrote in my journal,

> Lord, give me a career that includes producing and directing films and TV programs that lead people to know and understand the love of Jesus Christ, that will support my family and help me provide for others.

I also asked Him for an unending deepening of my love, faith and dependence on Him and a mind continually one with His—a heart set on fire with love for God.

As the years came and went, God answered that prayer in ways I could never have imagined. (Writing this book, I look back and think that you, too, cannot help but be excited when you discover the ways in which He brings His plans to pass. He can do the same in your life.) For seven years, I became the producer of a television program that was seen throughout most of the world. Translated into ten languages, it accomplished the very things I prayed for that night. As the psalmist says in Psalm 37:4–6,

> Delight yourself in the LORD, and he will give you the desires of your heart. Commit your way to the LORD; trust in him, and he will act. He will bring forth your righteousness as the light, and your justice as the noonday.

Before all that came to pass, however, I had to spend some time "in the wilderness" first.

— 21 —

The SECRET
COMES OUT

During those bittersweet years, from time to time I appeared on a TV or radio program to give my testimony, but I always kept my sexually broken past a big secret. It bears repeating that I was quite sure that most believers, including pastors, who knew about my scandalous past would turn away from me in fear and disgust. One day I received an invitation to appear with Pat Robertson on *The 700 Club*. I told the tale of being a Hollywood actor and a member of a cult, but I still kept secret my years of sexual addiction, homosexual confusion and prostitution.

Three months later, I was attending a conference called "Sex and Shame" at my church. I sat in the back row, listening carefully but minding my own business. During a lunch break, the associate pastor's wife came rushing up to me. "David," she said rather breathlessly, "the Holy Spirit just told me that you are to give your testimony before this crowd!"

Terror struck my heart. I recoiled, thinking, *Right. Well, when He tells me, then I'll consider it. And only then.*

Nonetheless, she was a pastor's wife, so I agreed to pray with her about it. As we prayed, the Holy Spirit fell on me powerfully. I knew then and there that she was right.

She ran off to try to get the one o'clock speaker to relinquish her time. Once she succeeded, I knew it was God's guidance at work for sure. Speakers spend weeks preparing for conference lectures and do not readily give up their time.

An hour or so thereafter, I found myself at the front of the audience. Somehow I had always known this moment would eventually come, but now that it had arrived, I felt overwhelmed. I must have been as white as a sheet. The sexual sins I had committed had been extremely shameful, and some of these Christians might never have imagined the sins themselves, much less that someone in their midst had actually committed them. Would anyone be my friend once I had bared my soul?

Scared as I was, I was conscious that there was really only an audience of One with whom I needed to concern myself. God had called me to share the good news of His power over sin. And now, with His help, that is exactly what I intended to do.

I began with some snippets from my childhood—the porn use, the addiction to masturbation from early on, the hetero-sexual immorality and then the homosexuality and prostitution. There was a decided hush in the room. People were definitely paying close attention. But as they began to see themselves in aspects of my story, sniffles began to erupt, followed by the sound of weeping. The Holy Spirit filled that small room, jammed with about one hundred attendees, with the weight of His presence. God was doing a mighty work.

As I drew to a close, I could feel the Lord inside me as though He were a child, clapping His hands and jumping up and down, exclaiming, "Yay, you did it! You did it!"

It stunned me because I never thought that someone like me could ever bring joy to God's heart. I was lucky just to get in—an example of His grace. But that He delighted in me? That was something unexpected and very special indeed.

I asked anyone who wanted prayer to come forward, and at least two-thirds of the crowd left their seats and crowded to the front of the room. Some of them were sobbing, some shaking uncontrollably. All of them had tears in their eyes. One young man came up and gave me a bear hug, saying, "I've never hugged a homosexual before, but come here!" Another took me aside and said, "I've never told anyone this before, but . . ." Then he confided his deep, dark, secret sin, which by comparison—after hearing about my sins—no longer seemed quite so bad.

I recognized then and there that I was being commissioned by the Lord. This was only the beginning. He was going to use me to tell my dark story, and in so doing, He would set others free to repent, follow Him and then share their stories. Those who heard me knew that if He could forgive what I had done, then He would forgive them, too.

What a wonderful day for me. It was glorious!

Later on, the speaker who had relinquished her time so that I could speak came up to me. She was also the wife of the pastor over pastoral counseling, and she placed her hand on my head and began to prophesy:

God says, "You are for the writing of books. And you will do seminars. I am giving you the keys to a ministry and have placed My power within you. I have a future for you that you've never dreamed of. I will take you places all over this land to carry out My work. I have well-placed humility in your heart, but it is not humility to refuse the keys that I am giving you. You are afraid of falling from high places, but I have placed you there."

Later, I wrote this in my journal:

> I feel free for the first time in my life. I feel as though I can now be a real person because I have nothing left to hide. God's power and His pleasure coursed through my body after the seminar was over.

The prophecy about writing books echoed explosively in my mind. I sat down to see if I could write one, and words began to flow effortlessly. Everything the Lord had taught me—all the visions and illustrations and passages of Scripture—seemed to line up in order. Unbelievably, within three and a half weeks, I had completed the first draft of a book called *Sexual Healing: God's Plan for the Sanctification of Broken Lives* (Mastering Life Ministries, 1995). The book spelled out in an orderly way the process through which all sexual sin and brokenness share common causal factors, and as a result, common paths for healing. I had written a book based not only on my experience, but on my walk of faith. It emphasized the centrality of intimacy with God the Father as the path to healing and transformation.

I wondered about the publication of the book and decided to set out a "fleece," as Gideon had done (see Judges 6:36–40), so I mailed a copy of the manuscript to John Wimber and to Dr. John White, a prolific author of Christian books. I prayed that God would inspire one of them to write the foreword. A few weeks later, I got a call from Dr. White, whom I had never met. "This is a marvelous book!" he told me. "It simply must be published!" Dr. White also heartily agreed to write the foreword, in which he said,

> David Foster's book is important. It is a book that sings with the joy of a man who has been delivered. It is a book that awakens us to an awareness of what is going on, and what God is waiting to do to correct the damage. I pray that this book will be widely read. Its contribution is unique!

269

It would be several years before the book was actually published. At the time I wrote it, Christian publishers still would not touch a book with "sex" in the title. But the process had begun.

A Team of Wild Horses

By then, having moved back to Chicagoland, I found myself house-sitting a beachfront penthouse on Lake Michigan for the summer, poor as ever, but now brimming with "a future and a hope" (Jeremiah 29:11). Perhaps I should have known that a test would come on the heels of such an outstanding breakthrough. And it did. How could I have imagined that the high-rises on the lakefront were filled with voyeurs and exhibitionists who liked to perform sexually for their neighbors?

It was hard enough not to look, and Satan tested me sorely with men who tried to lure me into exhibitionist behaviors. They stared at me through binoculars and placed signs in their windows, telling me what they wanted me to do. It catapulted me back to the time not so long before, when men would pay me to perform for them. My deep hunger to have a father figure who wanted me swept back into my heart. I was forced to cling to God as never before.

It was frightening. Desires that I had not felt for years revived, and feelings I thought were permanently under control suddenly returned. Like a team of wild horses, the old temptations came stampeding through my brain unbridled. I felt powerless to resist. My credo that "we needn't fight against something once victory is won" was dashed. Instead, I realized that I would be vulnerable to certain temptations for the rest of my life. My goal in life was not to be freed from being tempted, but to find God more attractive than the temptation. Above all, I needed to rely on His power to resist rather than my own power.

Fortunately, God was in control. He turned this demonic assault into an object lesson. He revealed that I had erected defenses of my own against such things—religious defenses—when only His power could quench them. Humbled, I sought His power. As I did, He promised that He was indeed going to deliver me from the demonic powers, but little by little instead of all at once (see Deuteronomy 7:22–23). In some cases, "little by little" is better.

My practice of spiritual warfare had sometimes been to repel attacking demons by sending them into uttermost darkness, or better yet, into the lake of fire. One night as I was doing this, the Lord spoke to me and said, "You don't have the authority to do that! That will be done by My angels at the end of the age."

In essence, He was letting me know that for me to cast demons into the lake of fire was to send them nowhere. So I said, "Where should I send them, Lord?"

He said, "Tell them to go where Jesus sends them."

I commanded the attacking demons to leave me and go where Jesus sent them, and I am here to testify that I don't know where Jesus sends them, but they definitely *don't* want to go there! The efficacy of my prayers picked up logarithmically from that point on.

This new understanding of how to pray also gave me a new awareness that Jesus does, in fact, stand beside me—that I am not alone. When I act according to His will, He has my back completely.

Not long after that, I had a vision of God putting His muscle into my arm, so that when I moved my arm, it would be His power within me carrying out the task at hand. He showed me that He intended to plant, cause the growth and create the fruit of everything in my life, and that I needed simply to keep my focus on Him, respond to His direction and trust Him to carry it out. He would do the work.

One evening as I gazed out on Lake Michigan, the full moon cast a golden path of light through the midst of the darkness. It was pitch-dark on each side, as well as at the end of the path. As I looked at the scene, the Lord spoke to my spirit, saying,

> Here is the path of glory where My power and presence dispel all evil and darkness. I set it before you to walk on. But notice that the glory and the ability to see are yours only as long as you walk in the light. The distance is not lit, because this is a walk of faith and you will not be able to see where you are going. You will be upheld and empowered only as long as you stay in the path of My glory.

It later occurred to me that if I did what He said, according to the vision, I would be walking on water.

During that battle with the forces of darkness, while I was worshiping the Lord, He gave me an incredibly powerful microsecond vision of His awesome authority. As I meditated on the way His power is displayed in the universe, in a new vision He suddenly sent a blast of powerful white light shooting into space—lighting up the entire universe, leaving not a single speck of darkness! In that instant, the universe went from being mostly dark to being fully illuminated. He helped me see that to fill the infinite trillions upon trillions of light-years of space was no more difficult for Him than flipping a light switch on was for me. Why, then, should I fear the circling demons in my high-rise?

During this same time, one of the most potent moments of my healing process came when I was practicing a besetting sin for the ten thousandth time. While I was committing the sin, the Lord spoke to me. That shocked me, because my assumption was that the Lord waited outside the room when I committed a sin—that He was too holy to actually be there while I did it.

I was wrong. He said to me, "David, if you turn to Me right now, I will love you, forgive you and embrace you."

I pretended not to hear and continued committing the sin. When I was finished, to my utter shock, the Lord spoke to me again, saying, "David, if you turn to Me right now, I will love you, forgive you and embrace you."

The second time He said it, He used the same positive, loving and inviting tone as the first time. It blew all my circuits. I was stunned! I had just ignored the Lord of all glory and had chosen a pathetic sin instead of Him. Yet He was still offering the same love and grace as before—and without the slightest change in His attitude toward me. It was a glimpse of the flawless grace of the Holy One.

Clearly, God was not someone I had to hide from. He did not look on me in disgust when I chose an idolatrous behavior over His glory. He was not trying to spoil my fun or take something good from me. He loved me, He loved me, He loved me! And there was nothing I could do to change that.

I said to Him, "Lord, if this is what You are really like, I *want* to follow You!" In that moment, I went from obeying Him because I was *supposed to*, to obeying Him because I *wanted to*. It was grace teaching me to say no to ungodliness (see Titus 2:11–14).

Lessons in Discipleship

In September 1990, I was on the move again. This time the Lord led me to Crossroads Discipleship Training School—two months of classes and ministry sessions, followed by two months on the mission field. Part of Youth With A Mission (YWAM), it took place in Kona, Hawaii, so I could not complain.

I had always admired YWAM as an organization, so I was glad to be there. Week after week, a different teacher flew in from some faraway corner of the world to impart his or her wisdom, often learned through a lifetime in ministry. The second week's sessions featured a Presbyterian minister from South Africa, Gus Hunter, who had the most amazing gift of prophecy I had ever encountered. One day in the midst of his lecture, Gus spun around on his heels, looked me straight in the eye and—in front of the entire class of 96 people—said,

> You are nothing like your father. God the Father has been and will continue to work on you to give you what your father never did. God is going to use you in a ministry of healing, and stuff like that, to certain kinds of people. It will be a much bigger ministry than you can now imagine. It will blossom. And I know that I know that I know that it will come to pass. It is the faith of God Himself speaking through me. A sensitive person like yourself will seek wisdom.

Several days later I was praising the Lord, dancing and singing some rousing Messianic songs. All at once, a picture of Jesus flashed into my mind. He was in heaven dancing with me, just as vigorously, with a tambourine in His hand. It was a sublime and exhilarating vision that lasted through two or three more songs. Jesus Christ, King of Kings and Lord of Lords, was rejoicing and exuberantly dancing with me. With *me*.

When you have rarely been affirmed, have committed terrible sins and have marinated yourself in self-hatred for a lifetime, such a vision is enormously healing.

Not many days thereafter, God asked me to begin a process of forgiveness. First, He showed me some painful memories from my childhood, reminding me of people who had hurt me. He asked me to forgive them. There were several instances, for example, of being beaten up by T.J., the neighborhood bully. It seemed easy to forgive such things, knowing that the infinite power and presence of God dwelt in me.

What I did not know was that God was setting me up for the big one—my father. I had "forgiven" him many times in prayer, saying the right words, but I had not done so at a deep level. Even after our reconciliation, acid still burned in my spirit at the thought of him.

Suddenly I saw Dad in my mind's eye, and the Lord said, "Time to forgive your father, David."

"I'll say the words if You ask me to," I told Him rather abruptly. "But You know that I won't mean them."

"Look at Me!" He commanded. I looked up and in a vision saw Jesus Christ standing in heaven with His arms outstretched.

"What do I have in My hand?" He asked while slightly moving His right hand.

Don't ask me how, but I knew what it was. I answered, "You have forgiveness in Your hand, Lord."

Jesus then said, "I can forgive your father. Why don't you take forgiveness from My hand and give it to your father?"

"Okay," I replied obediently, reaching up and taking the forgiveness from the hand of Jesus. Then, turning to my father, who stood next to me in the vision, I handed it to him, saying, "Father, with the ability that Jesus has to forgive you, I forgive you."

Instantly, a current of energy poured from Jesus' hand down my arm, into my heart and back out to my father's heart. In a second, it was done. The power of God extinguished a lifetime of anger, bitterness, hatred and unforgiveness. God had done for me what I had long been unable to do for myself. The acid was gone. The hatred was gone. All that misery was brought to its conclusion by the power, completeness and perfection that only God can provide.

That week, I exposed my past as a male prostitute to the entire class during a time of group confession. I had had enough of wondering what people would think if they knew—which ones would reject me and which would encourage me. My secret life of sex and shame was over. I could no longer deny that it had been part of my life.

After class, a woman with a prophetic gift spoke out, saying I was going to suffer many rejections and much resistance in the ministry ahead. I might even face physical injury. And God was giving me the option not to move ahead with such a ministry if I would rather avoid all that. He was making it clear that it would be okay to say no to the call. "But if you say yes," this woman went on to say, "then He has prepared you for a ministry of suffering through rejection."

This gifted woman continued, "Your talents and abilities will not see you through the task. Only a total dependence on the Lord will." She concluded, "If you take this road of rejection, there will be great reward for you in heaven."

This was not exactly the positive "word from the Lord" that most people get. But I already knew in my spirit—even before she uttered a word—that what she was saying was true. I was already prepared to go for it. I had given my all to the devil for 29 years. The Lord deserved the rest.

Another healing moment during the YWAM training session took place when our group shared a time of prayer for the release of deeply rooted anger. As you might guess, I had a veritable stronghold of anger that had built up over decades of hurt and trauma. I appeared calm most of the time, but was quite capable of exploding in rage if I was slighted. I had prayed for years that God would remove it, and now my day of deliverance had arrived.

As the leader prayed, I could sense the Holy Spirit working inside me, positioning Himself under the very root of the anger, lifting it up and removing it from my soul. I could actually feel it lift and exit my body. It really was the end of the fiery anger that had for too long dominated my life.

After so much deep, soul-searching ministry, it was time for our class's mission outreach. Our first stop was in Ginowan City, Okinawa, where we lived and served in a church for a while.

Then we went to Hong Kong, where the infamous "Walled City" was still standing. I took a walk through the narrow streets, once dominated by ruthless gangs and still steeped in unimaginable poverty. A modern-day saint of the Lord, Jackie Pullinger, had introduced this turbulent section of Hong Kong to Christian readers in her book *Chasing the Dragon* (Regal, 2007). She wrote about leading drug lords to Christ—men who had once made the Walled City so dangerous that the police refused to even enter it.

I was now assigned to the famous Hang Fook Camp, where former gang members, drug addicts and others came for rehabilitation. Each day, I worked at whatever task was given me. Many nights, I joined teams that went out several times a week to take food to the "street sleepers"—homeless people who lived in abject poverty. Our job was simply to love them and give them a hot meal.

I cannot forget one street sleeper who wept as we prayed for him. He lay surrounded by the rats, filth and squalor of his cardboard box home down one of Hong Kong's darkest alleys. Even more amazing was the sight of a beggar lady at the Star Ferry pier. Her eyes and face seemed to light up the universe as she opened the simple rice box we had given her to see what was inside. Rice, of course. She was so grateful! She had the countenance of a child receiving the Christmas present of her dreams, which gave me a whole new understanding of thankfulness. Watching her, I hoped that I would never have another ungrateful moment as long as I lived.

The food at camp was . . . interesting. I am sure we ate things that were never meant to be eaten. We ate alongside those to whom we were ministering. Needless to say, they were very hungry. At a given moment, everyone frantically drove their chopsticks into the plate of food at center table. Every animal still had its head, eyes, feet and various other parts intact. The eyes were the most sought-after commodity, and I was happy to let others go ahead of me. Within minutes, the entire plate of food was completely laid bare. I was constantly searching for the nearest grocery store.

It was a joy to see the hungry fed, the addicts delivered and the lost souls saved. And I have never seen more amazing baptisms in all my life, before or since. When men and women who have been hopelessly addicted to opium, heroin and other drugs receive deliverance and cleansing through the supernatural power of God and follow Jesus into the waters of baptism, their joy is boundless.

I was assigned, on one occasion, to sit up with a "new boy" who had just come in off the streets. He was still addicted to opium, and my job was to sit next to his bed while he slept. I was to pray in tongues over him every time he began to struggle with withdrawal pains. Jackie Pullinger and her team have a special anointing for this very ministry. They believe that when someone prays in tongues over an addict suffering from withdrawal symptoms, the Holy Spirit comes and removes the suffering. It was true. Every time the new boy squirmed and I prayed in tongues, he stopped squirming. It was amazing.

My trip to Hong Kong was revolutionary for me, much more so than my visit to Nigeria in 1982. Hong Kong was a game changer for my worldview. I found that I loved cleaning the gutters for the men at the camp and rearranging their meager library. I even praised God for the urine on my hands from nursing an old bedridden man who had once been addicted to opium. This is the work of Jesus Christ. This is His heart, and in finally doing it myself rather than admiring those who did, I was changed forever.

After completing my time with YWAM, I began to pray and ask the Lord where I should go next. To my utter surprise, He spoke clearly to my spirit *Nashville*. I had never had God tell me where to live before, and I did not know a soul in Nashville, so I asked for a confirmation. To my delight, several weeks later I ended up sitting next to a couple from Nashville at a conference in Honolulu. God had instructed them to come because there was someone there whom they were supposed to help. As it turned out, I was the one. After we got acquainted, they arranged for me to have the use of a house and a car in Nashville until I could find my own. As quickly as possible, I sold almost everything I owned, got on a plane and moved to Nashville.

— 22 —

SEXUAL HEALING
in NASHVILLE

The move to Nashville turned out to be a critical flash point for the ministry I had founded back in 1987, Mastering Life Ministries. I originally had intended to use the ministry to make a movie about the life of Christ that was Steven Spielberg worthy, with lots of special effects meant to draw in a young audience. One day as I was busy trying to raise money to produce the script I had written, the Lord spoke to me and said that I was trying to make it happen by my own wisdom and power and that I should stop. He reminded me that only what He called for and empowered would last into eternity. I had then decided to allow the ministry to become inert until God gave me further orders.

During the conference in Chicago a couple years later, God called me to minister to sexually broken people, and I realized that that was the raison d'être for Mastering Life Ministries. The call to move to Nashville in 1993 became the critical flash point for bringing the ministry back to life. Now, for the first time, I would operate as its director on a full-time basis. I had a meeting with Nancy Alcorn at Mercy Ministries of America, who promptly handed me a check for $1,000, exclaiming, "This is seed-faith for your ministry!" It was more than a financial blessing. God was confirming His word to me.

By the end of 1993, I had taught my first "Sexual Healing" seminar in Tennessee. Leanne Payne, author and founder of Pastoral Care Ministries, gave me three hours of her time for an interview, resulting in a three-part series for our newly revived "Mastering Life" newsletter. In the last half of 1993 alone, the mailing list for the newsletter topped one thousand, and I was given almost fifty opportunities to teach, preach and testify at various conferences, in churches and colleges and through different media venues.

One invitation in 1994 took me to a church near Orlando. By then, my presentation was well developed and included every major area of sexual sin from homosexuality to sex addiction, from pornography to masturbation and from child sexual abuse to voyeurism. On this occasion, the church inadvertently booked me into a hotel surrounded on every side by strip clubs and porn stores. When I walked into my hotel room, I immediately noticed two hardcore pornographic magazines neatly stacked next to the freshly made-up bed. *Looks like the maid must have left them here for the last guest,* I thought to myself.

Reaching for the magazines, I recognized one of them from my old life, and a thought entered my mind: *Porn must be way worse than it was when I was addicted to it. Maybe I should take a peek so I'm up-to-date about what I'm preaching against.*

I was about to crack open the magazine when the Holy Spirit screamed in my soul, *"STOP! Satan is trying to take you out!"*

It is always a bit disconcerting to be reminded that God is watching you when you are sinning, but for Him to scream a warning is something else again. I instantly recognized what an idiot I had been, and I threw the magazines into the garbage can and crushed them to the bottom with my foot. The second my foot hit the bottom of the trash can, the Holy Spirit thundered, *"I will crush him under My feet!"*

That is my God! He is my protector. He is my provider. He is the One who will keep me from falling. It is He "who is able to keep you from stumbling and to present you blameless before the presence of his glory with great joy" (Jude 1:24).

It is His power that will crush the enemy beneath my feet: "The God of peace will soon crush Satan under your feet" (Romans 16:20).

And He will trample down all my enemies: "With God we shall do valiantly; it is He who will tread down our foes" (Psalm 108:13).

He will do all these things just as long as I want Him to. And He will do the same for you.

The Ministry Explodes

Media opportunities also blossomed that year. Even the Catholic TV and radio networks invited me to share what the Lord had done in my life. I decided to produce a radio program called *Mastering Life,* and before long we went on the air in Key West and Nashville. Soon we were invited to be broadcast on the Focus on the Family Satellite Radio Network, where our program was made available to over two hundred radio stations nationwide. During those years, we amassed an audio library of interviews with Christian leaders that served as the foundation for a substantial teaching tape ministry.

Invitations to speak also came in from overseas, and before the year was out, I had traveled to England, Scotland and France to share the good news of God's grace for sexually broken people. The trip to France was arranged by Molly D'Andrea, who had a new TV program for homosexuals called *Set Free If You Want to Be* on the Christian Television Network, which she and her husband had founded. I had already been a guest on her program and went on to do a regular Q&A segment for the show. She decided to use my "Sexual Healing" materials as a basis for her ministry, too, and she eventually had me teach an entire in-studio "Sexual Healing" seminar for distribution on video.

So many prophecies about my ministry were all finally coming true. It was marvelous to see God take the disaster of a life like mine and turn it into a tool for rescuing those who had been broken in the same ways.

Financially, however, it was still very much a struggle. One August, I had to take out a $1,000 loan to pay my rent. I had always believed that God pays for what He calls for, so I figured something was seriously wrong. Maybe it would be best for me to close down the ministry and get a regular job. But the next day, a check for $1,000 came in the mail. As I looked at it, I could sense the Lord saying to me, "I can pull money out of the air for you if I want to. So don't mistake the lack of financial support as a sign that I don't want you to continue."

That was an important lesson I have tried to remember during many lean periods over the years.

By this point, Mastering Life Ministries had a board of directors made up of my ministry colleagues, and it became clear to us that God had called us to be a teaching ministry—media fluent, interdenominational and international, with a primary focus on the training of both leaders and laity. He was calling us to minister redemptively to sexually broken people of every kind.

I remember a signature moment in the refinement of our call. One night, I was complaining in prayer that I felt as though I were spitting in the wind with my efforts in comparison with the enormity of the problem. "Plus," I said to God, "most people will never go to a counselor or a pastor for help with sexual sin because it's too embarrassing. The most they will ever do is to share their struggle with a best friend."

The Lord immediately replied, "So train all the best friends so that they know what to do when that happens."

Good advice from a wise Father!

The year 1995 brought a similar blitzkrieg of ministry opportunities. Our board of directors and I began the new year by officially publishing *Sexual Healing: God's Plan for the Sanctification of Broken Lives*. Meanwhile, "Sexual Healing" seminars continued, with conferences in Idaho, California and Florida. Canada was added to our international reach. Having already joined the American Association of Christian Counselors, we now joined the National Religious Broadcasters, and within the year we would also join Exodus International.

I hesitated to join Exodus because I had already been finding it difficult to get pastors to understand that our ministry was called to reach *every kind* of sexually bound and broken person—heterosexuals included. I feared that by joining Exodus, which was known primarily for helping homosexuals, the problem would be exacerbated. But in the end, I decided that the widening of our interaction with the sexually broken community should include ex-gay groups.

Also during 1995, I busied myself networking with local pastors by attending prayer groups, rallies and the like. Additionally, I networked with Christian media and Christian counselors so that our services would become known throughout the Body of Christ. By that year's end, Mastering Life Ministries had held seminars in many of the largest churches in our area and was known and respected throughout Nashville's Christian community, as well as by the secular media.

Church Recognition

Because the media and the Church were such a large part of our calling, I knew that credentials were important; they could open doors of opportunity more easily and quickly. Although I had been ordained in the past, it was not through a recognized denomination. And although I desired ordination with the Vineyard Christian Fellowship, my unmarried status made that undoable according to their rules.

For quite some time, meanwhile, God had been showing me the beauties of the sacramental Church, and I had been praying for ways to get connected with a congregation like that. About that time, I discovered a new denomination called the Charismatic Episcopal Church (CEC) and arranged a meeting with the diocesan bishop. I was impressed with the way the CEC attempted to blend the charismatic, evangelical and sacramental into one holistic approach to worship. One thing led to another, and by the end of the year I was ordained a priest in the Charismatic Episcopal Church.

One of the lovely aspects of the sacramental Church is that it includes a category for God ordaining single men. The apostle Paul talked about it, as did Isaiah, but most of the Protestant world remains clueless as to the legitimacy of such a calling. As a priest, I was allowed to continue working as the director of Mastering Life Ministries, and it was not long before the bishop formalized that arrangement by appointing me a "Canon" of the church (someone appointed by the bishop for a particular task). This development brought further credibility to the ministry and opened up many new doors of opportunity.

The fellowship I shared with fellow priests, deacons and laypeople in the CEC was wonderful—we were a band of brothers. It was healing for me and was perhaps the first time that I began

Taken in 1999 during the ceremony at Cathedral Church of the Messiah in Jacksonville, Florida, when I was named a "Canon" in the Charismatic Episcopal Church by Bishop Dale Howard.

to believe I was *inside* the Body of Christ—not just outside looking in, or being dragged along.

There were a few painful moments as well, like the time I gave my testimony before a gathering of diocesan leaders. While several priests went out of their way to let me know that they felt closer to me than before because of my honesty about my struggle, some of them avoided me from that point on. Their rejection was a stinging reminder of the pain I had felt as a child, when my father had turned from me in disgust on so many occasions. But

Taken for a 1999 front-page article in the *Florida Times-Union* (Jacksonville, Florida) that featured my work to help sexually broken people.

overall, the good outweighed the bad, and I enjoyed being in that company.

The year 1996 brought even more new and unexpected opportunities for broadening our outreach. We began winning Angel and Covenant awards for our radio program and video course. Prison Fellowship became the newest major organization to place us on its recommended list. I started writing magazine articles for national Christian magazines like *Charisma*, *New Man*, *Touchstone* and others. We also launched our first ministry website. A particular thrill for me was speaking at George Washington's old church, The Falls Church Episcopal, although I suspect he would have been apoplectic over the need for such a ministry as ours in the country that he fathered.

In 1997, Mastering Life exploded internationally. I traveled to England, Canada, France and several times to South Africa to teach on sexual brokenness. *Sexual Healing* was finally published as a trade paperback, and its first printing sold out in short order. The local newspaper, *The Tennessean*, began using me as a source for articles on homosexuality, as did the local secular TV news channels. Summarizing the events of the year in our newsletter, I wrote,

> If there has been one central message that God has given me to proclaim—it is that we have been born for holy and heavenly purposes; that God will empower and direct the keeping of all His commandments toward that end; that He will forgive anyone of anything and radically transform the most broken areas in people into areas of great strength and fruitfulness; that the church is weak and defeated primarily because the church is filled with moral compromise and a lack of passionate desire for the purity of Christ; and that the only thing keeping us from an incredible impartation of God's power to set us aright is our love of sin, our slothfulness in the things of God and our love of the world. There is no overwhelming, pervasive power

of evil keeping us in bondage. It is our compromised motivations, our compromised will and the pride of self-sufficiency that keeps us from throwing ourselves on the mercy of God so as to be empowered to walk the kingdom walk that He promises in Scripture (Galatians 5:16; 2 Peter 1:3–10; Titus 2:11–14, etc). We desperately need to know how desperately we need Him. It is only from that knowledge that true wisdom comes—wisdom that persuades us once and for all to forsake the independent, religious spirit that keeps us performing for God, distant from His intimate heart, rather than perpetually abiding in weakness, need and passionate love.

— 23 —

ABOVE ALL
I COULD ASK or THINK

In 1998, I accepted an invitation from my bishop to move Mastering Life to CEC Cathedral Church of the Messiah in Jacksonville, Florida. It was the first time that a large church had ever expressed a desire to fully back our ministry, so it was a difficult invitation to turn down. It also put me right in the midst of the band of brothers who were my fellow clerics.

Working out of the Cathedral for the southeast diocese of the CEC in Jacksonville created interest in our ministry within an entirely new sector of the Body of Christ. Although we lost some evangelicals along the way—those who did not realize that we were as biblical as ever—we gained new interest from those in the sacramental communions.

My involvement with Molly D'Andrea's TV program *Set Free If You Want to Be* now included a regular segment and a repeating leadership training seminar, as well as guest appearances. I was asked to write several more articles for various

With my mother in 2001 on the campus of Trinity Episcopal School for Ministry (now known as Trinity School for Ministry) in Ambridge, Pennsylvania, just after receiving my doctorate.

Christian magazines, and my *Sexual Healing* book came out in Spanish.

In 2001, I was awarded a doctor of ministry degree—a degree that almost did not happen—at Trinity Episcopal School for Ministry (now known as Trinity School for Ministry). The head of the oversight committee initially turned down my dissertation, and I was instructed to remove large sections of it that were distasteful to her and to the academic dean. For example, they objected to my quotations of Saint John of the Cross and other famous mystics of the church, whom they considered unreliable sources. I refused to remove them, which created a campus-wide crisis. I had not realized that no one said no to a doctoral oversight committee, who had the power with the wave of a pen to void your entire multiyear, pricey investment in obtaining a doctorate.

The committee did not do that to me, however. My dissertation was instead sent out to every professor on campus. It so happened that all but those two professors supported me in my contention that my sources were orthodox and reliable. So the head of the committee graciously stepped down and allowed another member to make the final vote in my favor, and I was approved.

But here was the *pièce de résistance.* The commencement speaker for the graduation was Dr. Richard Foster, who, without knowing anything about the controversy, proceeded to quote Saint John of the Cross in his address, with the protesting professors sitting merely feet away. Oh, how I love it when God Himself arranges a vindication!

Looking back on the incident, it impresses me that the professors who held all the power necessary to deny me a degree chose instead to consult their colleagues and yield to their recommendations. For that, I am deeply grateful.

One extra-special moment during my doctoral studies was the week of teaching from Dr. J. I. Packer, author of *Knowing God* and other classic books, and arguably the greatest living theologian of our era. At one point, he threw out this age-old question to the class: "Could Jesus have actually sinned, and was His temptation therefore really a valid temptation?"

After a few brave souls tried their hand at it, I hesitantly proffered this thought: "Since Jesus was perfectly holy, He could not have sinned. But for that very reason, temptation was more difficult for Him than it is for us. We can relieve the pressure of temptation by giving in to it, whereas Jesus had to endure the pressure of it without any such release valve."

The room went silent while everyone awaited the verdict of the most brilliant theologian of our time. Packer gazed at me over his glasses with a curious look, mouth wide open.

Oh no, I thought to myself, *I've probably just uttered a heresy from the sixth century, and he's trying to figure out how to embarrass me as little as possible with his reply.*

"What a great thought!" Packer exclaimed.

My mind suddenly began to spin and reel. *Lord,* I silently cried, *You can take me home now. J. I. Packer just said that I had a great thought!*

From that moment on, my classmates treated me with a level of deference I had not experienced before. I cannot decide which was the greater moment, actually—the day I made the triple play in college or the day J. I. Packer said I had a great thought.

By 2002, I had finished revising my doctoral dissertation into a trade paperback book, which was published by the ministry. I titled it *Transformed into His Image: Hidden Steps on the Journey to Christlikeness.* A rather complex book, but rich in practical information, it quickly became a favorite among the more scholarly supporters of the ministry. Rather than a book about sexual sin, it is a broader look at the road to sanctification that every believer must traverse, and it includes wisdom from Leanne Payne, Dr. Larry Crabb and Benedict Groeschel—as well as a foreword by Dr. J. I. Packer.

Then one day, I received an unexpected phone call. The caller was a woman whose voice I did not recognize. Her first words to me were, "I'm Doris Wagner. How come I've never heard of you?"

I thought of several quick comebacks, but thankfully chose to be polite instead. I soon learned that Doris is the wife of Dr. C. Peter Wagner, of whom I knew a great deal. He had taken the courageous step of welcoming my former pastor, John Wimber, to teach a class called "Signs and Wonders" at Fuller Seminary in California. At the time, Peter had been the head of the church growth department at Fuller, and before long, healings were taking place in the classroom. This, to put it mildly, caused a great stir. I had a lot of respect for Dr. Wagner, who was a well-known seminary professor. He took radical risks, stepping into a realm that few seminaries wanted to enter.

Peter and Doris eventually had me speak at many of their conferences and serve as a professor at their Wagner Leadership Institute in Colorado. By that time, I had taught as an adjunct professor for Asbury Theological Seminary and Trinity Episcopal School for Ministry, but this was my first invitation from a Pentecostal group. Happily, their invitations led to another huge sector of the Body of Christ, the Apostolic Pentecostals, opening their door to our ministry.

The Wagners also invited me to be part of their International Society of Deliverance Ministers (ISDM) that met every year in Colorado Springs. I had never considered our ministry a "deliverance" ministry per se, but they wanted me to take part because I believed in deliverance, and they wanted an expert on sexual sin on the team. Besides, it was a great opportunity to rub shoulders with the likes of Peter Wagner, John and Paula Sandford, Peter and Fi Horrobin and other giants of the faith.

Our lineup of "partners in ministry" saw a big upsurge that year, from Roman Catholic to Pentecostal to Southern Baptist. I loved it because the Lord had let me know soon after I got saved that He was going to use me across all denominational lines. It was part of my father's legacy, I would later learn, since he had also been involved in ecumenical partnerships, mostly in an attempt to bring integration to the Church in the South back in the 1950s and '60s.

We inaugurated our first support group in 2003, Hope for the Broken Heart. It was a gathering for those whose loved ones were struggling with homosexual confusion. One of our board members had a son who had been murdered by his gay lover just as he was trying to leave the lifestyle and return to the Lord, so this was an area of great interest for us.

That same year, I taught my seventeenth "*Set Free If You Want to Be* Sexual Healing Leadership Training Seminar" for Molly D'Andrea, which would turn out to be my last. Molly had contracted Lou Gehrig's disease and would be in heaven within a year's time.

The year 2004 brought me into yet another new sphere of influence—this time with Ellel Ministries, an organization that spans the globe with high-quality discipleship training centers. I began to teach at their bases in England, Scotland and Australia. In the years that followed, I taught in those countries on a number of occasions and was deeply impressed with the scope and biblical depth of their ministry. They were essentially doing for discipleship what YWAM had done for evangelism. My association with Ellel Ministries has become a great friendship and ministry partnership.

I also took time that busy year to revise *Sexual Healing* for a new publisher, Regal Books, who wanted it narrowed down from 400 to 250 pages. It was an arduous task, but it gave me the opportunity to add things the Lord had taught me in the years since 1995, the year it had first been published by our ministry. Providentially, the income from the sales of the book has kept the ministry afloat ever since.

— 24 —

PURE PASSION

Molly D'Andrea passed away in October 2004. There was to be a telethon the next week for the Christian Television Network (CTN) that she and her husband, Bob, had founded. Bob and others decided to honor Molly by making the telethon a retrospective of her many years of ministry and hard work. Since I had been part of her *Set Free If You Want to Be* TV program, I did not miss one broadcast. While I was watching one night, the Lord said to me, "I want you to contact Bob and tell him that you would be willing to carry on Molly's work."

I thought, *That's crazy. The woman has just died. I can't contact Bob right now. What if he thinks I'm being opportunistic and taking advantage?* I put it out of my mind.

I was watching the telethon again the next night, and one of the main network-sponsored program hosts, Herman Bailey—who was a straight-arrow, non-charismatic evangelical—looked straight into the camera and said, "God is telling someone out there to pick up where Molly left off!"

Herman was the last guy you would expect to talk like that. That was all the confirmation I needed. I waited a week and then emailed Bob D'Andrea, saying that if he ever needed help in continuing Molly's work, I would be happy to help. I did not hear a word back from him. Finally, six months later, Bob called and said that he thought God wanted me to pick up where Molly had left off.

"So you got my email?" I asked.

"What email?" he replied.

I told him about the email I had sent months before. He explained that he had received so many thousands of emails after Molly's death that he had never seen it.

Now I was thinking, *This is really God.* I asked him how much it cost to produce a year of programs.

"Molly used to do it for about $50,000," he told me.

The next day, I was telling a former board member what had happened. He immediately offered to put up $25,000. No one had ever given such a large gift to the ministry before. Interestingly enough, this same man had also provided the seed money to publish *Sexual Healing* in 1995. Now God was using him again to do the same for the TV program.

I used the $25,000 to buy cameras, lights and sound equipment. Between speaking trips to Australia and Scotland, I set out to tape some interviews. My first interview was with Os Guinness at a retreat center in Saint Michaels, Maryland. I hired a video crew from the local cable access TV station, and we were on our way.

Then we taped multiple interviews at an Exodus International conference in Asheville, North Carolina. I was able to cut the cost down considerably by taping a dozen or so people in two days while they converged at this conference for ex-homosexuals.

After that, we set up our recording equipment at the American Association of Christian Counselors Worldwide Conference in

Nashville. God opened up the most amazing doors for me so that I could interview experts in counseling about a range of sexual problems. These interviews turned out to be some of the best expert testimonies available.

I still did not know when and where I would complete the shows, so in the meantime I was searching for the city where it would cost the least to produce our program. As it turned out, Nashville was the best place to do it. I talked with my bishop, obtained his permission and moved back to Nashville in October—right after a speaking trip to Hawaii and a guest appearance on the *Dr. Phil* show.

Return to Nashville

Shortly after I moved back to Nashville, the Lord spoke to me again. He said to stop accepting all speaking engagements outside the Nashville area. I wondered if I had I heard Him correctly. This was a rather frightening prospect. Without the income from speaking engagements far and wide, I did not think Mastering Life would have enough income to exist, much less produce a television program.

Still, I remembered the $1,000 check that God had sent through Nancy Alcorn in 1993 and the other $1,000 check He had sent through a YWAM friend a year later, just when it appeared that we could not survive. I also recalled the two millionaires He had sent my way when I began my studies at seminary, who had paid off all my debts and all the expenses of a three-year M.Div. degree program. I also remembered the two large gifts that the former board member had given to seed the last two great projects of the ministry. So I said yes to God and stopped accepting all speaking invitations. He tested me sorely on this one, as my favorite people in my favorite places persisted with their invitations for years to come. But I held my ground.

I suspected that God's request had something to do with the amount of work it would take to produce a TV program, not to mention my personal stamina as an individual. That guess turned out to be spot-on, because once I began the production of *Pure Passion*, sixty-hour workweeks became among the shortest, and seventy- to eighty-hour workweeks became the norm. This also helped me understand why God had called me so many years before to remain single.

There was more to this new beginning than met the eye. Not only was I facing an overwhelming workload, but I also was dealing with loneliness—a particular form of loneliness specific to my situation. Since learning to live in communion with the Lord, I had not suffered the nearly unbearable loneliness felt by many who live alone. My peculiar loneliness comes about as a result of the rejection (perceived and real) from those who hear my story.

As surprising as it may seem, I have noticed that once I give my testimony to any group, about a third of those present go out of their way to let me know that my personal history does not affect their desire to be around me. But another third turn their faces away. Some are undoubtedly trapped in one or more of the same behaviors I once practiced, and they do not want to stop. They fear I will somehow discern their struggle and upset their lifestyle. There are also those who genuinely look down on me because of my past. They simply do not want to know me. Still others are afraid that if they are seen with me, onlookers will think that they share the same struggles, since I am known for helping sexually broken people—basically a fear of man. Encountering these forms of rejection created in me an unexpected sadness.

By the time I got settled in Nashville, I had been a priest in the Charismatic Episcopal Church for twelve years and had enjoyed regular and ongoing peer fellowship while attending clergy meetings and retreats. There was no CEC presence in the Nashville area, however, and I certainly did not have the time to start a new church. In fact, I was beginning to hear the Lord speak to me about leaving the sweet "band of brothers" fellowship I enjoyed in the CEC in order to spread the message He had given me to a new sector of the Body of Christ. I contacted the bishop and told him I believed God was leading me out of the CEC. After much discussion, he reluctantly released me from my vows "without prejudice," which meant that I could return if I ever wanted to.

By September 2006, our TV program, *Pure Passion*, was on the air in the United States and all of Canada. By year's end, we were gearing up to be shown throughout Europe, Asia and the Middle East on Russian Christian TV (in Russian). Soon other networks were added.

We were also now part of the Charismatic Leaders Fellowship (a group led by Dr. Francis MacNutt), the International Society of Deliverance Ministers, the American Association of Christian Counselors and the National Religious Broadcasters. But our eleven years as an affiliate ministry of Exodus International came to an end when it became clear to me that it was no longer the right place for us to be.

The Lord led me to a new church home, Grace Chapel, which was part of the Calvary Chapel group of churches. The pastor embraced our work and gave me permission to minister however I saw fit at the church. He also agreed to replace my ordination in the CEC with one from Grace Chapel. At that time, I officially said good-bye to the Charismatic Episcopal Church.

Our first conference at Grace Chapel was a lalapalooza. I asked Peter and Fi Horrobin, founders and directors of Ellel Ministries International in England, to be keynote speakers for our first-ever *Pure Passion* conference. It was an information-packed event with great variety and an expansive look at healing the sexually broken that is not often seen.

Soon after that, I created a workbook to accompany all of the *Pure Passion* TV programs from the first year and turned it into an 18-week "Pure Passion Equipping Class." The combination of a video followed by classroom discussion was a great success, so as the number of *Pure Passion* episodes grew, I determined to create a much larger, topically arranged course for the future.

About this time, *Charisma* magazine published one of my most controversial articles to date, called "The Judas Church." In it, with great fear and trembling, I described the demise of the Episcopal Church and other mainline denominations as evidence that we are in the last days and are witnessing the great apostasy prophesied in the Bible for the time just before Christ's Second Coming. Happily, the letters to the editor affirmed my prophetic insight. I eventually sent a copy of the article to every bishop in the Episcopal Church, hoping that at least some could be rescued from the judgment God will bring on those who live in rebellion to His Word. All I got in return was silence.

As has so often been the case—and even more so with a TV program to fund—financial struggles came along, but the Lord helped us meet them. Before long, letters of gratitude began pouring in from Romania, Russia, Iraq, Israel, Spain, Italy, England, Canada and the United States. I was touched by the words of a middle-aged lady from Romania who wrote that ours was the first voice in her entire life that had provided information about how Christ can heal the sexually broken. She said that not even the churches in her country would talk about such a subject.

I remember thinking after that, *The first voice in her life! Wow! This is a much bigger deal than I had ever imagined. It's just like Gus Hunter's prophecy given during my YWAM training said it would be.*

One day, the Lord spoke clearly to me that *Pure Passion* would be seen throughout the world. Not long thereafter, America was hit by the great recession of 2008. Our situation seemed much more precarious than ever, especially since our costs were escalating. A number of regular givers had to withdraw their support. Yet God was there, and through the generosity of many, including a committed, long-term major donor, the hand of the Lord kept moving us forward.

As the months went by, I began to worry that since God told our major donor to give to us so generously, He could also tell him to stop and to give somewhere else. I knew that if God did that, we would go under almost immediately, not only as a TV production, but as a ministry. Alas, I am not the great man of faith and power I would like to be.

I did not confide my fears to anyone, yet within 24 hours, I got a call from that donor. Without even a hello, he said, "God told me last night to tell you that I am to stick with you for the duration." He added, "I don't know if that means anything to you, but I just thought I'd tell you what He just said to me."

I was flabbergasted—not only at the faith of this man and his willingness to do whatever God told him, but at God's effort to let me know that He was not going to let everything collapse the way I feared. In the very moment when I was doubting God's faithfulness, He was taking steps to alleviate those doubts.

I am sane today only because of God's unfailing provision and the faithfulness of His servants to let our voice continue to broadcast the message of His powerful grace. To my knowledge, even now we continue to be the only nationally distributed, weekly program that focuses exclusively on how God saves, sets free and heals sexually bound and broken people—of every kind.

A Wider Outreach

Since our founding as a ministry in 1987, we had never had a promotional video, so that became one of our major projects for 2009. When it was finished, I mailed it out to three thousand pastors and leaders around the country and posted it on our website. I believe it has gone a long way toward increasing our visibility in the eyes of leaders everywhere. It also has been used by God to rouse the troops—to get pastors to more actively minister to sexually broken people than they have in the past.

The sad truth is that most pastors are doing nothing about the epidemic of sexual brokenness around us. If they have one seminar or give one sermon a year on sexual sin, they think they are doing something great. Yet day in and day out, their congregants are facing an onslaught of sexual temptation. It is almost as if the evil one has placed a spell on the Church.

In our promo video, I point out to pastors that six out of ten of their church members are sexually bound or broken. Yet at times I wonder if pastors are even listening. Recently one of the local churches in my area—the church everyone would name as the most cutting edge—had a guest speaker who used the word *masturbation* in his message. The pastor later apologized to the congregation that such a word was spoken from the platform. *Unbelievable* does not even begin to describe that.

In 2010, Arabic and Spanish language opportunities opened up for us, so our program was being translated, subtitled and dubbed for those markets. As it happens, our main network (CTN) owns a Spanish-speaking sister network (CTNi) that covers the entire Spanish-speaking world by satellite. They began airing the program at no charge to us, an amazing opportunity that came with the full support of the man who has been funding all of our foreign language opportunities. This was utterly wonderful in my eyes.

My book *Sexual Healing* officially went out of print after fifteen years on the market, but it still remains available through Mastering Life Ministries. The Spanish version sold out, but we revived it as an e-book, and there are also Korean and Chinese versions. My second book, *Transformed into His Image*, also has a Chinese version that sells out of Taiwan. With all the new venues for our teaching that help take it all around the world, emails have been coming in from places like Israel, Cyprus, Estonia and Japan thanking us for making our life-changing ministry available to them.

In 2010, we created an annual award to be given to an unheralded ministry on the front lines of what God is doing on the earth for sexually broken people. We named it the "Pure Passion Award." Our first recipient was Treasures Ministries, a ministry outreach to strippers, and its director, Harmony Dust, who has twice been a guest on *Pure Passion*.

It had been a secret dream of mine since childhood to become rich and then secretly find worthy people who needed help so that I could help them. With the funding of a generous donor, that dream has come true in a way that I never expected. I now look forward each year to discerning which ministry God would like us to honor as the next Pure Passion Award recipient. Since ministries to sexually broken people are among the least heralded and least funded outreaches, it is especially rewarding to offer an award that is focused on them and that is presented in combination with a generous financial blessing.

In 2011, we gave the Pure Passion Award to New Creation Ministries and its founder/director, Russell Willingham. His is an outstanding counseling ministry for sexually bound and broken people—one that has stood the test of time. Russell has also twice been a guest on *Pure Passion*.

In 2012, we gave the Pure Passion Award to Agape International Missions and its founders/directors, Don and Bridget Brewster. Don has also been a guest on *Pure Passion*. His outreach to underage children in Cambodia who are being sex-trafficked is one of the most impressive ministries I have ever seen. What an incredible blessing to give an award to such a ministry.

In 2013, we gave the Pure Passion Award to Be Broken Ministries and its founder/director, Jonathan Daugherty. Jonathan has been a guest on *Pure Passion*, as well as serving as its cohost for several years. He has one of the most effective outreaches that I am aware of to sex addicts and their wives.

By the time of this book's publication, *Pure Passion* could be seen in eleven languages on ten networks covering practically the entire world, with two smartphone apps available (iPhone and Android), two Roku channels (U.S. and Europe) and a myriad of other ways to reach every place on the globe. What's even more amazing is that, despite our tiny workforce, the program has won three Telly Awards for excellence.

In 2013, after we had completed two hundred *Pure Passion* TV programs, the Lord made it known that He wanted us to move on. We have now ceased production of the program, but it is scheduled to air for two more years as a *Best of Pure Passion* series. Beyond that, we expect that all the networks currently carrying *Pure Passion* will continue to air the program.

In addition, we have posted all the programs on the Internet so that they are available for everyone to see until such time as Jesus returns. *Pure Passion* will always be available online, on Roku and as a smartphone app.

Our new assignment is to produce documentaries on how God sets free the sexually bound and broken. The first one came out in 2014. It is called *Such Were Some of You* and is a documentary that gathers a "cloud of witnesses" to testify to the fact that Jesus Christ can and does transform the lives of those who struggle with homosexuality and who seek Him for a way of escape.

Past, Present and Future

My mother died in 2012. The death of a parent can be a much more powerful event than one might imagine. Our family had been anticipating her passing for some time. But when someone is gone who was the physical source of your life and has been a prime former and shaper of your character, the lost weight of her presence is palpable. I still have moments when I reach for the phone to call her, before remembering that she is not there.

I have been doing family genealogical research for several years now, studying the lives of those who have gone before me. I had a cousin who died in the Battle of Franklin during the Civil War, whose body was never recovered. My mother's first husband died while serving in World War II. His plane was lost at sea, and his body also was never recovered. I became better acquainted with the ancestor who was president of the United States—I discovered that I am the half-fifth great-grandnephew of President Andrew Jackson. And I have learned more about my great-grandfather, who traveled the country in the late 1800s as a Covenanter preacher and teacher. He wrote books and spoke against slavery and the ill-treatment of the Indians, while defending temperance, the keeping of the Sabbath and the creation of a State of Israel.

I have thought long and hard about what my first meeting with such family members in heaven will be like (assuming they will be there). Will we have long talks in which they regale me with their life stories? Will God have videolike images that stream through our minds so we can actually see what happened? Will I be able to know and thank one of my ancestors from countless generations ago, who lived such a righteous life in the eyes of God that his descendants up to a thousand generations after him were blessed as a result? After all, God had to reach pretty far down into the pit to pull me out. Perhaps it was to keep His promise to an ancestor. Or maybe it was His response to the prayers of my father, my mother or my grandmother.

One thing is clear, however. Our time on this earth is racing to its conclusion at light speed, and only what we do for God will last. That, and the work of Christ on our behalf, will be the foundation for what we do for the rest of eternity.

My Message to You

As I look over more than sixty years of life, I am quick to remember that I never expected to live this long. Now I can see God's wisdom, His timing and His hand at work in all the suffering and trials I endured.

I brought much of my misery on myself through my own sinful choices, but even so, God took what I have been through, turned it around and used it to give me a voice of redemption and hope for sexually broken people. I know that some people will listen only to someone who has been through what they are going through. That is why I have told you my story.

I want you to know that I have been an expert in rebellion against God. I should have received ten Ph.D.s for what I know about rebellion.

I also know sexual brokenness from one end to the other, from heterosexual to homosexual, from voyeurism to exhibitionism, from compulsive masturbation to obsessive bondage to porn, from promiscuity to prostitution. I know what it is like to sell your body to the highest bidder and feel worthless as a result.

I know bondage and addiction, uncontrollable lust and obsession. I know what it is to be hopelessly addicted to drugs and alcohol, and to feel desperately unloved.

I know the unspeakable pain behind intense self-hatred and failed attempts at suicide. I know what it is like to be the target of vicious murder attempts.

I know the hypocrisy of religious people and the deceiving miracles of false gods.

I know the poverty and weakness of self-righteousness, and I know the undefiled purity of the Lord. I have felt His river of living water pouring into my heart—a river of liquid love that completes every hope and dream that anyone could ever have.

I know the power of God that is able to keep me from falling. I know the love and grace of God that has so transformed my heart that I no longer want to commit the sins that once possessed me.

I know the God who can set *anyone* free from *anything*—and without exception. The greatest sinners in history could have been saved if they had only repented and turned to Jesus Christ for His forgiveness and cleansing.

And *you* are no exception.

I *know* that God loves you. And He has declared in His Word that anyone who calls on the name of the Lord Jesus Christ will be saved.

EPILOGUE

You might be wondering, now that I am sixty-something, how it all worked out for me with regard to my drug, alcohol and sexual sobriety. Maybe you would like to know if there really is freedom from such addictive behaviors, or if the healing of the emotional wounds that caused them was permanent. You might want to know if there is any hope for you, and whether I have been exaggerating the changes in order to make God look good.

The first and most important thing I want to say is that God heals and delivers people only as they pursue and maintain an intimate relationship with Him. It is when we pursue Him, and as a result, fall more deeply in love with Him, that He reveals more of His glory (see Jeremiah 29:11–14). It is that glory that purifies our motivations, causes us to see things as they really are and persuades us to continue further pursuit of Him.

Our goal must never be perfect behavior, and the means must never be our own wisdom and power. The goal is to know God and be transformed by that relationship. Revelation and freedom come as a byproduct of intimacy with Him. When we live in that abiding relationship with Him (see John 15:5–8), only then does God reveal the secrets of our bondage. Only then does He send His power to heal the wounds and to keep us from falling (see Jude 1:24). It is in that context that He works in us to will and to do His purpose (see Philippians 2:13). It is through our *knowledge* of Him, both intellectual and intimate, that we receive everything we need for godliness (see 2 Peter 1:3). It is then that we walk according to the Spirit and are kept from carrying out the desires of the flesh (see Galatians 5:16).

Most people want to skip the "intimacy with God" part. That is why they keep falling back into sin.

Surprisingly, living free from bondage is not the sign that we have discovered God's way of escape (see 1 Corinthians 10:12–13). Most people "in recovery" achieve some measure of progress in maintaining their sobriety by following the rules of their program. But to the degree that they see results by following that program, their sense of a need for God diminishes. What they end up with is a *maintenance* program based on self-effort rather than the *transformation* that God wants to give them.

That is not to say that there is not any value in some of those programs. God has used many of them to keep disaster at bay. But they are not the way to transformation, and if mistaken as such, can actually create a barrier to what really does transform the heart.

Fortunately, I was able to learn from the start that the only way that I could be healed, delivered, transformed and kept free from falling back into sin was to depend completely on God's power to keep me from falling. I also learned that that meant I needed to be in close fellowship with Him so that I could receive from Him the revelation and direction I would need in the moment of trial.

You see, He did not permanently remove the temptations. Oh, He took some away for a season so that I would not have more than I could handle. I quickly learned, however, that my transformation was going to be a matter of learning to love Him more than the things of the world, so that when the world's siren song began to wail, the choice would be obvious. I needed to make up my mind before the temptations came, so that my decision, once I was tempted, would not be based on the feelings and emotions of the moment, but on my love and commitment to the One who suffered a horrible death in my place.

So, how did it go? you ask.

On that day in the office at Hollywood Presbyterian Church in 1980, when the pastor encouraged me to believe that God would do for me what I realized I could not do for myself, my simple, childlike faith brought about several rather dramatic deliverances. Instantly, my desire for drugs and alcohol vanished. I did not even have to struggle with wanting them. And that freedom from temptation continued for a good ten years before it finally returned.

Satan was allowed to test me once again—not because God knew that I would fall, but because God knew that by then I was mature enough and in love with Him enough not to return to the habits of my past. For the victory to be complete, however, I needed to choose Him instead of those things, *even while being sorely tempted by them.*

As for my homosexual inclinations, they underwent a gradual reduction that was in direct proportion to the healing of their root causes—a healing led by God Himself over a period of about ten years. Periodically, He would reveal a root cause such as unforgiveness, idolatry or a father wound and tell me how to find healing or deliverance for it. (You can read more on the root causes of sexual sin in my book *Sexual Healing.*)

I have never returned to homosexual behavior. From the first day of my salvation walk until now, God has kept me from falling in that area. I know that I am fully capable of falling without Him. But in relationship with Him, He will not allow me to be tempted beyond what I am able to withstand. While my head can still be turned by someone, I do not pursue the temptations at any level. They no longer interest me, nor do they define me.

Additionally, my fear of women has been erased by the healing process. The natural heterosexuality that was always there, though damaged and unformed, has emerged as my true identity. Due to my unique calling to remain single, I have not pursued marriage. I easily could have, though, if God had had other plans for me.

As for my former bondage to pornography and various other sexually addictive behaviors (voyeurism, exhibitionism and the like), God has brought a great victory there as well. I have been tempted, of course, and often, but except for one brief glance at a magazine in an airport 25 years ago, and the struggle that I had in the Chicago high-rise that I mentioned earlier, I have not returned to those activities.

Like anyone else, I have happened upon sexual scenes in R-rated movies or seen nude pictures online while doing a search for something, and I have struggled with looking away or turning it off. But there has been no pursuit and no deliberate return to looking at those materials. When you get serious with God, He will get very serious with you. When temptations come and you never even consider following them as an option, then you are on the right track.

When I get close to giving in to such temptations, I literally can feel the grief of the Holy Spirit within me. The thought of causing the Lord who died for me more suffering is now even more grievous than the torment of having to say no to a sexual temptation.

Once again, let me emphasize that I am capable of committing all the sexual sins that I used to do. I just do not want to anymore. My love for Jesus has grown greater than my love for cheap sensual thrills. My reliance on His power to carry me through the times of deep trial is resolute and absolute. And most importantly, when I am faithful in such a battle, I am really clear on who won the victory for me.

The most difficult area for me to stay faithful in these past 34-plus years has been with masturbation and its accompanying fantasies. They come at me in the morning, as though arriving on the morning train, and I have to get out of bed quickly so that they do not overtake me.

Having said that, however, let me add that the victory over this sinful brace of behaviors has been far greater than I could have ever imagined. Masturbation was something that took hold of my life from the age of eight or nine and held complete control for decades. It is also the kind of temptation that can have its tentacles in a myriad of hidden root problems, which can take a long time to uncover and find deliverance from. The ambiguity in the Church over its sinfulness also feeds its intransigence, although it must be acknowledged that, biblically, its sinfulness is found in the embracing of the idols of the heart that feed it more than in the act itself. (For example, look at what Jesus said in Matthew 5:28.)

Nevertheless, I have experienced periods of complete victory over this bondage that have lasted ten years and more at a time, so I know that the full victory is there to experience. And the grace of God is there in the moments of defeat.

We must always remember that it is the grace of God that teaches us to say no to ungodliness and to live upright and godly lives in this present age (see Titus 2:11–14).

Another thing I have learned is that God causes everything to work for good for those who love Him and are called according to His purpose (see Romans 8:28). He can take even your failures and turn them into victories. And He can also take your broken places and turn them into healing balm for the nations.

But the most important lesson I have learned is that the purpose of life, for all of us, is to seek and to find Jesus Christ, who created all things, to turn from our sinful lifestyles in repentance and to give ourselves fully into His care.

We were born to fall in love with God as a response to our Savior's supreme act of love in dying on the cross to pay the penalty of our sins. We were born to enter into a union with Him (like unto a marriage) and to give ourselves completely to Him, even as He gives Himself completely to us.

The reality is that we live in the midst of a great love story. Every romantic hope and dream that we have ever chased in life, or longed for while reading or watching a love story, is the manifestation of our eternal DNA—put there by God Himself for the day when our eyes would be open and we would see Him as He really is, a river of liquid love desiring to fill us and live in union with us forever.

There is a famous image in the book of Revelation where Jesus Christ is revealed in all His power and glory, with eyes "like blazing fire" (Revelation 1:14 NIV1984). One night as I was singing love songs to Him, Jesus suddenly appeared in a vision, and I saw Him in that revealed glory, eyes aflame with fire. Until that moment, I had always avoided that passage of Scripture because I had mistaken it as being a fire of judgment. But as I looked into His eyes, I saw for the first time that the fire was a fire of burning desire. It was an overflowing of His passion for me and the revealing of His fierce determination that no one would ever be allowed to snatch me out of His hand. In that moment of being fiercely loved and absolutely protected, the idols of this world became ridiculous to me in comparison.

In short, my advice to you is this: Seek Him! Find Him! Love Him! Follow Him! And don't ever look back!

Dr. David Kyle Foster struggled with a serious bondage to pornography and other sexually addictive behaviors before his salvation in 1980. The founder and director of Mastering Life Ministries, David has produced and hosted two hundred episodes of the television program *Pure Passion*, an outreach designed to equip believers to redemptively minister to those trapped in sexual sin and brokenness. Each episode is freely available online for anyone to access (visit www.masteringlife.org). David has also appeared on *The 700 Club*, *Dr. Phil* and many other television and radio programs around the world, always witnessing to the power of God to set anyone free from anything. He was also host of the Covenant Award–winning *Mastering Life* program on the Focus on the Family Radio Network.

With an M.Div. from Trinity Evangelical Divinity School and a D.Min. from Trinity School for Ministry, David has served as adjunct professor at Asbury Theological Seminary, The Bible Institute of Hawaii, Trinity Episcopal School for Ministry, Logos Christian College and Graduate School and the Wagner Leadership Institute. He has authored three books, and his articles have appeared in numerous journals and magazines. He has been a speaker on five continents for Youth With A Mission, Ellel Ministries and others.

Currently, David is directing a series of documentaries on how God sets free the sexually bound and broken. The first one is called *Such Were Some of You* and gathers a "cloud of witnesses" to testify to the fact that Jesus Christ can and does transform the lives of those who struggle with homosexuality and who seek Him for a way of escape.

Making his home in the Nashville, Tennessee, area, David loves hanging out with Jesus during the autumn in a quiet mountain cabin and being in the company of people who cannot stop talking about how much they love God.

To learn more about David and his ministry and materials, contact

Mastering Life Ministries
P.O. Box 770
Franklin, TN 37065

www.masteringlife.org
www.facebook.com/purepassiontv
www.twitter.com/purepassiontv